Praise for *The Ages of Globalization*

"This dazzling book makes an invaluable contribution to the debate about the future of globalization by brilliantly summarizing humanity's existential challenges and providing bold ideas for ensuring our survival. Sachs makes a persuasive argument that applying the concept of sustainable development must be today's essential mission. His thoughtful proposals for reforming key international institutions, starting with the UN, merit particular attention. *The Ages of Globalization* is required reading for our times."

—**Vuk Jeremić**, former president of the United Nations General Assembly

"In this erudite yet accessible book, Jeffrey D. Sachs traces the history of modern humans from our migration from Africa some 70,000 years ago to today. In a pathbreaking account, he shows how geography, technology, and institutions drive change. His analysis is indispensable for understanding current global predicaments. A tour de force."

—**Prasannan Parthasarathi**, Boston College

"As it comes from Jeffrey D. Sachs, I had expected this book to be analytical, punchy, and readable, and so it is. But it is a pleasure to be able to report that it is also a book by a superstar economist that takes both history and geography seriously and that allows the past, with all its complexities and contingencies, to speak for itself. Impressively broad in both temporal and geographical scope, this is a masterpiece of concision and a great introduction to global economic history."

—**Kevin O'Rourke**, author of *A Short History of Brexit: From Brentry to Backstop*

"*The Ages of Globalization* is not just a book for the modern citizen. It is an essential survival kit for the twenty-first century. At the same time that humanity was amassing wealth, it was also creating the means of its own destruction. Now we are facing forces none of us can counter alone, such as climate change and environmental degradation. Sachs's call for action resonates with vigor and urgency. With this book, we can better explore, learn, and act."

—**Miroslav Lajčák**, minister of foreign and European affairs
of the Slovak Republic

"At a time when the foundations of the world economic order are being challenged, we must rely on the knowledge accumulated throughout history to make wiser choices for the future of our societies. In *The Ages of Globalization*, Sachs offers a superb and unique historical and analytical framework for understanding the process of globalization, highlighting its dynamic nature and addressing its social and economic implications. From the Paleolithic Age to the current digital age, this book examines the interplay of geography, technology, and institutions to achieve a comprehensive explanation of how globalization emerges and evolves. Analysts, policy makers, social and political leaders, interested citizens, and anyone concerned with the future of the global economy can draw invaluable lessons from this book."

—**Felipe Larraín B.**, former minister of finance of Chile

"Few scholars have the breadth of knowledge with which to cogently weave insights from such wide-ranging fields such as agronomy, economics, archeology, anthropology, and engineering to recount the layered story of how globalization and development unfolded. As always, Sachs is a treat to read."

—**Gordon McCord**, University of California, San Diego

The Ages of
Globalization

For Nina

Our family's newest arrival to the Digital Age, with our hopes and aspirations for peace, prosperity, and environmental sustainability.

Jeffrey D. Sachs

The Ages of Globalization

Geography, Technology, and Institutions

Columbia University Press / New York

Columbia University Press
Publishers Since 1893
New York   Chichester, West Sussex
cup.columbia.edu
Copyright © 2020 Jeffrey D. Sachs

Library of Congress Cataloging-in-Publication Data
Names: Sachs, Jeffrey, author.
Title: The ages of globalization : geography, technology, and institutions /
Jeffrey D. Sachs.
Description: New York : Columbia University Press, [2020] |
Includes bibliographical references and index.
Identifiers: LCCN 2019038327 (print) | LCCN 2019038328 (e-book) |
ISBN 9780231193740 (cloth) | ISBN 9780231550482 (e-book)
Subjects: LCSH: Economic history. | World history. | Globalization—History.
Classification: LCC HC21.S224 2020 (print) | LCC HC21 (e-book) |
DDC 909—dc23
LC record available at https://lccn.loc.gov/2019038327
LC e-book record available at https://lccn.loc.gov/2019038328

Columbia University Press books are printed on permanent
and durable acid-free paper.

Printed in the United States of America

Cover and title page images
The SDG logo (wheel) is the logo for the Sustainable Development Goals
Please note: The content of this publication has not been approved by
the United Nations and does not reflect the views of the United Nations
or its officials or Member States. United Nations Sustainable Development
Goals web site: https://www.un.org/sustainabledevelopment.
All other symbols are royalty free.

Cover design: Lisa Hamm

Contents

Contents

Contents

Contents

Preface

The COVID-19 epidemic hit as this book was going to press. A most global phenomenon—a pandemic disease—was suddenly provoking the most local of responses: quarantines, lockdowns of neighborhoods, and the closure of borders and trade. In just three months, the virus spread from Wuhan, China, to more than 140 other countries. In the fourteenth century, the bubonic plague spread the Black Death from China to Italy in the course of some sixteen years, 1331 to 1347. In our time, the pathogen arrived within days by nonstop flight from Wuhan to Rome.

This book is about complexities of globalization, including the powerful capacity of globalization to improve the human condition while bringing undoubted threats as well. The interconnections of humanity across the globe enable the sharing of ideas, the enjoyment of diverse cultures, and the exchanges of diverse and distinctive goods across vast geographies. I savor my morning coffee, which arrives not from the coffee shop across the street but from the sloping tropical hillsides of Ethiopia, Indonesia, and Colombia, thousands of miles away. I delight in having visited these places as well, and have enjoyed their rich cultures and great natural beauty. I have learned from such visits and my work that human kindness, our aspirations for our children, and our enjoyments of life are common to all humanity, no matter how diverse our backgrounds and our material conditions.

The new coronavirus reminds us yet again that the benefits of global trade and travel have always been accompanied by the global spread of disease and other ills. In this book, I will discuss how Adam Smith, the father of modern economics, viewed the voyages of discovery of Christopher Columbus and Vasco da Gama. He wrote that the discoveries of the sea routes from Europe to the Americas and to Asia were the most important events of human history, because they linked all parts of the world in a web of transport and commerce, with vast potential benefits. Smith also wrote, with dismay, that the new sea routes occasioned a massive repression of native societies by European conquerors and colonizers.

Because Smith lived a century before Robert Koch, Louis Pasteur, Giovanni Grassi, Ronald Ross, Martinus Beijerinck, and others who elaborated the bacterial and viral transmission of disease, he did not realize the key role that Old World pathogens played in devastating the Native American societies. Columbus brought to the Americas not only conquerors but also a massive biological exchange. The Europeans brought horses, cattle, and other plants and animals to the Americas for farming, and also many new infectious diseases, including smallpox, measles, and malaria, while bringing back to Europe the cultivation of the potato, maize, tomatoes, and other crops and farm animals. This "Columbian Exchange" united the world in trade while dividing the world in new kinds of inequalities of wealth and power.

The excess mortality of Native Americans caused by Old World diseases was devastating. The native populations were "naïve" to the Old World pathogens, and hence unprotected immunologically. In the same way, the world population today is immunologically naïve, and hence vulnerable, to the new coronavirus sweeping the planet. It is highly likely, thank goodness, that the illnesses and deaths caused by COVID-19 will be far less severe than the epidemics that ravaged Native American societies in the sixteenth century. Nonetheless, the current pandemic will influence global politics and society as other diseases have in the past.

In fact, we don't have to go back to the fourteenth-century Black Death or the sixteenth-century Columbian Exchange to recognize the profound role of diseases in shaping societies and economies. Until late in the nineteenth century, Africa's heavy burden of malaria created a kind of protective barrier against European imperial conquest. West Africa was known as the "white man's grave," since European soldiers succumbed in such high proportions to malaria. This barrier fell when the British learned to extract an antimalarial treatment, quinine, from the bark of the Andean cinchona tree. Gin and tonic (containing quinine) thereby became the beverage of British imperial conquest. Since then, Africa's malaria burden has stood as an obstacle to child survival and economic development, though new drugs and preventative measures are enabling humanity to fight back against this age-old scourge.

More recently, another killer pathogen circled the globe and caused devastation and havoc: the human immunodeficiency virus, HIV, the cause of AIDS. HIV, like COVID-19, is a zoonosis, that is, a pathogen of animal populations that jumps to human populations through some kind of interaction and perhaps genetic mutation. AIDS entered the human population most likely from West African apes that were killed for bushmeat. COVID-19 entered the human population most likely from bats. In the case of AIDS, the virus apparently spread among Africans for decades in the middle of the twentieth century, then was transmitted internationally in the 1970s and early 1980s. HIV/AIDS was diagnosed for the first time in San Francisco in the early 1980s, decades after its first introduction into the human population. By that time, many millions of Africans were already infected by, and dying from, the HIV virus.

AIDS marked another major event of globalization, at both its most devastating and its most inspiring. The deaths from AIDS quickly mounted into the tens of millions, with vast attendant suffering. Many of those with HIV infection were from socially marginalized groups: the very poor, ethnic minorities, the LGBT community, intravenous drug users, and others. This delayed the response of many governments, but civil society groups, led first and foremost by people infected with HIV, demanded action and step by step moved the world's governments, although after costly delays.

Impressively, the scientific community sprang quickly into action, making rapid and fundamental discoveries about the nature of the virus, the causes of disease, and the ways to fight both. Within roughly a decade of the identification of HIV as a new zoonotic disease, scientists discovered a number of antiviral medicines that could turn the HIV infection from a nearly certain deadly ailment to a chronic and controlled infection. In these breakthroughs and the subsequent distribution of the new medicines, globalization played a huge role. The science of discovery was global, with new scientific knowledge moving rapidly across all continents.

The distribution of the new medicines was also a coordinated global effort. A notable initiative was the launch of a new Global Fund to Fight AIDS, TB, and Malaria, in which I was thrilled and honored to play a role during its early formulation and development. The speed of policy implementation and health interventions was greatly spurred by rising public awareness and the crucial activist leadership of civil society.

COVID-19 similarly provokes the reckoning of the balance sheet of globalization, and the policy challenge of promoting the positive sides while limiting the negative consequences. The early steps in fighting COVID-19 have involved closing down international trade and travel, and even restricting the movements of people between and within cities of single nations. Quarantines are back, the word itself referring to the forty days (*quaranta giorni* in Italian) that Venetians held ships away from the port when the ships were suspected of carrying plague. The policy of quarantine dates back to the late fourteenth century. As did the AIDS crisis, the COVID-19 pandemic will require great attention and sensitivity to social justice in implementing measures to confront the disease.

Some concerns are being raised once again in our own time: that open trade is simply too dangerous, that we should revert to closed borders and national autarky (self-sufficiency). This is an illusion. While quarantines may indeed limit the spread of disease, they rarely stop the spread of the pathogens entirely. And their successes surely come at very high cost. Closures of trade bring their own kinds of miseries, starting with the massive losses of economic output and livelihoods. Throughout history, it has been important to understand the threats arising from globalization (disease, conquest, war, financial crises, and others) and to face them head on, not by ending the benefits of globalization, but by using the means of international cooperation to control the negative consequences of global-scale interconnectedness.

This has entailed the invention of new forms of global cooperation, one of the most important themes of this book. From the late eighteenth century onward, philosophers, statesmen, politicians, and activists have sought new ways to govern globalization in order to promote its benefits while controlling its many potential harms. The fight against pandemic disease has loomed large in the efforts at cooperation. Indeed, the International Sanitary Conferences that began in 1851 and continued until 1938 were among the first modern efforts at intensive global scientific and policy cooperation. These efforts at disease control gave rise to the World Health Organization in 1948, one of the first major agencies of the new United Nations, which was founded at the end of World War II in 1945. WHO, of course, is currently at the center of the global fight against COVID-19. WHO has helped to coordinate scientific information about the pathogen and how to control it, and to coordinate and monitor the global push to contain and end the pandemic.

Globalization enables one part of the world to learn from others. When one country shows successes in containing the spread of COVID-19, other parts of the world quickly aim to learn of the new methods and whether they can be applied in a local context. The development of new drugs and vaccines to fight COVID-19 is also a global effort, as was the case with HIV. The clinical trials to test the new candidate drugs and vaccines will involve researchers spanning the world. The distribution and uses of the new drugs and vaccines will also require cooperation on a global scale.

Disease control is not the only area where global cooperation is vital today. The case for global cooperation and institutions extends to many urgent concerns, including the control of human-induced climate change; the conservation of biodiversity; the control and reversal of the massive pollution of the air, soils, and oceans; the proper uses and governance of the internet; the nonproliferation of nuclear weapons; the avoidance of mass forced migrations; and the ever-present challenge of avoiding or ending violent conflicts. All of these challenges must be confronted in a world that is too often divided, distrustful, and distracted, and now, preoccupied with a new zoonosis that has suddenly become a new pandemic.

This book will not provide simple answers or antidotes to these ills and threats. The history of globalization is a history of humanity's glorious achievements, cruelties, and self-inflicted harms, and of the great complexities of achieving progress in the midst of crisis. Globalization, we shall see, involves the intricate interplay of physical geography, human institutions, and technical know-how. COVID-19 is at once a physical phenomenon, a sudden intruder into our politics and social life, and a target of scientific discovery. It is, therefore, the kind of phenomenon of globalization that has been part of human experience from the very start of our species. I hope this book will shed light on that long experience of global interconnectedness, and on the role of globalization in shaping our humanity and lives.

1

Seven Ages of Globalization

Humanity has always been globalized, since the dispersals of modern humans from Africa some seventy thousand years ago. Yet globalization has changed its character from age to age. Those changes have often come quickly and violently. In the twenty-first century, we need to change peacefully and wisely; in the nuclear age, there may be no second chances in the event of global war. By studying the history of globalization, we can arrive at an informed understanding of globalization in the twenty-first century and how to manage it successfully.

In my interpretation, we have passed through seven distinct ages of globalization from the deep past to the present day. In each of these seven ages, global change emerged from the interplay of physical geography, technology, and institutions. Physical geography in this context means the climate, flora and fauna, diseases, topography, soils, energy resources, mineral deposits, and Earth processes that affect the conditions of life. Technology refers to both the hardware and software of our production systems. Institutions include politics, laws, and cultural ideas and practices that guide society. Geography, technology, and institutions are subject to remarkable variability and change, and they interact powerfully to shape societies across place and time.

Understanding the interplay of geography, technology, and institutions is fundamental to understanding human history. This understanding is also fundamental to navigating the changes under way in the twenty-first century. By examining the history of globalization, we can make wiser choices for our societies and economies in our own time.

Philosophers, historians, theologians, and others have long asked: Is there a direction to history? Can we speak of long-term change or only of repeating cycles of history? Is there long-term progress? I will suggest that, yes, there is an arrow of history. In each age, human beings have become more aware of the wider world. Technological advances—especially in transport and communications—and demographic changes in the size and structure of human populations have intensified our global-scale interdependencies and awareness. As a result, politics too has gone from being very local to being global, never more so than in our own time.

Let us keep our eye on five big questions. First, what have been the main drivers of global-scale change? Second, how do geography, technology, and institutions interact? Third, how do changes in one region diffuse to others? Fourth, how have these changes affected global interdependence? Fifth, what lessons can we glean from each age to help us meet our challenges today?

The Seven Ages

Globalization signifies the interlinkages of diverse societies across large geographical areas. These interlinkages are technological, economic, institutional, cultural, and geopolitical. They include interactions of societies across the world through trade, finance, enterprise, migration, culture, empire, and war.

To trace the history of globalization, I will describe seven distinct ages: the Paleolithic Age, our prehistory when humans were still foragers; the Neolithic Age, when farming first began; the Equestrian Age, when the domestication of the horse and the development of proto-writing enabled long-distance trade and communications; the Classical Age, when large empires first emerged; the Ocean Age, when empires first expanded across the oceans and beyond the accustomed ecological zones of the homeland; the Industrial Age, when a few societies, led by Great Britain, ushered in the industrial economy; and the Digital Age, our own time, in which nearly the entire world is instantaneously interconnected by digital data.

In the Paleolithic Age, which I date from 70,000 BCE to 10,000 BCE, long-distance interactions were by migration, as small groups migrated from one place to another. As these groups moved, they carried with them their tools, their know-how, and their emerging cultures. As migrating groups of *Homo sapiens* (anatomically modern humans) entered new regions, they had to fend for themselves in new ways, confronting other hominins (members of the genus *Homo*) such as Neanderthals and Denisovans, new predators and pathogens, new ecological conditions (such as living at high elevations), and of course, other competing groups of modern humans. That competition contributed to cultural patterns that have continued to the present day.[1]

The end of the last ice age and the onset of a warmer climate enabled the next phase of globalization, the Neolithic ("new stone") Age, which I date from 10,000 BCE to 3000 BCE. The fundamental breakthrough was agriculture, both crop cultivation and animal husbandry. As foraging gave way to farming, nomadism gave way to sedentary life in villages. The range of human interaction widened from the clan to the village and to politics and trade between villages. Trade in precious items—gemstones, shells, minerals, tools—was pursued at distances of hundreds of kilometers.

The domestication of the horse ushered in a third age of globalization, the Equestrian Age, which I date from 3000 BCE to 1000 BCE. This period is typically labeled the Copper and Bronze ages, though I prefer to emphasize the role of the horse over that of the minerals. With the domesticated horse, rapid, long-distance overland transport and communications became possible. The horse served several basic roles: animal traction (horsepower), communications (conveying messages), and military (cavalry). In modern jargon, we would say that the domesticated horse was a "disruptive technology," somewhat like the invention of the steam engine, locomotive, automobile, and tank combined. In politics, the horse hastened the arrival of the state, by enabling the reach across much greater distances of public administration and coercive force.

The next age, known to us as the Classical Age, which I date from 1000 BCE to 1500 CE, marked the rise and intense competition of large land-based empires. Starting around 1000 BCE, some states—such as the neo-Assyrian state in Mesopotamia and, soon after, the Achaemenid state of Persia—embarked on vast territorial expansions, which succeeded as the result of advantages in governance, both military and political.

Ideas mattered enormously in the rise of the empires. The major empires were spurred by new religious and philosophical outlooks, such as the new philosophies of the Greco-Roman world, that profoundly shaped the outlooks of these societies. The imperial age ushered in trans-Eurasian trade, such as between the Roman Empire in the west and the Han Empire of China in the east, carried out both overland and by sea routes along the coastlines of the Indian Ocean and the Mediterranean.

By around 1400 CE, advances in oceangoing navigation and military technologies led the transition to a new era, the Ocean Age, which I date from 1500 to 1800. During this new age, empires became transoceanic, indeed global, for the first time, with temperate-zone imperial powers of Europe conquering and colonizing tropical regions in Africa, the Americas, and Asia. Revolutionary changes in global trade ensued, such as the rise of multinational corporations, the vast expansion of transoceanic trade, and the mass movement of millions of people across the oceans, including the forcible enslavement of millions of Africans bound for American mines and plantations. Politics also became global in scale for the first time, leading to the first global wars fought simultaneously across several continents.

The Industrial Age, which I date from 1800 to 2000, marked another profound acceleration of global change. Changes that used to take place over the course of centuries or even millennia now occurred over just a few decades. The Industrial Age was marked by remarkable waves of technological advance, and a powerful new alliance of science and technology. With the tapping of fossil fuels, made possible by the invention of the steam engine and the internal combustion engine, industrial production soared. Global populations soared too, as the result of massive increases in food production. While the Ocean Age gave rise to transoceanic empires, the Industrial Age gave rise to the first global hegemon, Great Britain, and later, the United States. These two powers bestrode the entire globe with unprecedented military, technological, and financial power. But, as the end of the British Empire demonstrated, even hegemons can quickly lose their place at the apex of the global competition.

We have now entered the Digital Age, from 2000 to the present, the result of the astounding capacities of digital technologies: computers, Internet, mobile telephony, and artificial intelligence, to name a few. The global transmission of data is pervasive: computational power has multiplied billions-fold, and information technologies are disrupting every aspect of the world economy, society, and geopolitics. We are moving from an era of hegemonic power to a multipolar world, in which several regional powers coexist. The ubiquitous flows of information have globalized economics and politics more directly and urgently than in the Industrial Age. We have seen how a hiccup in one part of the world economy, for example, the failure of the Wall Street investment bank Lehman Brothers on September 14, 2008, can within days create a global-scale financial panic and economic crash.

Table 1.1 summarizes the seven ages, with their time intervals, major technological changes, and scale of governance.

The Acceleration of Change

At the dawn of human history, all humans were foragers, engaged in hunting and gathering food for their survival. There was no urban-rural divide, as there were no villages, much less cities. The Neolithic revolution in agriculture gave rise to farm villages and sedentary life, mostly (but not completely) displacing foraging and nomadism. For thousands of years, up to the start of industrialization itself, almost all of humanity lived in rural areas, and most engaged in subsistence agriculture. Each farm family struggled to feed itself, with only a tiny margin of surplus, if any, sold in the marketplace or used to pay taxes.

Up until the twentieth century in much of the world, and until today in the poorest countries, agricultural production was so meager that the risk of famine and mass hunger was ever present. The French Revolution in 1789 was partly provoked by widespread hunger during attempts by the government to raise taxes to cover public debts. The Irish famine of the 1840s claimed around 1 million deaths. In the second half of the nineteenth century, repeated famines in British India and other colonized regions killed tens of millions.[2]

Industrialization and the accompanying advances in farm mechanization and agronomic know-how vastly expanded the food production per farmer in the industrial economies. Where it was once necessary for almost all households to be engaged in farming in order to grow enough food for the population, it became possible for a smaller and declining share of the workforce to feed the rest. The expanded food output led to sharply

Table 1.1 Ages of Globalization: Dates and Breakthroughs

Globalization age	Approximate dates	Primary energy	Information, media	Agriculture	Industry	Transport	Military	Governance
Paleolithic: global dispersal	70,000–10,000 BCE	Human, ocean currents	Language, petroglyphs	Hunting, gathering	Stone tools	Foot, raft, canoe	Stone weapons, bow and arrow	Clan
Neolithic: farming and villages	10,000–3000 BCE	Oxen	Hieroglyphs	Crops, animal husbandry	Bronze, copper	Foot, sail	Bronze weapons	Village
Equestrian: horse-based state	3000–1000 BCE	Horse	Early writing system, stela	Plow	Iron, wheel, cart	Horse, donkey, sail	Cavalry	State
Classical: imperial-scale governance	1000 BCE–1500 CE	Windmill, waterwheel	Alphabet, book	Large-scale grain trade	Engineering, infrastructure	Horse, road network, sail	Infantry, cavalry, gunpowder	Empire
Ocean: global empires	1500–1800	Ocean, wind	Printing press	Global trade of crops	Ocean navigation	Transoceanic sail	Cannon, musket	Global empire
Industrial: industrial mass production	1800–2000	Fossil fuels: coal, oil, natural gas; hydroelectric	Telegraph, telephone, broadcasting	Use of chemical fertilizers	Steam engine, textiles, steel	Ocean steamer, railroad	Machine gun, air, tanks, nuclear, space	Global empire, constitutional government, high capitalism
Digital: connectivity, computation, artificial intelligence	Twenty-first century	Solar, wind	Internet, artificial intelligence	Precision agriculture	Digital networks	Virtual, space	Cyberwarfare	Global rule of law?

lower risks of generalized famines and widespread hunger. The "surplus" agricultural workers, replaced by farm machines, left for the cities to find employment. Britain, the world's first industrial society, became more than half urban around 1880, at a time when most of the world was still overwhelmingly rural. As industrialization spread, albeit very unevenly around the world, urbanization and living standards began to rise.

The remarkable fact is how long it took for humanity to break free of omnipresent and nearly all-encompassing poverty and hunger. Looked at in the long sweep of the human experience, most economic and demographic change has occurred in the blink of an eye, during the past two hundred or so years of our roughly three hundred thousand years as a species. The first lesson of long-term global change, then, is that it has been super-exponential, meaning that it has come at a rising rate, with the largest changes occurring in the very recent past.

Let us consider three dimensions of long-term change. The first is the total human population. The second is the rate of urbanization—that is, the share of the global population residing in urban areas. The third is the global output per person. The Hyde 3.1 Project has heroically worked to construct consistent estimates of population and urbanization globally and by region during the period since 10,000 BCE.[3] It is a remarkable accomplishment and a vital body of evidence. The estimates of output per person come from a similarly remarkable effort, that of Angus Maddison, a late and great economic historian.

The estimated total world population over the past twelve thousand years is shown in figure 1.1. Between 10,000 and 3000 BCE, during the Neolithic Age, the estimated population rose from 2 million to 45 million, an annualized growth rate of just 0.04 percent. Between 3000 and 1000 BCE, the Equestrian Age, the growth rate rose slightly to 0.05 percent. From 1000 BCE to 1500 CE, the Classical Age, the growth rate rose again to 0.06 percent. During 1500 to 1800, the Ocean Age, the annualized growth rate rose further to 0.25 percent, and the global population doubled from an estimated 461 million to 990 million. Then, during 1800 to 2000, the Industrial Age, the growth rate jumped to 0.92 percent, resulting in a more than sixfold increase in world population—from 990 million to 6.145 billion. Thus, for most of human history, the rise of population year to year, even century to century, was imperceptible. With the Ocean and Industrial Ages, the global population soared.

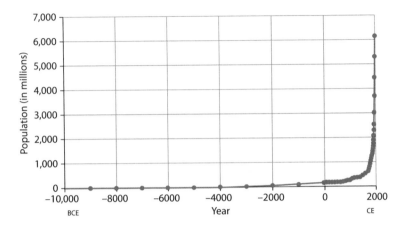

1.1 World Population, 10,000 BCE to 2000 CE

Source: Kees Klein Goldewijk, Arthur Beusen, and Peter Janssen. "Long-Term Dynamic Modeling of Global Population and Built-up Area in a Spatially Explicit Way: Hyde 3.1." *The Holocene* 20, no. 4 (2010): 565–73.

The estimated urbanization rate is shown in figure 1.2. The graph looks nearly the same. At the start of the Neolithic period, almost all humans were still foragers. Urbanization was zero. Yet even ten thousand years later, in 1 CE, while most of humanity lived in small agricultural settlements, the proportion living in cities was still only 1 percent. A thousand years later, in 1000 CE, urbanization had reached around 3 percent. By 1500, the urbanization rate stood at a mere 3.6 percent. As late as 1900, the global urbanization rate was only 16 percent. It is only in the twenty-first century that more than half of humanity lives in urban settings (an estimated 55 percent as of 2020). Though we marvel at the magnificent urban remains of ancient Rome and delight in the dazzling urban achievements of Renaissance Florence and Venice, the world's cities in total were home to only a very small share of humanity until very recently.

Maddison's estimates of global output per person from 1 CE to 2008 are shown in figure 1.3. Again, we see the same pattern as with population and urbanization: no perceptible change in global output per person before 1500, with annual growth at 0.01 percent; a tiny rise in output between 1500 and 1820, with annual growth at 0.05 percent; and then, with the onset of industrialization, a decisive turn upward, with annual growth between 1820

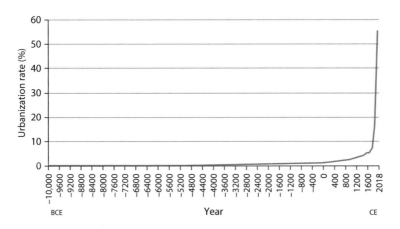

1.2 World Rate of Urbanization, 10,000 BCE to Present

Source: Kees Klein Goldewijk, Arthur Beusen, and Peter Janssen. "Long-Term Dynamic Modeling of Global Population and Built-up Area in a Spatially Explicit Way: Hyde 3.1." *The Holocene* 20, no. 4 (2010): 565–73.

and 2000 at 1.3 percent. During the 180 years from 1820 to 2000, world output per person increased roughly eleven times, leading to an equally dramatic fall in the global rate of extreme poverty—from around 90 percent in 1820 to roughly 10 percent as of 2015.[4]

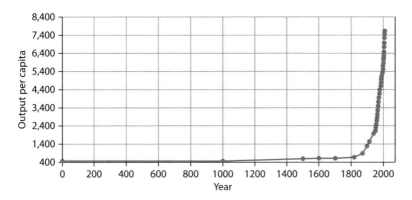

1.3 World Output per Person, 1–2008 CE. Output in 1990 International Geary-Khamis dollars.

Source: Angus Maddison. "Statistics on World Population, GDP and Per Capita GDP, 1–2008 AD." *Historical Statistics* 3 (2010): 1–36.

These three cases of super-exponential growth are dramatic. They remind us of the dramatic changes in the world since the onset of industrialization. Yet we should not infer that societies were static before 1800. The long period until the start of industrialization was an active and necessary runway for the eventual liftoff of the world economy. The preceding ages of globalization set the essential foundations of science, technology, governance, commercial law, and sheer ambition that ultimately gave rise to the Industrial Age.

Economic Scale and the Pace of Change

There is a basic idea in economics that a larger market leads to higher incomes and more rapid growth. With a larger market, there can be more specialization in job tasks, leading to greater skills and proficiency of the workforce in each line of economic activity (farming, construction, manufacturing, transport, healthcare, and so forth), and falling costs of production. With a larger market, there are also greater incentives to invent new products—because they reach more consumers—and more inventors are available to produce breakthroughs.

The most fundamental reason for the takeoff of economic growth around 1800 is therefore scale. World population had reached nearly 1 billion people by 1800, and humanity was increasingly interconnected through trade, transport, migration, and politics. Of course, some parts of the world, notably the North Atlantic, were the biggest beneficiaries of this new scale, and some places, notably sub-Saharan Africa and India, succumbed to brutal and debilitating imperial conquest. Yet the scale of global enterprise by 1800 was incomparably larger than, say, in 10,000 BCE, when an estimated 2 million widely-dispersed human beings constituted the entirety of humanity.

One can therefore see the history of globalization as a series of scale-enlarging transformations. In the Paleolithic Age, modern humans enlarged the scale of human settlement through migration across the world, yet most individuals spent their lives within a band of some thirty to fifty people.[5] In the Neolithic Age, the global population rose roughly twenty-two times, from around 2 million in 10,000 BCE to around 45 million in 3000 BCE, and individuals lived in villages of several hundred persons. In the Equestrian Age, the population rose from around 45 million in 3000 BCE to 115 million in 1000 BCE, with the vast majority in an increasingly interconnected east-west band of Eurasia. Now, for the first time, humanity was organized into recognizable states, no longer merely interspersed villages. In the Classical Age, the human population soared to 188 million by 1 CE, 295 million by 1000, and 390 million by 1400. Human beings increasingly lived in large multiethnic, multireligious empires covering vast land areas including the Roman, Han, Mauryan, Persian, Byzantine, Umayyad, Mongol, and other empires. These empires not only fought with each other, but also traded with each other over vast distances.

With the voyages of Christopher Columbus and Vasco da Gama, and the transition to the Ocean Age, scale increased yet again, this time to a global reach that reconnected the Old World and the New World through ocean navigation. The world population soared again as food varieties were exchanged across the oceans, such as wheat from the Old World to the Americas and maize from the Americas to the Old World, permitting a vast increase in food production and populations. By 1800, the population stood at 990 million. The Industrial Age decisively intensified global interconnections—by rail, ocean steamer, automobile, aviation, telegraph, telephone, satellite, and eventually the Internet and the global population soared. For the first time in human history, there were truly hegemonic political powers with sway over much of the globe: first the British Empire and then, after World War II, the United States. With the transition to the Digital Age, global power is shifting again, and the intensity of global interactions continues to rise, this time with pervasive, real-time flows of data across the planet.

In this sense, the ages of globalization both explain and are explained by the rising scale of global interactions. Each boost in global scale has given rise to new technologies that have expanded populations and production. Each boost of scale, in turn, has changed the nature of governance and geopolitics. We are now reckoning, however, with a phenomenon unique to our time. In 2020, with the population now at 7.7 billion and rising by 75–80 million each year, and with output now at around $17,000 per person on average (measured at purchasing-power-adjusted prices), the sheer scale of human activity is dangerously impinging on fundamental environmental processes: climate, water, air, soils, and biodiversity. We have reached a scale

11

at which human activities taken as a whole are dangerously changing the climate, biodiversity, and other Earth systems such as the water and nitrogen cycles. We take up that theme later in the book.

While scale is crucial for productivity and innovation, geography is often decisive in determining scale. The scale of an economy, or a group of interconnected economies, depends on the ability to trade, and therefore on the geographic conditions for the movement of goods, people, and ideas. Places that are remote or isolated will not benefit as much from trade and the diffusion of ideas and technologies as places that are more accessible. The Americas, for example, lagged far behind the Old World in technological advances until the two hemispheres, separated for ten thousand years, were reconnected by ocean-based transport after 1500. Remote mountainous societies and small island societies far from the mainland and from shipping lanes typically lag technologically behind more coastal and therefore accessible regions. Eurasia long had vast geographical advantages over the Americas, Africa, and Oceania in achieving scale—through more connected trade, easier communications, and shared ecological niches that facilitated the diffusion of technologies, institutions, and cultural practices.

Malthusian Pessimism

The basic history described so far seems to be one of unfolding progress, albeit progress repeatedly marked by injustice, inequalities, and extraordinary violence. Yet there have long been powerful voices of caution regarding the sustainability of progress. The most influential pessimist in modern economic thinking has no doubt been Thomas Robert Malthus, an English pastor writing in the late eighteenth and early nineteenth centuries. Malthus famously warned against trying to improve the lot of the poor, and even against the chances for long-term economic progress. He argued that following any rise in productivity, the world would simply end up with more poor people, but with no long-term solution to poverty. Malthus's provocative pessimism became known as the Malthusian curse. He raised the fundamental question as to whether long-term gains in living standards can be sustained.

Here is Malthus's reasoning. Suppose that farmers learned to double their output. It would seem that everybody could eat twice as much, and that hunger and poverty would plummet. But what if the population were to increase as a result, as more children survived to adulthood and more young people could afford to start families? If the population doubled while the farmland remained unchanged, the amount of food per person would be back where it started. And if the population were to more than double—that is, if the population were to overshoot—then living standards could actually fall below the starting point, until new bouts of hunger and disease reversed the overshooting.

Malthus made a provocative and important point, but fortunately for us, his conclusions were far too pessimistic. When living standards began to rise globally in the nineteenth and twentieth centuries, and as more people moved to cities, families chose to have fewer children and to invest more in the education, nutrition, and health care of each child. They shifted, in the jargon of demography, from "quantity" to "quality" of child-rearing. As living standards, literacy, and urbanization have risen worldwide, fertility rates have declined in most parts of the world to "replacement rate," two children per mother, or below.[6] As a result, productivity improvements are not being offset by rising populations. There are still a few regions with very high fertility rates—notably in sub-Saharan Africa—and as a result, living standards are not yet rising at the rates needed to end poverty in those places. The expectation is that with more urbanization and longer years of schooling, especially for girls, fertility rates will decline in those places as well.

Yet Malthus's pessimism is still all too relevant for us today; we have not yet *fully* disproved his warnings. With nearly 8 billion people on the planet, and with population projected to rise to around 9.7 billion by 2050, and the massive environmental dangers ahead—climate change, loss of biodiversity, mega-pollution—we have not yet shown that we can *sustain* the progress to date. To do so will require not only stabilizing the global population but also ending the massive environmental harms we are now causing. We must still make the transitions to renewable energy, sustainable agriculture, and a circular economy that safely recycles its wastes. Until those transitions are accomplished, Malthus's specter will continue to loom large.

13

The Gradual Transformation to Urban Life

Across the ages of globalization, we have seen not only an increase in scale—of the human population, of economic production, and of politics—but also a decisive shift from rural to urban life. It is only in recent decades that a significant proportion of humanity has resided in cities and engaged in nonagricultural activities. To understand this change, we should examine in more detail the structure of an economy.

Economic activities are usefully categorized into three productive sectors, called the primary, secondary, and tertiary sectors. The primary sector includes the production of food and feed crops, animal products, other agriculture (such as cotton, timber, fish, and vegetable oils), and mining products (such as coal, oil, copper, tin, and precious metals). The secondary sector, or industrial sector, involves the transformation of primary commodities into final products (such as buildings, machinery, processed foods, and electric power). The tertiary sector involves services that support productive activities (freight transport, warehousing, and finance), individual wellbeing (education, health, leisure), and governance (military, public administration, and courts).

The primary sector requires large inputs of land and marine resources per worker and therefore takes place mainly in rural areas, where population densities are relatively low. Tertiary, or service production, on the other hand, requires extensive face-to-face interactions and therefore takes places mainly in urban areas, where population densities are high. Industrial production can be located both in rural areas (in the case, say, of a smelting operation close to a mine) and in urban areas (in the case, say, of a construction site or a garment factory close to customers).

The production of goods (in the primary and secondary sectors) and of services (in the tertiary sector) uses both human effort and machines. The human effort can be mainly physical, as in weeding a field by hand or clearing a forest, or cognitive—for example, a medical doctor diagnosing a disease or a judge deciding a case. Generally, physical labor requires good health, youthful vigor, and adequate nourishment, while cognitive labor also requires formal schooling, training, mentorship, and experience.

Over time, humanity has built more and more powerful machines to substitute for human brawn. In ancient societies, almost all production was achieved through human physical labor aided by a small range of tools such as flints, awls, bows and arrows, containers, and hammers. Transport was accomplished by carrying goods from one place to another. Communication was by word of mouth. Today, machines have replaced physical labor in most arduous activities, and work is increasingly cognitive, based on human thought. Smart machines will substitute for that kind of work, as well, in the coming decades.

Economists have identified a basic recurring pattern of change among the three sectors. In the Paleolithic Age, before the advent of agriculture, all humans were part of the primary sector. Productive activity involved hunting and gathering. The industrial sector occupied a tiny proportion of activities: making tools and weapons, building shelters, sewing clothing, preparing food. Services were performed within the household or shared within clans. In the Neolithic Age, with the advent of agriculture, around 90 percent of humans remained engaged in the primary sector, with up to 10 percent engaged in industry (construction, metallurgy) and services (religion, public administration). Indeed, for most of human history, the primary sector occupied 80 percent or more of human activity, with the rest divided between industry and services.

With the advent of scientific farming beginning in the eighteenth century (including early mechanization and scientific knowledge about soil nutrients), the proportion of employment in the primary sector began to decline. The reason is simple. Society must devote enough labor effort to feed the population. When agriculture is rudimentary, each household feeds itself with almost no surplus for nonfarm households. Almost every household must therefore engage in agriculture to provide the food needed for survival. When agriculture is modernized and yields per farmer rise, one household can feed itself and many others. In the United States today, one farmer can feed around seventy families, so that employment in agriculture accounts for just 1.4 percent of the workforce.

The global result is the time pattern illustrated in figure 1.4, which uses very approximate numbers to illustrate the key points. In the Paleolithic Age, all work—hunting and gathering—was in the primary sector. Today, primary employment (agricultural and mining) is around 28 percent of worldwide employment, and secondary employment is now around 22 percent, while tertiary (service) employment is now around 50 percent of total employment. In the future, both the primary and secondary sector shares

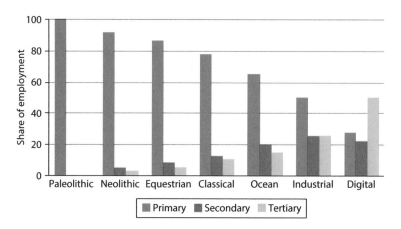

Seven Ages of Globalization

1.4 Estimate of Employment Shares by Major Sector in the Seven Ages of Globalization

will continue to decline as jobs continue to shift toward services. In the United States, the shift from primary to tertiary employment is much further along. U.S. primary-sector employment is now a mere 2 percent of the total, with industry (construction and manufacturing) accounting for only 13 percent and services accounting for 85 percent of all jobs![7] In the course of the twenty-first century, global employment will continue to shift relentlessly to the service economy as machines increasingly take over the tasks of agriculture, mining, construction, and manufacturing.

The Interplay of Geography, Technology, and Institutions

The economic system of any time and place rests on three foundations: geography, technology, and institutions. The three are, of course, mutually dependent. Consider the coal-burning steam engine, the most important invention of the Industrial Age. The steam engine offered a brilliant new way to create motive force in factories and transport, leading to industrialization and eventually to a vast increase in productivity and living standards (while displacing and even impoverishing many people in the short term).

The invention of the steam engine in eighteenth-century Britain depended on geography—specifically, the presence of coal in England that could be mined and transported at low cost. Its invention and deployment also depended on Britain's economic institutions. The inventor of the modern steam engine, James Watt, was out to make a profit, and he expected to do so in part because Britain offered legal protection for intellectual ideas and a market to sell the product. Watt patented his invention and successfully defended his patents from those who tried to cash in on his invention. Moreover, industrialists purchased and deployed Watt's steam engines because they could readily establish their own companies under British law.

Economists have long debated whether economic wellbeing and progress are the results of geography, technology, or institutions. Some have argued vociferously that institutions are the key: without patents, there would have been no steam engine. Some have argued that technologies are the key: without Watt's ingenuity and skill as a craftsman, there would have been no patent and no industrial revolution. Others have that geography is decisive: without the physical accessibility of coal, Watt's ingenuity would have been theoretical at best.

Clearly this debate is misguided. The industrial revolution emerged as a result of the *interaction* of geography, technology, and institutions. That complex interaction, indeed, is why the industrial revolution was such an extraordinary event. Many factors had to combine to produce the breakthrough of the commercially successful steam engine. To understand the dynamics of change, we need to think interactively among the three pillars of geography, technology, and institutions, as illustrated in figure 1.5. These three domains are interdependent; we cannot understand economic history and economic change without taking all three into account.

Let us look at some of the detailed dimensions of geography, technology, and institutions. Geography involves at least six major factors. The first is climate, meaning the year-round typical patterns of temperature and rainfall that shape the kinds of crops that can be produced, the kinds of farm animals that can be raised, and the suitability for human work and habitation. The second is biodiversity, including the presence or absence of particular species of plants and animals. The third is patterns of disease incidence, transmission, and prevalence, which are shaped by climate, biodiversity, human population densities, and the accidents of evolution

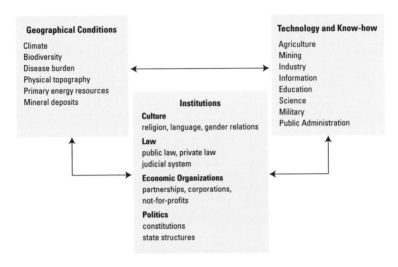

1.5 Geography, Technology & Institutions

and history. The fourth is physical topography and proximity to coasts, rivers, and mountain passes. The fifth is primary energy resource availability. The sixth is deposits of copper, iron, tin, gold, and other minerals.

These geographical factors must be considered in light of existing technologies. An economy depends both on its physical resource base and on the know-how to use those natural resources. Since each age of globalization has been characterized by advances in know-how, the implications of geography have changed along with the advances of knowledge. The great grasslands of the steppe region meant a lot more after the domestication of the horse than before. The presence of coal and oil reserves meant a lot more after the invention of the steam engine and the internal combustion engine, respectively. The intense sunshine of the deserts will mean a lot more in the future with the deployment of low-cost photovoltaic energy.

Such examples run deep throughout the human experience. The control of fire enabled early humans to move to colder biomes; the multisite invention of agriculture enabled dense human settlements in alluvial plains; the domesticated horse expanded the zones of agriculture; Columbus's voyages of discovery ultimately led to massive European migrations to the Americas; the Suez and Panama canals deeply altered the costs and patterns of global trade and, with global warming, new trade routes in the Arctic Sea may do the same; the British mass production of quinine to control malaria enabled the European conquest of tropical Africa; the railroad opened up the interiors of continents for food production and trade. The economic importance of geography is therefore constantly reshaped by changing knowledge and technologies.

We should keep in mind that the Earth's physical geography is itself subject to long-term change, and indeed that humanity is dangerously changing the Earth's physical geography in the twenty-first century. Human evolution and the ages of globalization have been fundamentally reshaped by natural changes in the Earth's physical geography. The end of the last ice age, paced by changes in the Earth's orbital characteristics, opened the way for agriculture, sedentism, and civilization itself, while raising sea levels and thereby submerging the Beringian land bridge between Asia and the Americas. The drying of the African Sahel during 5000–3000 BCE created the vast Sahara and perhaps caused the densification of human settlements along the Nile that gave rise to pharaonic Egypt. The little ice age in Europe in the 1600s, possibly the result of the steep decline in the indigenous populations of the Americas in the sixteenth century that led to reforestation and a reduction of atmospheric carbon dioxide, may have helped to spur Europe's Thirty Years' War and other political upheavals.[8] Other examples of environmental changes and their impacts on human society include the depletion of soil nutrients by overexploiting farmlands; the spread of pathogens into new populations; the human-driven extinctions of plant and animal species (such as the horse in the Americas); and siltation and other changes in the flow of rivers and the location of natural harbors.

Social institutions, the third fundamental driver of societal change, include the range of cultural, legal, organizational, and political rules of daily life. Cultural practices include religious observance, use of languages, adherence to philosophical ideas, and patterns of gender relations. Legal practices include commercial law (for establishing businesses and entering into contracts), private law (for marriage and inheritance), public law (for public administration), and systems for adjudicating conflicts and enforcing the laws. Economic organizations include business partnerships, corporations, and not-for-profit associations. Political rules, such as a constitution, define the organization of state power, backed by the state's "monopoly of the legitimate use of physical force," to use Max Weber's terminology. Institutional innovations are of course essential determinants of human history. Like technological innovations, they flow across the globe, carried by migrants, conquering armies, and scholars, diplomats, travelers, and even spies reporting on developments in other parts of the world.

The Favorable Geographies

Unfair as it is, certain parts of the world have been more favorable for economic development than others throughout most ages of globalization. Eurasia has been advantaged relative to Africa, the Americas, and Oceania. Temperate climate zones have been favored relative to other climates. Coastal regions have been favored relative to hinterlands (in the interior of continents). Places with accessible primary energy resources have also been advantaged. Let us consider these advantages in turn.

○ ○ ○

The Advantages of Eurasia

The Eurasian landmass, combining Europe and Asia, makes up 43 percent of the world's land area, not including Antarctica, and is currently home to around 70 percent of the world's population. For the past two millennia, it has consistently been home to around 80 percent of humanity, falling below 75 percent only around 1980. Throughout most of history, until the rise of the United States in the late nineteenth century, Eurasia consistently led the world in technological innovations and economic activity. As shown in figure 1.6, using the production estimates of Angus Maddison, Eurasia accounted for around 90 percent of world output during the long period from 1 CE to 1820.[9] With the industrialization of the United States after 1820, Eurasia's share of world production declined to around 58 percent as of 1950, then rose again with the post–World War II growth of East Asia and South Asia, reaching around 67 percent in 2008, the last year of Maddison's data.

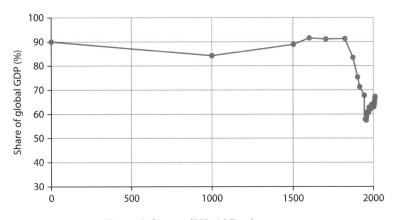

1.6 Eurasia's Share of World Product, 1 CE to 2008

Source: Angus Maddison. "Statistics on World Population, GDP and Per Capita GDP, 1-2008 AD." *Historical Statistics* 3 (2010): 1–36.

During most of human history until very recently, the rest of the world—the Americas, Africa, and Oceania—were generally far behind the leaders of Europe and Asia in the deployment of technologies and economic development. Once the sea level rose at the end of the last ice age, the Americas and Eurasia were separated for around ten thousand years, until Columbus's voyages. As of 1000 CE, Eurasia had 77 percent of the world's population, while the population of the Americas amounted to a mere 8 percent, far too small and dispersed to develop technologies at anywhere near the pace of Eurasia. Africa's population was a mere 14 percent of the world total, and while northern Africa and the Horn of Africa were actively linked with Eurasia, sub-Saharan Africa was effectively cut off by the vast desert, not to mention ecological barriers such as endemic malaria and trypanosomiasis (sleeping sickness that afflicts livestock, as well as people). Oceania, too, was cut off from Eurasia, with a population under 1 percent of the world total.

The United States is the exception that proves the Eurasian rule. Today, it is the world's richest economy, but for most of human history, North America was poor and sparsely settled. North America has unparalleled geographical bounties: a temperate climate, vast and fertile lands, navigable rivers, a vast coastline, and enormous mineral and energy resources. Yet without the benefit of Old World technologies—horsepower, metallurgy,

21

wheat cultivation, writing systems, science and mathematics, and more—economic development stopped at hunting, gathering, and a bit of agriculture. After Columbus's voyages, North America was increasingly settled by European colonists, who inflicted horrific violence on the native populations in the process of spreading across the continent. By the late nineteenth century, the United States had become the world's richest economy, in line with its geographic bounty. The gains were entirely appropriated by the European settlers and their descendants.

The Advantages of the Temperate Climate

According to the very useful Köppen-Geiger climate system, the world's climates are categorized into six main zones: tropical, dry, temperate, cold, highland, and polar. The tropical zones are hot year-round, with adequate rainfall for farming; the dry regions are dry all year long, resulting in deserts or grasslands suitable for livestock rearing, but not for much crop production (except in irrigated river valleys); the temperate zones have winters and summers, with adequate rainfall for crop production; the cold regions have long, cold winters; the highlands and polar regions are sparsely populated, at high elevations or high latitudes (near the North and South poles).

These climate zones are shown in figure 1.7. Let us start at the equator, in the tropics (shown in red and pink), and move poleward (toward the North Pole in the northern hemisphere and the South Pole in the southern hemisphere). We first pass through the dry zones (yellow and beige), then through the temperate zones (shown in green), then through the cold zones (shown in blue), and finally to the polar zones (shown in gray). The highland (or mountainous) regions are shown in darker gray.

The temperate zones, in green, have long enjoyed a remarkable advantage in economic development compared with the other climate zones. With a mix of summers and winters, and adequate year-round levels of precipitation, the temperate zones at midlatitudes have been the preeminent regions for grain production (wheat, maize, rice) and mixed farm systems (combining food crops and farm animals). The temperate climate is hospitable to horses and other beasts of burden, such as donkeys and oxen. The winter season breaks the transmission of many vector-borne diseases, such as malaria. Most of Eurasia's population has always been concentrated

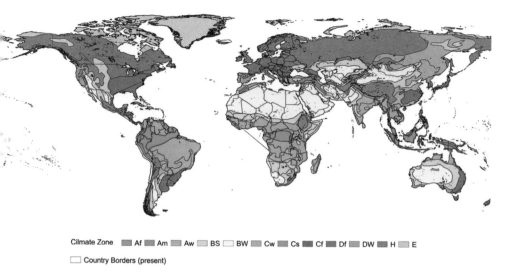

Cilmate Zone ▨ Af ▨ Am ▨ Aw ▨ BS ☐ BW ▨ Cw ▨ Cs ▨ Cf ▨ Df ▨ DW ▨ H ▨ E

☐ Country Borders (present)

1.7 The Köppen-Geiger Climate Classification System

in the temperate climate zones, notably in eastern China, northern India, and western Europe.

The Cw temperate monsoon climate deserves special mention. The monsoon climate, covering much of south, southeast, and east Asia, is characterized by the wettest months of summer bringing more than ten times the rainfall of the driest months of winter. The monsoon rains are the lifeblood of Asia's highly productive rice-growing agriculture, which in turn feeds much of humanity. It is because of the temperate-zone monsoons of Asia that Southern, Southeastern, and Eastern Asia are home to 55 percent of the world's population in 2020.

Tropical climates are home to rain forests and savannas, the ancestral homes of humanity in Africa. Yet the very high year-round temperatures give rise to many great difficulties for long-term economic development. These include the difficulties of heavy physical labor at high temperatures; the year-round transmission of vector-borne diseases in humans, such as malaria, and in farm animals, such as trypanosomiasis; and the rapid proliferation of pathogens in food and water. Moreover, many tropical soils are easily depleted of their nutrients as soil organic matter decomposes very quickly. Throughout history, these tropical disadvantages weighed particularly heavily on Africa, which lies mostly in the tropics.

The dry climate zones are too dry for most crop production except with irrigation, or the production of short-season, low-yield crops such as sorghum and millet. Population densities are therefore typically low with the exception of river valleys like the Nile, the Tigris, and the Indus, where the rivers enable irrigation and also replenish the soil nutrients with alluvium. Most dryland agriculture other than in the river valleys is based on animal herding in the wetter part of the drylands, called steppes or grasslands. The Eurasian steppes were home to the wild horse and were the original sites of horse domestication. Before the Industrial Age, the steppes were for millennia the vast east-west "highway" for horse-based transport and communication, known today as the Silk Road (a name given to these ancient trade routes in the nineteenth century).

The cold zones have growing seasons that are too short and too cold to support high-yield crop production, other than some wheat-growing areas in the more hospitable parts of the cold zones, such as in Canada and Russia. As with the dry climates, population densities tend to be low. Other agriculture includes logging, trapping animals for furs, fishing, and reindeer herding.

Mountain zones are distinctive because of their very high transport costs and often difficult terrain for crop production because of their alpine climates and steep slopes, though specialty crops such as coffee and tea often thrive in such high-elevation zones. More favorably, mountainous regions are often rich in minerals, and societies in mountain regions often have a decisive advantage in defending themselves against attackers from the lowlands. The typical outcomes are a low population density, cultures that are quite distinct from those of lowland populations, many distinct languages or dialects within a small geographic area, fierce traditions of independence, high attractions for mining, and in the twentieth century, high suitability for low-cost hydroelectric power, as in Switzerland.

Population density is a useful shorthand indicator of the relative agricultural productivity of the different climate zones. Favorable climates support more people per square kilometer than harsh climates. Let us consider, therefore, Eurasia's population distribution by climate zone at four dates: 3000 BCE, 100 CE, 1400, and 2015, as shown in table 1.2. These four dates have been chosen to represent the end of the Neolithic Age, the

Table 1.2 Population Distribution of Eurasia by Climate Zone

	Density (persons per km²)			
Year Zone	3000 BCE	100 CE	1400	2015
A	1	4	11	243
B	1	2	3	66
C	2	10	17	252
D	0	1	1	29
E + H	0	2	2	33
Total	1	3	5	94

Source: Author's calculations using HYDE and CIESIN data. See data appendix for details.

high Classical Age of the Roman and Han empires, the world just before Columbus, and the modern era. In each period, the population density of the temperate regions (C climate) was by far the highest, followed by the tropical regions (A climate), the dry regions (B climate), the highlands and polar regions (E + H climates), and finally the cold regions (D climate) with their low crop yields and frigid winters. Even as Eurasia's overall population density rose more than a hundredfold between 3000 BCE and 2015 CE, from one person per km² to 94 persons per km², the relative ranking of density by climate zone remained the same.

The Advantages of Proximity to Coasts and Rivers

Economic prosperity depends on trade, because no place can produce on its own the range of goods and services needed for wellbeing. Yet the feasibility of trade depends on low transport costs. To move bulk freight, transport by water has long been by far the lowest cost method. Even in ancient times, grains were shipped across the Mediterranean to feed and provision the Roman Empire. Overland transport is far more expensive, taking into account the cost of not only the transport itself (horses, cars, trucks, rail), but also the necessary infrastructure (roads, rail lines) and security along the route.

Regions along navigable waterways, including rivers, lakes, and oceans, have therefore long been favored in economic development. Living far from waterways has always been a huge disadvantage and living in the high mountains in the interior of continents has been nearly a sure obstacle to economic development. (The highland civilizations of the Americas are a partial exception to this rule.) Adam Smith, in his *Wealth of Nations*, famously put it this way:

> As by means of water-carriage a more extensive market is opened to every sort of industry than what land-carriage alone can afford it, so it is upon the sea-coast, and along the banks of navigable rivers, that industry of every kind naturally begins to subdivide and improve itself, and it is frequently not till a long time after that those improvements extend themselves to the inland parts of the country.[10]

There is another crucial advantage to settlements in river valleys: agricultural productivity. Rivers provide fresh water for irrigation, and in traditional riverine farm systems, such as along the Nile, the Tigris, and the Euphrates, annual flooding replenished soil nutrients thanks to the fine-grained sediments carried by the river flow from the mountains to the river valleys. The earliest states were formed along riverways, with the dual benefits of low-cost transport and high food production. In 3000 BCE, for example, around 30 percent of the Eurasian population lived within twenty kilometers of a river, though the river valleys constituted only around 18 percent of Eurasia's land area. Put another way, the population density near rivers was roughly twice the density farther from rivers.

Indeed, from ancient times until today, most of the world's major settlements and cities have been built along riverways or ocean coasts. Riverine cities have been the centers of agriculture, and coastal cities have been the centers of industry, trade, and innovation and the hubs of global networks of knowledge and culture. As of 2015, around 38 percent of the world's population lives within 100km of the oceans and 28 percent live within 20km of rivers, though the land area near the coasts is only around 20 percent of the total, and the land around rivers is only around 16 percent of the total. Throughout the course of civilization, back to at least 3000 BCE, roughly 30 percent of the world's population has lived near the oceans and another 30 percent or so has lived near rivers.[11]

The continents differ markedly in their coastal proximity and the extent of their river basins. In this respect, Europe is especially blessed: 51 percent of Europe's land area is within one hundred kilometers of the oceans, and 25 percent of Europe's land area is within twenty kilometers of a river. Around 80 percent of Europe's population lives near a waterway (2015 data), either a coast or a river. Europe has had the advantage of a temperate climate and a great proximity to water-based trade. On the other hand, only around 16 percent of today's Commonwealth of Independent States (CIS), essentially the former Russian Empire, is within one hundred kilometers of the oceans, and around 19 percent within twenty kilometers of a river. Only 14 percent of the CIS population lives near the oceans, while 39 percent live near a river, roughly half in total. The CIS is northern, cold, and far from ocean sea routes. The rivers and overland routes, rather than the oceans, have been Russia's pathways of trade. These characteristics have long defined Russia's history. In Asia, around 40 percent of the population lives near the coasts and another 30 percent near rivers, in between the high coastal proximity of Europe and the low coastal proximity of the CIS.

The Advantages of Primary Energy Reserves

Economic development is limited by the availability of energy for work, including for industry (e.g., metallurgy), farm production (e.g., plowing), transport, and communications. Primary energy resources include biomass, fossil fuels (coal, oil, and natural gas), wind, water, solar, geothermal, nuclear (uranium), and ocean power. The ability to tap them, of course, depends on technological know-how. For most of history, energy depended on animal power and hard human labor, and therefore ultimately on the supply of foods for human beings and feed grains for beasts of burden. The great Eurasian empires that conquered on horseback did so, ultimately, based on the solar energy captured by the vast grasslands that fed the hundreds of thousands of horses in the conquering cavalries.

From ancient times, such energy was abetted by wind power for sails and windmills and waterpower to turn waterwheels. From the steam engine onward, fossil fuels came to economic preeminence in the nineteenth and twentieth centuries. Those places lucky enough to have economically accessible coal tended to industrialize well before those that did not. In the twenty-first century, we will have to turn to zero-carbon energy—wind, solar, hydro, geothermal, and ocean—to avoid the great risks of human-induced global warming caused by the fossil fuels, and geographical advantages will shift once again. We will also depend on great advances in technological know-how, such as utilizing solar energy through photovoltaics.

Geopolitics and Globalization

Since the great dispersal from Africa, and surely before that within Africa, human groups have battled each other for territory and to secure their basic survival needs (including water, food supplies, shelter, and minerals). Indeed, human nature was forged in the cauldron of territorial competition, which instilled in our genes and our cultures a remarkable capacity to cooperate within a group, combined with a deeply rooted tendency toward conflict and distrust between groups (according to race, religion, language, national origin, and other markers of identity).

Since at least the second millennium BCE, globalization has involved intense geopolitical, economic, and military competition among rival empires. The first great Western historian, Herodotus, described the competition between the Greek city-states and the Persian Empire. Since then, globalization has entailed the rise and fall of competing empires: Assyria, Macedonia under Alexander the Great, the Hellenistic empires, Rome, Persia, Chinese dynasties, Indian empires, Arab caliphates, the European empires, the Soviet Union, the United States. Since around 1600, the European empires increasingly gained sway over other parts of the world, and during the Industrial Age, Britain and the United States became global hegemons.

One of the crucial links among geography, technology, and institutions is the interplay of military technology with physical geography and political institutions.[12] The ages of globalization are marked by technological innovations in the areas of transport, communications, energy, food production, public health, construction, and others that typically have included significant changes in military technologies and relative power. The innovators have often gained a decisive, albeit temporary, advantage in military force, which led to upheavals of global power through military conquest. Typically, the innovations would sooner or later diffuse to the adversaries, often causing a decisive reversal of fortunes of the conquerors and the conquered.

Of course, military technology is multidimensional and highly complex, involving offense and defense; land, air, and sea; light, heavy, and now nuclear weapons; tactics, logistics, transport, communications, deception, psychological warfare, and much more. We will have occasion to mention some of the key military breakthroughs that helped launch new ages of globalization. The horse-drawn chariot enabled Mesopotamian cities to become states and Egyptian kingdoms to unify and control Upper and Lower Egypt. The Greek and Roman massed infantry, the phalanx, supported by the cavalry, achieved major victories in land battles. The Macedonian phalanx was empowered by the innovation of the sarissa, the long spear, giving Alexander a decisive advantage in his Asian conquests. Greek and Roman oar-powered galleys were effective battering rams against opposing navies. The steppe-region archers sweeping in on horseback landed decisive blows on opposing infantries.

China's invention of gunpowder gave rise, centuries later, to the musket and other firearms that, in turn, decisively ended the advantages of the archers. The cannon artillery enabled by gunpowder helped to account for the spectacular successes of the Ottoman, Mongol, and Timurid empires. When the Atlantic powers, including the Spanish, Portuguese, Dutch, and English, successfully added cannon power to their ocean vessels, they were able to dominate the Indian Ocean trade routes. Britain's early industrialization tremendously spurred its military power, through a steam-powered navy, mass-produced firearms and heavy artillery, machine guns, logistics and transport supported by rail and telegraph, and in the early twentieth century, armored personnel carriers and tanks. The invention of powered flight in the first decade of the twentieth century led to bombardments by plane as early as 1912 in the first Balkan War, and then at a much greater scale in World War I. World War II introduced ballistic missiles and the atomic bomb in 1945.

A constant theme of history is that major changes in military technologies almost inevitably lead to deep changes in political institutions, as well. Larger empires, for example, facilitated by a new military advantage, often have led to new forms of political control in order to govern a larger population and territory. Weapons systems that require vast state outlays have given advantages to larger states over smaller states. Some military innovations, by contrast, are cost-saving, thereby giving a relative boost to smaller and poorer nations.

In the early twenty-first century, we are again entering into a new geopolitical era; power is becoming more diffused, most notably with Asia joining Western Europe and the United States in technological, economic, and military preeminence. China, India, North Korea, and Pakistan are nuclear powers. The new age of digital technologies is abetting the global shift in power relations generally, but also through the advent of new forms of cyberwarfare.

What is notable about geopolitics is how rapid global change can be. Empires rise and fall with stunning speed. In 1914, Britain still ruled the world. By 1960, Britain's empire had essentially vanished and the Soviet Union seemed to challenge the United States for hegemonic leadership. By December 1991, the Soviet Union too had vanished from the map. In our own time, the rise of China, the rapid growth of India, and the soaring population of Africa all portend a remarkably different world in the twenty-first century. Bob Dylan's lyrics certainly ring true:

> For the loser now
> Will be later to win
> For the times they are a-changin'.

Looking Back to See Forward

Many of these decisive changes were ushered in by technological changes that produced new inequalities of power that, in turn, led to new wars. This is a reality of globalization that must be fundamental to our investigation. Yet we cannot afford another global war. Our technologies today mean that another such war could be the end of our species.

We may refer to the wise words of President John F. Kennedy, who defined our modern existential reality in his 1961 inaugural address: "The world is very different now, for man holds in his mortal hands the power to abolish all forms of human poverty and all forms of human life." That is our own truth about globalization. We cannot afford to have the kinds of disruptions that we had in the past, lest we lose everything.

With that in mind, I want us to consider three great issues for our time as we use our backward gaze at history to gain insights for the future. First, can the world choose a path of shared prosperity, social inclusion, and environmental sustainability in this seventh age of globalization? We can call this the challenge of sustainable development. Second, how should our global governance be organized if, as seems likely, the Anglo-American age has ended and we are now in a truly multipolar world? We can call this the challenge of multilateral governance. Third, is global peace possible, and if so, on what model of human understanding and ethics could this be accomplished? We can call this the challenge of universal values.

The successive ages of globalization have expanded our outlook and our interdependence. We have learned to think globally. By understanding our common history, and our common vulnerability, we can also grasp our common interests and values. In that way, we can also find a path to shared prosperity and peace.

2

The Paleolithic Age

(70,000–10,000 BCE)

Our species, *Homo sapiens*, traces its evolutionary past to around 6 million years ago in Africa, when our ancestral line of great apes diverged into two branches, one that would evolve into modern humans and the other that would evolve into modern chimpanzees and bonobos. The human genus *Homo* emerged around 4 million years ago, when humanity's biological ancestors began to walk on two feet. The first great dispersal of hominins from Africa occurred around 2 million years ago, or even earlier, when an early *Homo* species left Africa for Europe and Asia. Premodern *Homo* species, including Neanderthals, Denisovans, and others, evolved in Asia and Europe before the arrival of anatomically modern humans. The remains of hominin hunters using stone tools hundreds of thousands of years ago have been found throughout Europe and Asia. This was truly the first globalization, but not by anatomically modern humans.

The great evolutionary advance of the genus *Homo* involved a massive increase in brain capacity, notably in the frontal cortex used for cognition. This evolutionary process, called encephalization, may have occurred as an early *Homo* species learned improved ways to hunt game and cook meat, giving a boost of concentrated energy that could support larger brains with greatly increased cognitive power. Hominin brains are voracious users of energy, not too different from the energy-intensive data centers of the big-tech companies. The brains of anatomically modern humans, or *Homo sapiens*, are around 2 percent of our body mass, but consume around 20 percent of our metabolic energy.

The best evidence suggests that *Homo sapiens* emerged first on the African savannah around two hundred thousand years ago, the start of a period known as the Middle Paleolithic, though we must emphasize that genetic and fossil discoveries continue to alter the estimated chronology.[1] According to the evolutionary biologist E. O. Wilson, the fundamental characteristics of human nature—including our capacity to cooperate within groups, which he terms *eusociality*, and our decidedly aggressive attitudes toward out-groups—evolved on the African savannah as a result of intergroup competition over territory and the resulting group-level natural selection between competing groups of *Homo sapiens*. The Paleolithic humans lived in small foraging bands of perhaps twenty-five to thirty members, with seasonally shifting base camps organized around the campfire.[2]

In Wilson's view, natural selection endowed humans with behavioral traits, including language and in-group cooperation, contributing to the defense of the base camp. Like some insect societies, but unlike other great apes, *Homo sapiens* became eusocial, or highly social. At the same time, in-group sociality was matched by aggression toward out-groups. Cooperation within the group was forged by war between groups. Thus, human cooperation, large brain size, more meat consumption, and campsite-based hunting societies coevolved to shape our distinctive human nature.

The First Age of Globalization

According to the most recent evidence, *Homo sapiens* may have begun to migrate from Africa as early as 180,000 years ago, or perhaps even earlier, reaching sites along the Red Sea and perhaps the Mediterranean coast of modern-day Israel.[3] Yet it appears that these first migrant groups outside of Africa did not survive. A second migration, known as the Great Dispersal from Africa, began fifty thousand to seventy thousand years ago; these groups did survive and continued to migrate and expand around the world. In this great dispersal, humans crossed the Red Sea into Arabia and crossed the narrow land bridge from Egypt to the eastern Mediterranean. From Arabia and the Levant, early humans spread toward Asia

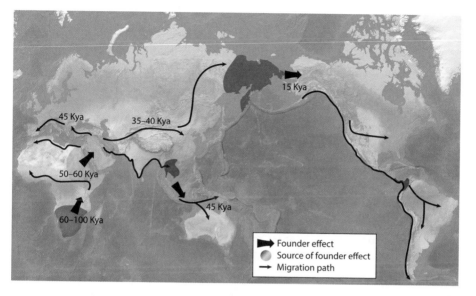

2.1 The Human Dispersal in the Paleolithic Period

Source: Brenna M. Henn, L. L. Cavalli-Sforza, and Marcus W. Feldman.
"The Great Human Expansion." *Proceedings of the National Academy of Sciences* 109, no. 44
(2012): 17758–64. doi:10.1073/pnas.1212380109.

and Europe, arriving in Europe some forty-five thousand years ago. Along the way, they encountered other hominins, the now-extinct Neanderthals and Denisovans.

Figure 2.1 summarizes one recent theory of the Great Dispersal from Africa. It shows the estimated timing of the arrival of the modern human species in the Near East 60-60 Kya (thousand years ago), in Europe and Australasia around 45 Kya, and in the Americas around 15 Kya.[4] The precise dates of the dispersion are still heatedly contested among experts, with geneticists, anthropologists, archeologists, and others all weighing in with the respective evidence and techniques. There are still basic questions as to whether there was one main dispersal or several, whether the descendants of humans who left Africa also returned to Africa in some numbers, and precisely how and where the modern humans met other hominins outside of Africa.

When humanity arrived in Australia around 45 Kya, the newly arrived foragers soon hunted to extinction many of the megafauna—the large animals weighing more than 44 kilograms.[5] Around 85 percent of the continent's large mammals went extinct soon after the arrival of humans, as did a number of birds and reptiles. It is currently debated whether these extinctions were caused solely by overkill by humans or rather by a mix of hunting and climate change. Recent evidence puts the blame largely, if not entirely, on overkill by hunters.[6]

In the Americas, the same thing occurred roughly 33,000 years later. The arrival of foragers across Beringia contributed to the extinction of the woolly mammoth, the mastodon, the Shasta ground sloth, the saber-toothed cat, and most consequentially, the wild horse. In the Americas, it seems likely that overhunting and climate change played a synergistic role in the extinctions. The wild horse and the woolly mammoth were most likely driven to extinction by humans hunting these animals for meat. The extinction of the saber-toothed cat was possibly more indirect, resulting from a decline in the saber-toothed cat's prey caused by human foraging. Other megafauna, including the giant sloth and the mastodon, may have been driven to extinction not by human hunters but by a sudden cold period known at the Younger Dryas that occurred toward the end of the Pleistocene, 12,900 to 11,700 years ago, just on the eve of the Holocene.

The extinction of the wild horse was a devastating blow for the Amerindian populations.[7] It meant that Native Americans would not have the vast benefits of horses for transport and animal traction for the following ten thousand years. The next time the native populations encountered the horse was with the arrival of European conquerors on horseback—but by then, it was too late. The Europeans arrived with an overwhelming advantage in military power, including horsepower, and with Old World pathogens that struck down the natives, enabling small numbers of Europeans to subjugate the far more numerous native populations.

It also seems likely that the arrival of *Homo sapiens* led to the rapid extinction of our closest relatives, the Neanderthals and Denisovans. *Homo sapiens* and Neanderthals coexisted in Europe and Asia for around ten thousand years, roughly forty thousand to fifty thousand years ago. The Neanderthals went extinct around forty thousand years ago, but the precise timing and causes remain a mystery. It seems likely that *Homo sapiens* outcompeted the Neanderthals, either directly in combat over territory or indirectly by achieving greater successes in hunting and gathering food, thereby depriving the Neanderthals of their subsistence—a process known to ecologists as competitive exclusion. Neanderthals had mental abilities and adaptive skills that had enabled them to survive for hundreds of thousands of years. The precise nature of *Homo sapiens'* advantages is uncertain, but they may have included language ability, a greater ability to handle fire, a greater capacity to cooperate, or other traits. Much remains uncertain.

What is now certain, though, is that *Homo sapiens* and Neanderthals interbred. Neanderthal genes entered into the human genome for populations living outside of Africa that encountered the European and Asian Neanderthal populations. Around 2 percent of the genomes of modern Eurasians are inherited from Neanderthals. Similarly, around 5 percent of the genomes of indigenous Australasians are inherited from Denisovans, as are some of the genes of Tibetans, who apparently encountered the Denisovans high on the Tibetan Plateau.[8] Even though only one species of the genus *Homo* remains, *Homo sapiens*, we literally embody our ancestral relatives as well.

Cultural Acceleration

During the last glacial period, known to Earth-system scientists as the Upper Pleistocene, *Homo sapiens* lived in small groups of closely related individuals. The economy was based on hunting and gathering in a nomadic setting. Population densities were inevitably very low, perhaps around one person per square kilometer. During the long haul of that nomadic life, commencing roughly 50,000 years ago, human societies advanced through a combination of biological evolution and cultural evolution.

A great acceleration in human cultural development, according to modern evidence, occurred around this time, the transition from the Middle Paleolithic to the Upper Paleolithic Period. The anthropological evidence suggests the emergence of art, language, and religious practices, or at least a great advance of such cultural practices. A partial list of significant achievements dated to around this time includes campsites and settlements, storage pits, cave paintings and petroglyphs, carvings of figurines, fishing, use of new materials such as bone, more differentiated toolmaking, body decoration, and long-distance exchange of precious objects.

The causes of this revolution in culture remain unknown and contested.[9] Some neuroscientists speculate that the advent of language and other cultural breakthroughs depended on biological changes in human neuroanatomy—in other words, an evolutionary change in the species.[10] Other scientists contest that conclusion, arguing that the Upper Paleolithic revolution was essentially a cultural revolution, not a biological one, and draw an analogy with the later Neolithic revolution of agriculture described in the next chapter. The Neolithic revolution most likely resulted from cultural and ecological factors rather than any biological changes in humans.

Whatever the causes, humanity achieved a measure of "modernity" in the Upper Paleolithic, in terms of language, arts, religion, and other aspects of culture. Human cultures began to flourish. Populations increased, which may have been both a cause and an effect of the cultural changes. Higher population densities may have increased the competitive struggle for survival between competing groups. That intensified competition, in turn, may have accelerated cultural and biological evolution toward within-group cooperation. The cultural breakthroughs, in turn, led to many other advances. Human migrations reached new regions, including farther north in Eurasia and finally across Beringia or along the Pacific coastal waters of Beringia and into North America some fourteen thousand to sixteen thousand years ago.[11]

Language, we can say with some confidence, was the greatest "technological" breakthrough of the Upper Pleistocene. It gave rise to a vastly more complex social life, a societal memory of cultural advances conveyed by word of mouth across generations, and a growing division of labor within society. In short, language provided the basis for high within-group sociality, complex cultures, advances in know-how, and intergenerational transmission of knowledge, all of which have defined our species ever since.

Human Society in the Upper Paleolithic

The contours of human society in the Upper Paleolithic are of great interest to us. Knowing more about these early societies would help us understand our core human nature, before the overlays of sedentism, agriculture, and modern culture. Most of this prehistory is lost in the mist of deep time. Nonetheless, intrepid scholars, using the tools of a variety of disciplines—prehistoric anthropology, archeology, prehistoric linguistics, genetics, and the anthropology of modern foraging societies—have been able to make informed judgments about key features of Upper Paleolithic foraging societies: the size of communities, their internal hierarchical structures, in-group versus out-group behavior, and war and peace.

Burial evidence, genetic analysis of ancient sites, and the patterns of modern foraging societies all suggest a hierarchical structure of the communities. The smallest unit is the band, around fifty people, gathered around the overnight campsite; the next level is the clan, roughly three times the size, or around 150 people; then comes the mega-band, once again roughly three times larger, or around five hundred people; and the highest in-group structure is the tribe, three times larger still, at around 1,500 individuals. Some scholars have suggested that clan sizes of around 150 reflect human cognitive constraints on the size of tight-knit groups. Even today, business teams and tight-knit social networks are generally of this size. The evidence from modern foragers and the ancient genomic record of at least one burial site, Sunghir, Russia, is that clans avoided in-breeding by maintaining wider social and mating networks.[12]

Within these societies, the evidence of modern forager societies suggests an egalitarian social structure. Unlike in other primate species, such as chimpanzees, that have a strong hierarchy of dominant and subordinate males, the structure of human forager societies appears to be essentially egalitarian. Gintis and colleagues suggest two main forces at play: the very strong benefits of cooperation within the clan in hunting, cooking, food-sharing, and child-rearing; and the widely distributed presence of lethal hunting weapons, which members of the clan could use to resist any attempts by individuals to dominate the clan.[13] This egalitarianism from below—the resistance to authority—has been termed a "reverse dominance hierarchy." Leaders were most likely still important, but they apparently had to win their position through persuasion and skills rather than brute force. According to this view, egalitarianism eventually gave way to hierarchical social structures in sedentary societies when the state amassed sufficient power to impose inequalities by force.

As Wilson has emphasized, the strong capacity for in-group cooperation in foraging societies is matched by their potential for extreme violence against out-groups. Forager groups maintain peaceful and cooperative networks across tribes, but revert to extreme violence against out-groups when defending territory. The presence of war is not foreordained but is contextual, readily arising when a group is under threat. In that circumstance, identity politics—belonging to one's group and fighting the other group—is part of humanity's deep human nature.

Some Lessons from the Paleolithic Age

The Paleolithic Age was the formative period for all of human history. It was the period in which human beings spread from Africa to all parts of the world, created the first cultures, invented the use of language, formed clans, and intensified the manipulation of nature, evident in improved hunting, advances in toolmaking, and the invention of the arts. Humans adapted to hugely diverse habitats and climate zones and carried their inventions—both technology and institutions—with them as they migrated. The evidence, albeit limited, is that these early societies were egalitarian rather than hierarchical. Moreover, cooperation extended across networks of foraging tribes, though war would also erupt among competing groups.

This overview of the Paleolithic Age offers some provisional lessons—indeed warnings—for us today. It forces us to abandon the quaint and soothing idea that human beings by our very nature live harmoniously and sustainably with nature, and that only modern capitalism has created environmental crises. Even hunter-gatherers, we now realize, were capable of massive environmental upheavals, to their great subsequent suffering. When humans populated Oceania fifty thousand years ago and the Americas some ten thousand years ago, they drove the large land animals to extinction. They also apparently drove our closest humanity relatives, the Neanderthals, to extinction as well, either through direct conquest or through competitive exclusion, beating the Neanderthals to the scarce resources of food and shelter. We can be our own worst enemy, or at least our cousins' worst enemy. Environmental sustainability and peace across cultures may not come naturally, but must be constructed using our abilities to reason and to look ahead.

3

The Neolithic Age

(10,000–3000 BCE)

The great dispersal from Africa, and migrations of modern humans across the planet, culminated in the birth of permanent settlements in dispersed villages and the so-called Neolithic revolution—the advent of farming around eleven thousand years ago. Initially, a small proportion of humanity took up the permanent cultivation of crops. Over time, more and more of humanity settled in permanent locations for farming, forsaking the nomadic lives of hunters and gatherers. Thus, the Neolithic Age became the age of globalization by farming.

The invention of agriculture in Western Asia was preceded by sedentism, which began roughly 14,500 years ago. The cause was a warming of the climate toward the end of the Pleistocene and the start of the Holocene. The rise in temperature increased the availability of food and enabled communities in the eastern Mediterranean to establish more permanent settlements even before they cultivated crops. Populations also began to increase. This early sedentism was apparently partly reversed with one final cold wave, the Younger Dryas, before the final end of the ice age and the beginning of the Holocene some 11,600 years ago.

Figure 3.1 shows in green the regions where agriculture first emerged, in purple where agriculture emerged a bit later, and in brown, where early agriculture can be biogeographically inferred.[1] What do we know about the rise of agriculture? We know that agriculture was a kind of invention,

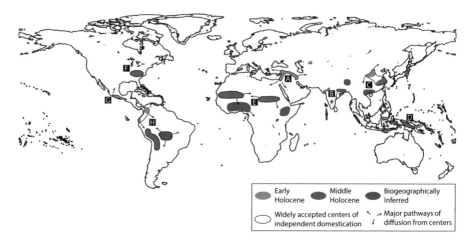

3.1 The Origins of Agriculture

Source: Greger Larson, Dolores R. Piperno, Robin G. Allaby, Michael D. Purugganan,
Leif Andersson, Manuel Arroyo-Kalin, Loukas Barton, *et al.* "Current Perspectives and the
Future of Domestication Studies." *Proceedings of the National Academy of Sciences* 111, no. 17
(2014): 6139-46. doi: 10.1073/pnas.1323964111.

one that occurred independently in several locations across the inhabited world. It involved a process of learning how to plant selectively the seeds of certain wild plant species, mainly grasses, to enable humanity to cultivate crops rather than simply to gather the natural outputs of these plants.

The near-simultaneous birth of agriculture is a striking case of multiple parallel discoveries over the course of a few thousand years, roughly coinciding with the end of the ice age. In the Eurasian context, there were two major early sites. The first was the Fertile Crescent extending from the Egyptian Nile to present-day Iraq, with wheat cultivation most likely beginning in southeastern Turkey. The second was China, in the Yellow and Yangtze river basins, where people began to cultivate millet in the north and rice in the south. In the Americas, agriculture began with the cultivation of maize in today's Mexico and the potato in the highlands of the Andes. Other early sites that followed include the Ganges River basin, the island of Java (now in Indonesia), and several locations in Africa and the Americas.

A puzzling and counterintuitive finding, based on archeological and anthropological evidence, is that hunters and gatherers seem to have had better nutrition, fewer diseases, more varied diets, less strenuous labor, and longer lives than contemporaneous farm households.[2] The evidence includes the larger stature of nomadic populations compared with early agricultural populations, as well as advantages of the nomadic life relative to early farming vis-à-vis disease burden, work effort, and aging. Yet despite these apparent advantages of a nomadic life, settled agriculture ended up winning out. The question is why.

Perhaps the key lies in the demographics of nomadism versus farming. Nomadism supports only a very low population density while farming supports a far larger population per unit area. Farming, after all, replaces natural ecosystems with human-made ecosystems that are engineered to yield far more foodstuffs per unit area. The plant and animal species not cultivated on farms are the sure losers, as humanity encroaches on the habitats of other species that are not directly conducive to food production or that compete directly with food grains and animal husbandry.

With farm villages supporting, say, ten individuals per square kilometer compared with nomadism that supports, say, one individual per square kilometer, it seems clear that farm-based communities would be able to take by force the land once used by nomadic hunters and gatherers. This, of course, is the history around the world, where hunter and gatherer populations (such as the Native Americans of the Great Plains) found themselves forced into smaller and smaller regions by farm communities expanding into the hunter-gatherer territories by force.

Yet the outcome may have been a lowering of average wellbeing in the process, perhaps the one described by the biblical "expulsion from Eden," in which a life of leisurely foraging in the garden was replaced by a life of arduous farm labor. God's punishment to Adam and Eve for eating the fruit of the tree of knowledge is stated: "By the sweat of your brow you shall eat bread, Until you return to the ground, from which you were taken."

If a life of foraging is really better than a life of farm labor, why wouldn't humanity find a path back from agriculture to hunting and gathering? The best guess is that early farm settlements faced a one-way demographic trap. Here is a simple illustration: Suppose that the first generation of farmers got a boost from farming. Instead of eating two thousand calories a day based on four hours a day of hunting and gathering, they enjoyed three thousand calories a day based on four hours of farming, with each farmer cultivating, say, two hectares of land. But then, with a sedentary life and higher caloric intake, fertility rose and infant mortality declined. The population doubled, with each household of the next generation having just one hectare of land. Perhaps the next generation now had to devote six hours daily to eke out 1,800 calories per day on the one hectare—more work for a poorer diet than in hunting and gathering.

Yet there would be no going back to nomadic hunting and gathering according to this example because the local ecosystem cannot support twice the population of hunters and gatherers. The second generation must farm merely to stay alive. The nomadic alternative, albeit superior to farming, would instead become a relic of myth and memory. With the higher population, Eden cannot be regained. Farming indeed helped the first generation but cursed the following generations with greater work effort for less result. And as the sedentary farm populations continued to rise from one generation to the next, the farm communities continued to encroach on the lands used by hunter-gathers.

Yet all was not lost. The densely settled farm villages eventually offered their own novel rewards. Sedentary lives within larger communities set in train new technological discoveries, in metallurgy, the arts, record keeping, ceramics, and eventually writing, first in cuneiform and pictographs and later with alphabets. Sedentary life in this way set off a chain reaction of endogenous growth, producing a gradual expansion of know-how and an accompanying increase in population. After some time, perhaps millennia, the living standards of the settled farm communities eventually outstripped those of the hunter-gatherer groups, and did so with vastly expanded populations. According to the HYDE 3.1 population estimates, Eurasia's population rose from just 2 million people around 10,000 BCE to 15 million in 5000 BCE, 60 million in 2000 BCE, and a remarkable 165 million people as of 1 CE.[3] Sedentary lives produced a bounty of food and other products that supported a hundredfold rise in population over roughly ten thousand years.

After agriculture's first successes, farming spread gradually to other regions. Over many millennia, in a process that has lasted until today, the expansion of farm-based societies squeezed out the places still devoted to hunting and gathering. There is another great debate about farming: did it spread through imitation, or did it spread because migrant populations of farmers displaced the hunter-gatherers?

The answer in Europe seems to be the latter. The provisional evidence suggests that the early agriculturalists from Anatolia arrived as migrants in

Western Europe around 6000 BCE and largely displaced the local populations of hunters and gatherers. This is shown by a genetic analysis of the early farmers found in archeological sites in Europe. Their genes are far more closely linked to those of the early farmers of Anatolia than to the genes of the preceding hunter-gatherer populations in Europe.[4] That displacement might have come by war or by the spread of pathogens from the arriving Anatolians and their farm animals to the hunter-gatherer populations who, not having been raised in the presence of these diseases, would not have acquired immunity to them.

This is not the end of the population story, however. It appears from the genetic record that Europe incurred a second massive upheaval with the arrival of populations on horseback from the Eurasian steppes, beginning around 3000 BCE with the Yamnaya people, who once again seem to have replaced large portions of the indigenous populations they encountered. There is a mystery as to how a small number of pastoralists from the steppes replaced the large number of sedentary farmers they found upon their arrival in Europe. One possibility recently uncovered in the genetic record is that the Yamnaya may have carried *Yersinia pestis*, the plague, with them.[5]

By 3000 BCE, small farm communities were strewn across all of the continents (save Antarctica). The vast majority of lives were lived within the narrow confines of these villages. Technological learning occurred, as did the gradual diffusion of new techniques, such as ceramics, early metallurgy, crop cultivation, domestication of farm animals, and cultural and religious practices. People could move long distances on foot, in horse-drawn carts, or by boat. Yet long-distance trade was still minimal, and the long-distance diffusion of techniques occurred over centuries and millennia, not years or decades.

Diffusion of Agriculture Within Ecological Zones

The diffusion of agricultural know-how is guided strongly by geography because specific crops have distinctive ecological ranges. Crops like wheat can grow only in cool places, not in the tropics. Grains such as rice grow especially well in the subtropics, notably in monsoon environments with plentiful freshwater for flooded fields. Maize, with its C_4 photosynthesis pathway, began as a subtropical grain. Within these ecological niches, technological diffusion occurs through migration of farmers, the spread of crop varieties, and imitation.

The diffusion of early agriculture naturally occurred within ecological zones, according to where specific farm techniques could spread. The largest contiguous zone of shared agriculture potential is the east-west axis of Eurasia, a wheat-growing belt that stretches ten thousand kilometers from the Atlantic coast of Portugal to the Pacific coast of China.

Jared Diamond, one of the great modern explicators of economic history and economic development, has emphasized in his wonderful book *Guns, Germs, and Steel* that Eurasia's long east-west axis facilitated the dissemination of technologies within ecological zones.[6] Wheat, which emerged originally in the Fertile Crescent (in today's Turkey, Iraq, and eastern Mediterranean), diffused west into Europe and east into Asia. Horse domestication, which emerged first in the Pontic-Caspian region (spanning the Black Sea and the Caspian Sea north of the Caucasus), diffused west into Europe and east into China. The Mediterranean basin offered a shared ecology for wheat, olives, vineyards, horses, donkeys, and other farm animals for the Roman, Byzantine, and Ottoman empires and the Muslim caliphates.

The Americas and Africa, by contrast, lie on mostly north-south axes, meaning that technological breakthroughs had a more difficult time disseminating across ecological zones. Consider the case of the llama and alpaca of the high Andes region of South America. These camelids were the only pack animals available to the Amerindians between the extinction of the horse some ten thousand years ago and the arrival of the European conquerors around 1500 CE. Yet they did not diffuse out of the Andes because of their limited ecological extent. Unlike the east-west Eurasian steppes, the Andean highlands could not offer an animal-based highway system for the north-south Americas.

The Early Alluvial Civilizations of Eurasia

Five early agricultural regions in Eurasia made fundamental and lasting contributions to technology, institutions, culture, and governance for all of humanity: ancient Egypt, Mesopotamia, the Indus Valley, the Yellow

River, and the Yangtze River. These early civilizations shared fundamental similarities. All were based on alluvial farming, wherein the rich soils of a river basin were replenished by seasonal flooding that delivered new topsoil and nutrients each year. On the basis of these productive soils, along with the other advantages of the riverine location in terms of transport, irrigation, and defense, the world's first city-states and then empires developed at these sites.[7] In the Americas, similar developments took place along rivers in the Peruvian Andes and in Mesoamerica.

The common features of the Egyptian and Eurasia riverine civilizations are striking. They arose and advanced roughly from 5000 to 3000 BCE. All were based on alluvial farming. In the case of Egypt, the Indus Valley, and the Yellow River, the river runs through a dry climate, making the river indispensable for irrigation. These rivers are dependent on the annual monsoon rains, which themselves are highly variable across seasons and at scales of centuries and millennia. Long-term changes in monsoon patterns paced by changes in the Earth's orbit, have had long-term consequences for the prosperity and decline of riverine civilizations.[8]

Each of the five riverine civilizations of the Old World used domesticated animals for food, transport, and traction. (In the Americas, the Andean civilizations relied on South American camelids, alpacas and llamas, as pack animals, while Mesoamerica lacked any large animals for pack or draft work.) In ancient Egypt, the domesticated donkey was used as early as 5000 BCE as a pack animal for desert transport between the Nile and the Red Sea, while oxen were used as draft animals. In Mesopotamia, between the Tigris and Euphrates rivers, the ancient civilizations of Akkadia and Assyria in the third millennium BCE similarly used donkeys and oxen as beasts of burden. Each of these civilizations used sailboats to navigate the river. All developed methods of irrigation and flood control; they were later termed "hydraulic civilizations" for their advanced technologies of water management.

These civilizations also invented forms of writing that became the precursors of modern scripts. The oldest writing systems in Mesopotamia date from the use of pictographs around 3500 BCE and then the great breakthrough to cuneiform around 2500 BCE. Hieroglyphics in the Nile River valley date from around 3100 BCE, possibly influenced by Sumerian writing or possibly an independent invention. Sumerian cuneiform and Egyptian hieroglyphics likely contributed to the later Phoenician writing system that in turn was adapted to become the Greek alphabet, the world's first alphabet with distinct characters for vowels as well as consonants. Chinese characters date from the second millennium BCE during the Shang Dynasty that controlled parts of the Yellow and Yangtze river valleys. In the Americas, Mayan writing began much later, with the earliest inscriptions dating from around 300 BCE.

The riverine civilizations are striking and vivid cases of the role of physical geography in economic development. The rivers served multiple indispensable purposes: soil replenishment, irrigation and freshwater management, aquatic-based nutrition, transport by ship, and military defense. They allowed astounding growth in the size and density of populations at a remarkably early period of civilization, with civilizations reaching several hundred thousand people in a number of city-states. In turn, the high productivity of agriculture, which supported these large populations, also made possible a sophisticated division of labor, the development of writing systems, the rise of scientific knowledge (mathematics, astronomy, metallurgy, agronomy), and the novelty of governance of large populations.

The Lucky Latitudes

The temperate-zone east-west swath of Eurasia has enjoyed a distinctive role throughout history. Some of Eurasia is desert and almost uninhabited. Some is tundra, frozen throughout the year, with very small populations herding reindeer in the far north. Most of Eurasia's population has lived in a subtropical band of latitude and climate zone that historians including Ian Morris have christened "the lucky latitudes."[9] They are lucky because they have been home to humanity's greatest technological and economic progress. I will define the lucky latitudes as the area from 25 degrees north to 45 degrees north in Eurasia, as shown in figure 3.2.

The lucky latitudes so defined constitute 28 percent of the land area of the Old World but have long been home to a far higher share of the population. In 100 CE, for example, the lucky latitudes were home to 64 percent of the total Old World population. Within Europe, the lucky latitudes are 30 percent of the land area but were home to 48 percent of Europe's population in 100 CE; in Africa, the lucky latitudes are 14 percent of the land but

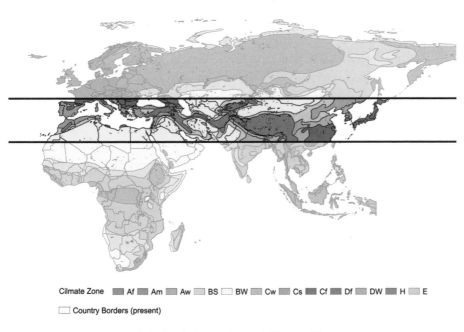

Cilmate Zone ■ Af ■ Am ■ Aw □ BS □ BW □ Cw ■ Cs ■ Cf ■ Df ■ DW ■ H □ E
□ Country Borders (present)

3.2 The Lucky Latitudes and Climate Zones

were home to 52 percent of the population; and in Asia, the lucky latitudes are 58 percent of the land but were home to 71 percent of the population.[10] (Data may be found in the appendix.)

Notice that the lucky latitudes also cover most of today's United States. Yet, as noted earlier, North America was not as lucky as Eurasia for most of economic history. For around ten thousand years, the Americas were cut off from the technological advances in Eurasia, until the Americas and the Old World were rejoined by trade and migration in the 1500s. After that, remarkable economic development of North America ensued, but in the context of brutal wars of conquest and genocide of the Native American populations.

Within the Eurasian lucky latitudes, countless innovations not only arose but also diffused throughout the long east-west band. The lucky latitudes shared a common and relatively hospitable climate, transport routes, and the absence or low intensity of tropical vector-borne diseases such as malaria, though bubonic plague was episodically transported long distances across the region. The lucky latitudes of Eurasia have long shared common crops, horse-based transport, sailing vessels in the Mediterranean and the Indian Ocean, a shared language Indo-European language family, long-distance migrations of populations, the flow of ideas, and long-distance overland trade stretching ten thousand kilometers from the west of Europe to the eastern seaboard of China.

In the Americas, higher population densities and greater technological development were concentrated more toward the equator, in the region from the Valley of Mexico through Central America and to the Andes of South America. This region was home to the great civilizations of the Olmecs, Mayas, Toltecs, and Aztecs of Mesoamerica and the Incas of the Andes. These civilizations produced wondrous advances in agriculture, stone construction, astronomy, and calendric and writing systems, yet they lagged far behind their contemporaries in the Eurasian lucky latitudes. The American civilizations had writing systems but no alphabets, lacked draft animals other than the llama of the Andean highlands, used no wheeled vehicles, and arrived much later than Eurasia to metallurgy.

The lucky latitudes of Eurasia are congenial for both animal husbandry and staple crop production, thanks to a Goldilocks climate: neither too cold, as in the higher latitudes nearer the poles, nor too hot, as in the equatorial tropics. These midlatitudes have growing seasons that are long enough to support high crop yields but are cold enough in the winters to break the transmission of vector-borne diseases such as malaria. The lucky latitudes do have seasonal transmission of malaria, but not the year-round crushing burden of tropical Africa. And luckily for Eurasia, trypanosomiasis, which kills domesticated animals as well as humans, is restricted to tropical ranges in Africa and Latin America (where it is known as Chagas disease).

The lucky latitudes were the site of early technological innovations and long-distance diffusion. Early technologies adopted by 3000 BCE included metallurgy (the Copper Age was underway and the Bronze Age was beginning); early writing such as hieroglyphics in Egypt, proto-cuneiform in Mesopotamia, and early pictographs in China; animal husbandry; the earliest domestication of the donkey and horse; pottery; viticulture (as early as 5000 BCE in the Caucasus region, present-day Georgia); and even the wheel and chariot. These technological advances outstripped contemporaneous developments in the Americas, Oceania, and Africa south of the

Sahara, where the innovations arose much later or arrived through diffusion from the lucky latitudes.

Not all parts of the lucky latitudes are equally blessed. Looking at the map in figure 3.2, we see that the western (Europe) and eastern (China) ends of the lucky latitudes are temperate regions while the middle stretch from Western Asia to Central Asia are drylands. The great empires of Western and Central Asia—the Persian, the Mongol, the Timurid—were dryland empires with relative low population densities (but lots of horses and grazing areas). The temperate-zone empires, such as the Roman and Han empires, were far more populous and, in general, far more technologically dynamic.

Interestingly, the lucky latitudes maintained their good luck even during the fossil-fuel era of the past two centuries. By sheer accident of geology, the lucky latitudes contain major geological reserves of coal. The reason is coincidental: Around 100 million years ago, much of today's lucky-latitude land was tropical swampland. Dead plant and animal debris were submerged in the swampland and, during the passage of geological time, transformed into coal—the fuel that would eventually power the industrial revolution.

Some Lessons from the Neolithic Age

Luck matters. In many ancient languages, the word for happiness is the same as the word for luck or good fortune. Being in the right place at the right time is sometimes the key to success. In the Neolithic Age, being in the right place at the right time was indeed critical. Early agriculture depended on a fertile environment, notably in alluvial floodplains, and with the flora and fauna that were the precursors to cultivated crops and domesticated animals. The long east-west extent of Eurasia's lucky latitudes meant that there was a vast area for both innovation and diffusion, giving rise to early civilizations and the proto-states that would emerge in the next age of globalization. The Americas also had their lucky sites, notably in Mesoamerica and along the Andes coastlines of present-day Peru. But the bad luck of the Americas was to be cut off from the technological advances of the far more populous Old World and to lack vital resources, such as domesticated large animals like the donkey and the horse, that would prove pivotal for long-term economic advancement. Africa too was deeply disadvantaged, largely cut off from Eurasia by the vast Sahara Desert and burdened by an exceptionally severe disease environment for both humans and farm animals.

4

The Equestrian Age

(3000–1000 BCE)

As a contiguous land area that has been home to most of humanity, Eurasia has long enjoyed the benefits of scale, long-distance trade, and the innovation and diffusion of technologies. For at least five thousand years, the horse has played a key, even decisive, role in Eurasia's development, offering unequalled transport services, horse power for agriculture, powerful military capacity, rapid communications, and the capacity to govern large areas in a unified state. This is why the domestication of the horse some fifty-five hundred years ago gave rise to the first empires of Eurasia, and also why I have chosen the Equestrian Age as the name of the third age of globalization.

Our examination of this age of globalization begins with the band of grasslands just to the north of the lucky latitudes known as the steppes of Asia (figure 4.1). These great grasslands include the western Eurasian steppes, spanning the northern Black Sea coast, the Caucasus Mountains, today's Kazakhstan and Uzbekistan, and the eastern Eurasian steppes, notably Mongolia and northern China, including Xinjiang, Inner Mongolia, and parts of northeast China. The steppes, classified as climate zone BS, are semiarid but not desert. This climate zone accounts for around 10.8 percent of the land area of Eurasia, and was home to a somewhat larger proportion of the population, around 15.1 percent in 3000 BCE and 14.5 percent in 1000 BCE.

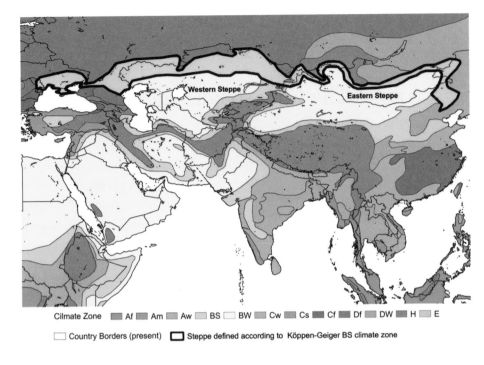

Cilmate Zone ■ Af ■ Am ■ Aw ☐ BS ☐ BW ■ Cw ■ Cs ■ Cf ■ Df ☐ DW ■ H ☐ E

☐ Country Borders (present)   ■ Steppe defined according to Köppen-Geiger BS climate zone

4.1 Eurasian Steppe Region

The steppes provided the abundant energy input—grass—and the hospitable climate for the most important transport vehicle for almost all of human history: the horse. The steppes also served as the great long-distance highways connecting Eurasia well before paved roads. Horse-driven transport was, in effect, the automobile, truck, railroad, and tank of the ancient empires. It was the only available high-speed option for land-based movements of traders, messengers, warriors, and explorers.

Animal Domestication

To understand the significance of the horse's arrival in human history, let us start with animal domestication more generally. Animal domestication was a long and complex process, starting in the Paleolithic Age with the domestication of the dog (around fifteen thousand years ago in China) and continuing in the Neolithic Age over many thousands of years. The archeological evidence suggests that the ruminants (goats, sheep, and cattle) were originally domesticated during the period from 10,000 to 8000 BCE in southwest Asia. The donkey was domesticated (from the African wild ass) in Egypt around 5000 BCE. Dromedary camels were domesticated in Arabia around 4000 BCE, and camelids (alpaca and llama) in the high Andes around the same time. Horses were domesticated late in the Neolithic, around 3500 BCE, in the western Eurasian steppes, the region spanning the north coast of the Black Sea, the northern Caucasus, and western Kazakhstan.[1]

Here is a staggering reality: The domestication of animals occurred almost exclusively in Eurasia and North Africa (in the case of the donkey). No large farm animals were originally domesticated in tropical Africa. Africa's own ungulates, including antelope and zebras, resisted domestication. Domesticated sheep and goats arrived to Africa from Southeast Asia, horses from the western Eurasian steppes, cattle from Southwest Asia, the dromedary from the Arabian Peninsula, and the donkey from North Africa.

In general, the African tropical environment proved extremely harsh for many farm animals. Cattle, sheep, goats, pigs, horses, and donkeys were vulnerable to trypanosomiasis within the vast tsetse belt of West and Central Africa (figure 4.2) and to other diseases such as the tick-borne east coast fever, caused by the protozoan pathogen *Theileria parva*, equine piroplasmosis, also transmitted by ticks, and African horse sickness, an orbivirus transmitted by insect vectors. Many domesticated animals did successfully adapt to the tropical African environment, at least in some places, and many African regions have had mixed crop-and-animal farm systems for thousands of years. Nonetheless, much of tropical Africa long suffered from the scarcity of horses, donkeys, and other pack and draft animals.[2]

The situation in the Americas was even more dramatic. Most domesticated animals reached the New World only upon the Columbian exchange of flora and fauna between the Old World and New World after 1492, when the Old World farm animals arrived with European conquerors. The hunter-gatherers of North America killed off the wild horse (*Equus occidentalis*) and other megafauna, including the woolly mammoth, and saber-toothed cat.[3] The only surviving candidates for domestication were the two

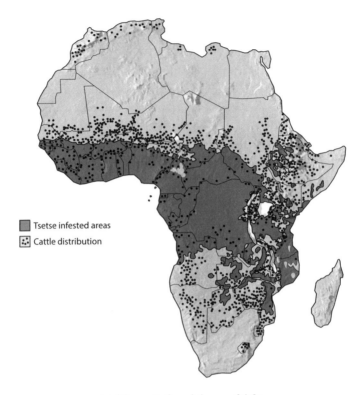

4.2 Tsetse-Infested Areas of Africa

Source: Food and Agriculture Organization of the United Nations, 1998, G. Uilenberg, A field guide for The Diagnosis, Treatment and Prevention of African Animal Trypanosomosis, www.fao.org/3/X0413E/X0413E00.htm#TOC. Reproduced with permission.

camelid species of the high Andes (the llama and the alpaca), two birds (the turkey and the Muscovy duck), and the guinea pig. Other than llamas and alpacas in the high Andes, the Amerindian populations had to make do for more than ten thousand years with no large domesticated animals for pack and draft work and without horses for long-distance transport and communications. The early extinction of the horse in North America was therefore a loss to the Amerindian civilizations of catastrophic dimension. The next time that Amerindians encountered the horse was when the Spanish conquistadores showed up on horseback at the end of the fifteenth century.

Domestication of the Donkey and the Horse

The horse is unmatched in its importance for economic development and globalization. Only the horse offered the speed, durability, power, and intelligence to enable deep breakthroughs in every sector of the economy: farming, animal husbandry, mining, manufacturing, transport, communications, warfare, and governance. Regions of the world that lacked horsepower fell far behind those that had it, and typically ended up being conquered by warriors on horseback. That ancient story was played out repeatedly in East Asia, South Asia, West Asia, Europe, Africa, and the Americas.

The horse is one of subgenera of the genus *Equus*, the others being the African ass, the Asian ass (onager), the Tibetan ass (kiang), and several subgenera of zebras. The native range of the horse, based on its distribution in the late Pleistocene, is shown in figure 4.3. In the late Pleistocene, the horse was native to most of the Americas and Eurasia other than South

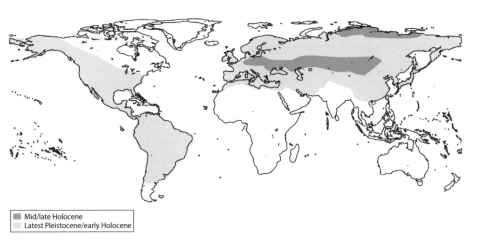

Mid/late Holocene
Latest Pleistocene/early Holocene

4.3 The Distribution of Wild Horses in the
Late Pleistocene–Early Holocene

Source: Pernille Johansen Naundrup and Jens-Christian Svenning, "A Geographic Assessment of the Global Scope for Rewilding with Wild-Living Horses (Equus ferus)," PLoS ONE 10(7): https://doi.org/10.1371/journal.pone.0132359

Asia, the Arabian Peninsula, and Southeast Asia. Horses were present in Africa only at the very northern tip of the continent, in the small temperate band north of the Sahara.

Figure 4.3 depicts the remarkable decline in the range of horses between the late Pleistocene (light) and the mid/late Holocene (dark). The main reason is that horses were hunted for meat in the early Holocene and driven to extinction throughout the Americas and in most of Eurasia other than the steppe region. The steppes, which were remote from the more populous concentrations of hunter-gatherers and early farmers, offered a refuge for the wild horse. It was therefore from the steppes that the horse would reemerge as the key technology for war and empire some eight thousand years after the start of the Neolithic period.

Of the other subgenera of the genus *Equus*, only the African wild ass was domesticated. The Asian and Tibetan asses and the various subgenera of zebras all proved resistant to domestication. The native range of the African wild ass was the drylands and deserts of North Africa and the Arabian Peninsula. Its domestication appears to have originated around 5000 BCE in Nubia, today's southern Egypt, perhaps 1,500 years before the domestication of the horse.

While cattle served as slow-moving beasts of burden (draft animals), donkeys served mainly as pack animals, carrying heavy loads. A recent study of early donkey domestication explains their pivotal role this way:

> Donkeys are tough desert-adapted animals, and their ability to carry heavy loads through arid lands enabled pastoralists to move farther and more frequently and to transport their households with their herds. Domestication of the donkey also allowed large-scale food redistribution in the nascent Egyptian state and expanded overland trade in Africa and western Asia.[4]

The domestication of the wild horse (*Equus ferus*) followed that of the donkey around 3500 BCE. Domestication occurred as farmer-herders pushed north from Mesopotamia into the western Eurasian steppes. There they encountered the surviving feral horses. The horse was clearly not easy to domesticate, and the process took a considerable amount of time. The horse is fast and aggressive and ready to attack if cornered. It was probably

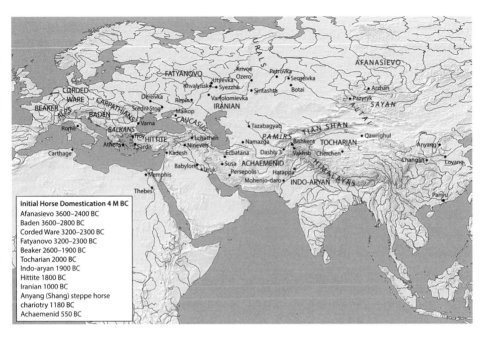

Initial Horse Domestication 4 M BC
Afanasievo 3600–2400 BC
Baden 3600–2800 BC
Corded Ware 3200–2300 BC
Fatyanovo 3200–2300 BC
Beaker 2600–1900 BC
Tocharian 2000 BC
Indo-aryan 1900 BC
Hittite 1800 BC
Iranian 1000 BC
Anyang (Shang) steppe horse
chariotry 1180 BC
Achaemenid 550 BC

4.4 Early Locations of Horse-Based Societies

Source: Pita Kelekna, *The Horse in Human History*, Cambridge University Press, 2009.

first cornered, trapped, and subdued in group hunts. The initial purpose of domestication seems to have been to use the horse as a pack animal to carry loads across the grasslands. What ensued was several millennia of gradual technological developments and adaptations for the effective use of horses, including the gradual improvement of halters to harness loads, saddles, stirrups, types of carts and chariots, and weapons that could be deployed by riders in combat. The sites shown in figure 4.4 are the steppe regions with early horse domestication.[5]

The result of horse domestication is an animal of remarkable versatility. It is a pack animal, able to transport goods long distances. It is a saddle animal, for use in warfare and farming (as in the herding of farm animals). It is a draft animal, able to pull wheeled vehicles. It has endurance, intelligence, and great speed. In short, it has played a decisive role in economic development.

The Domestication of the Camel and Camelids

Species of the camel family (*Camelidae*) have also played an important role in the more extreme climates of deserts and high plateaus. In the Old World, two species predominate: the one-humped dromedary of the Arabian Peninsula and North Africa, and the two-humped Bactrian camel of Central Asia, including Turkmenistan, Afghanistan, and Mongolia's Gobi Desert. In the New World, two wild Andean camelids, the guanaco and vicuna, were domesticated to the llama and the alpaca, respectively. All of these species have played an important economic role, though to a lesser extent than the horse.

The Old World camels are distinctive for their ruggedness and ability to endure extreme temperatures, hot in the case of the dromedary and cold in the case of the Bactrian. Camels can go long periods, even weeks under certain circumstances, without drinking, and their humps store fat for long periods without food. Crucial as pack animals through deserts and high-steppe regions, they played an integrative role in long-distance trade as early as ancient pharaonic Egypt. The Old World camels were domesticated later than the horse, probably between 2000 and 1000 BCE.

The camel played multiple roles: as a source of milk and meat; as a pack animal in long-distance caravans across the Arabian Peninsula, the Egyptian desert west of the Nile, and later the Sahara Desert; as a battle animal; and as an animal for sport racing. The camel's ability to carry heavy loads of up to five hundred pounds for fifteen to twenty miles per day over the course of a hundred days meant that camel transport across the Arabian Peninsula between Asia and the Mediterranean was competitive with travel by sea. The camel was also an important complement to the warhorse in Bedouin campaigns of raiding and conquest. Although camels could not stand up to horses in shock combat, they could powerfully aid the cavalry by carrying war supplies and water over large distances. One scholar summarizes the camel's role in Mideastern nomadic societies as follows:

> It seems clear the camel is the key without which there could have been no nomads in the hot deserts of the Old World. This one domestic animal provided food, transportation, and a basis for military power, and continued to do so under conditions no other animal of comparable capabilities could endure.[6]

The Andean camelids, the llama and the alpaca, were domesticated in the high Andes around 3000 BCE. The llama, the larger of the two species, served as a pack animal as well as a source of wool for coarse fabrics, milk, meat, and hides. The alpaca, smaller and with long, finer fibers, was used to produce fine fabrics, as well as for milk, meat, and hides. Recent research suggests that agriculturalists in the high Andes engaged in mixed-crop and animal-husbandry agriculture and that the llama served also as a vital pack animal for exchange between the highlands and the coastal lowlands of Peru. These camelids, the dog, and the guinea pig were the only domesticated animals available in the Andes.

The Metal Ages

Alongside the domestication of the horse, donkey, and camel, the advance from the Neolithic Age to the Equestrian Age occurred on other fronts as well. Most importantly, the New Stone Age gave way to the Metal Age, making possible new and stronger tools, weaponry, and artisanal products. The Copper Age commenced around 4000 BCE, though copper ornaments are known from earlier millennia. Copper is widely accessible in elemental form and can be melted at a relatively low temperature, 1085°C. Smelting of copper ores requires a higher temperature, around 1200°C. These temperatures are hotter than campfires and therefore required new methods of heating.

Copper is relatively soft in pure form; it becomes stronger and more durable as an alloy with tin, making brass, or with arsenic (though dangerous in the metalworking). The Bronze Age arrived with the discovery of the copper-tin alloy, beginning around 3300 BCE in the Near East, the Indus Valley, and the Yellow River valley. The problem with bronze was the scarcity of tin. There were few accessible tin deposits in the region of the Fertile Crescent. Tin mines were established in parts of Western Europe (Germany, Iberia), but the tin had to be transported long distances to the Near East. Other tin arrived from mines in Central Asia along the Silk Road.

Iron is superior to bronze in many ways, notably in strength per unit weight. Iron is also far more plentiful than tin. The problem with iron, however, is its very high melting point, around 1530°C, almost 500°C higher than copper. The vast amount of energy needed to melt iron ores drastically limited the large-scale production of iron products and delayed the onset of iron production. The Iron Age commenced around 1500 BCE, roughly 1,800 years after the start of the Bronze Age.

Comparing Old World and New World Developments

The extinction of the wild horse in the early Holocene meant that the Amerindians were bereft of horses until the arrival of the European conquerors. Nor did they have the benefit of the donkey, which originated in North Africa and did not arrive to the Americas until the Colombian exchange. The absence of equids certainly did not stop many remarkable advances of civilization in the Americas, but it did fundamentally alter, and limit, the civilizational advances that occurred. The Americas lacked the potential for long-distance overland transport, communications, agricultural productivity, and aspects of large-scale governance made possible by the horse and donkey. The llama served this purpose, but only to a limited extent, in connecting the high Andes with the lowlands of Peru.

The implications were profound, as cogently argued by the anthropologist Pita Kelekna in her magisterial account of *The Horse in Human History*. I summarize her conclusions in table 4.1, comparing long-term development in Eurasia and the Americas, the first benefiting from the horse and the latter bereft of the horse.

The Yamnaya Breakthrough in Eurasia

Perhaps the first major horse-based society in Eurasia was the Yamnaya people, hypothesized to have emerged as an admixture of hunter-gatherers from the Caucasus and Eastern Europe. Their territory was the northern Caucasus between the Black Sea and the Caspian Sea (known as the Pontic-Caspian Steppe). What is notable about the Yamnaya civilization,

Table 4.1 Comparing Eurasia and the Americas

Dimension of social life	Americas (without the horse)	Eurasia (with the horse)
Agriculture	American steppes (prairies and pampas) remained most undeveloped and unpopulated	Adoption of agriculture throughout the steppes, intensification in the temperate zones
Metallurgy	Little transport of metals, very slow uptake and diffusion of metallurgy	Long-distance transport of metals, more rapid diffusion of metallurgy
Trade	Short-distance trade	Long-distance trade, with horse-based trade encouraging other modes as well (e.g., canal building)
Diffusion of ideas and inventions	Little diffusion of technologies such as writing, counting devices, arithmetic (e.g., role of zero)	Extensive diffusion of technologies, including alphabets, arithmetic, use of the wheel
Warfare	Small polities, governed as confederations	Large empires, secured by horseback
Religion	Little diffusion	Long-distance diffusion
Language	Little linguistic interaction	Long-distance linguistic interaction

Source: Data from Pita Kelekna, *The Horse in Human History*. Cambridge: Cambridge University Press, 2009

dated around 3500–2400 BCE, is their early domestication of the horse and their apparent remarkable success in migrating westward toward Europe. The Yamnaya civilization is closely linked in technologies and genetics to the so-called Corded Ware culture of northern Europe around 3000 BCE (named for the corded decoration of its pottery). Paleo-geneticists suggest that much of Europe's population in fact reflects the admixture of two populations: the first originating with early farmers from Anatolia and the second with the Yamnaya people, itself an admixture of hunter-gatherer populations.[7] The hypothesized dual origin of early Western European farm populations is illustrated in figure 4.5, showing two key migrations into Western Europe, the first from Anatolia dated around 7500–6000 BCE and the second from the steppes, dated around 4000–3000 BCE.

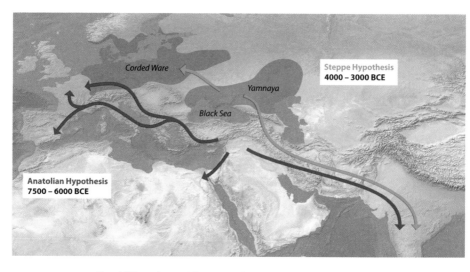

4.5 Rival Hypotheses: Neolithic Age Migrations from the Steppes
and from Anatolia

Source: Wolfgang Haak, Iosif Lazaridis, Nick Patterson, Nadin Rohland, Swapan Mallick, Bastien Llamas, Guido Brandt, *et al*. "Massive Migration from the Steppe Is a Source for Indo-European Languages in Europe." *bioRxiv* (2015): 013433. doi:10.1101/013433.

In support of the hypothesized migrations from the western steppes, archeologists point not only to the genetic record but also to the remarkable and rapid dissemination of major horse-related technologies—including the wheel, ox-driven carts, and depictions of horseback riding—through the vast area of Mesopotamia, Eastern Europe, northern Europe, and the Indus region. The domestication of the horse, with the unmatched mobility that it brought, enabled a dissemination of basic technologies over a huge area of Eurasia at a speed that was unprecedented in comparison with prior human experience.

One other fundamental cultural breakthrough apparently arrived with the Yamnaya and related peoples: Indo-European languages. As with the genetic code, the language code of western Eurasia and South Asia suggests a crucial admixture of languages from Anatolia and the western steppes, which together gave birth to the Indo-European languages, the family of almost all of today's European languages (other than Basque, Estonian, Finnish, and Hungarian) and many of the languages of western

Asia and northern India. Paleogeneticist David Reich offers a fascinating hypothesis based on the genetic record:

> This suggests to me that the most likely location of the population that first spoke an Indo-European language was south of the Caucasus Mountains, perhaps in present-day Iran or Armenia, because ancient DNA from people who live there matches what we would expect for a source population both for the Yamnaya and for Ancient Anatolians.[8]

Reich also describes how the genetic record in India suggests that present-day Indians are an admixture of two ancestral populations, from northern India and southern India, with the northern Indian ancestral population genetically related to the populations of the Eurasian steppes, the Caucasus, and the Near East (Anatolia).

The Early Equestrian States

From the original domestication in the Pontic-Caspian steppes, the horse and horse-based civilizations spread throughout the temperate and steppe regions of Eurasia. The Eurasian steppes would remain regions of low population density in fierce, horse-based warrior societies. Their names would be dreaded among the sedentary societies of Eurasia, North Africa, the Middle East, South Asia, and East Asia for 3,500 years, from roughly 2000 BCE to 1500 CE. The first groups included the Hyksos, who conquered ancient Egypt around 1580 BCE and ruled for around 130 years, and the Scythians, who controlled parts of the ancient land routes between Asia and Europe from around 900 BCE to 400 CE. Later steppe conquerors include the Goths and Huns, between 400 and 600 CE; the Magyars and Bulgars, who settled Hungary and Bulgaria around 1000 CE; and the Seljuks and Mongols, who conquered vast territories of Asia from 1200 to 1400 CE.

The horse was also adopted by the far more populous agricultural societies after their early and often brutal encounters with the peoples of the steppes. The horse became a mainstay of farming, transport, and war for the early equestrian empires from Egypt to Mesopotamia, Persia, South Asia, and East Asia, and then later for the vast land empires of Alexander the

Great, Rome, Persia, China, and India of the Classical Age of globalization. The land-based empires of the Classical Age would have been impossible but for the communications, transport, and military might of the horse.

Key Development Breakthroughs in the Fertile Crescent

The period from 3000 to 1000 BCE marked decisive civilizational advances in the Fertile Crescent, including Egypt, the Levant, and Mesopotamia. Similar advances occurred in other riverine civilizations (the Indus, the Yellow River, and the Yangtze). Breakthroughs included technological and institutional advances in agriculture, public administration, writing and communications, engineering, and long-distance trade. These breakthroughs gave rise to city-states and to larger political units.

The earliest kingdoms of a unified Egypt were founded around 3000 BCE, roughly contemporaneous with the rise of the first dynasties in Mesopotamia, beginning with the early dynasty of Sumer around 2900 BCE. Both Egypt and Sumer had early writing systems, the hieroglyphics of Egypt and the cuneiform (wedge-shaped) writing of the Sumerian language, which provided an invaluable tool for public administration. Unified dynasties ruled Egypt for most of the period until the neo-Assyrian conquest of Egypt around 670 BCE, followed by brief conquests by Babylonians and afterwards by Achaemenid Persia. In Mesopotamia, a number of dynasties rose and fell during this same period, including the first empire of Mesopotamia, the Akkadian Empire (c. 2350–2100 BCE), followed by Assyrian and Babylonian kingdoms. The largest of the Mesopotamian kingdoms would be the neo-Assyrian empire (tenth to seventh century BCE), which conquered the Levant and Egypt and which in turn was conquered by the Persians.

These Fertile Crescent civilizations achieved an astonishing number of breakthroughs during this period. They created early written legal codes, including the Code of Hammurabi (Babylonia, c. 1790 BCE), which became models of legal codes throughout the classical world. They created grand public structures, not least the pyramids, and considerable public infrastructure. They built cities and established methods of public administration and tax collection. They made breakthroughs in writing systems and historical documentation. They created new philosophies and religions that would profoundly influence Judaism and Christianity. They made great advances in a range of scientific fields, including mathematics, astronomy, engineering, metallurgy, and medicine. And, of course, these kingdoms engaged in long-distance trade and long-distance warfare, both dependent on the horse. Chariots and cavalry became core features of the Near East military from around 1500 BCE. Horses and donkeys as pack animals were vital for long-distance trade, transporting precious stones, spices, gold, other metals, cloth, and artisanal works.

By the end of our period, 1000 BCE, a large number of urban centers dotted the lucky latitudes of Eurasia. A recent study of ancient cities documents twenty-six Eurasian cities with populations of ten thousand or more between the years 800 BCE and 500 BCE, the legacy of the Equestrian Age.[9] Strikingly, as we see in figure 4.6, all of these urban sites except one (Marib, Yemen) lie in the lucky latitudes, a vivid illustration of the uniquely favorable development conditions in that narrow band, and almost all are either in the temperate zones in China and the Mediterranean littoral or along river valleys in the drylands (notably in Egypt and Mesopotamia).

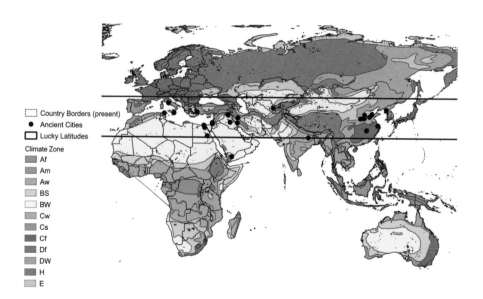

4.6 Ancient Urban Centers Were Concentrated in the Lucky Latitudes

Some Lessons from the Equestrian Age

The period from 3000 to 1000 BCE was transformative for the major civilizations of Eurasia. Three profound technological breakthroughs were most decisive: the domestication of the horse, the development of writing systems, and the breakthroughs in metallurgy. These were accompanied by dramatic advances in public administration, religion, and philosophy, especially in the Fertile Crescent. By the end of the Equestrian Age, around 1000 BCE, large land empires were beginning to emerge beyond their riverine home base. The first was the neo-Assyrian empire, which would briefly conquer Mesopotamia, the Levant, eastern Anatolia, and Egypt. Yet that empire merely set the stage for even larger empires that would arise across the lucky latitudes of Eurasia. That is the story of the Classical Age, to which we now turn.

5

The Classical Age

(1000 BCE–1500 CE)

The period between 1000 BCE and 1500 CE gave rise to civilizations so dynamic that they set a standard of achievement hailed ever since as the Classical Age. Many of the world's major religions— Judaism, Christianity, Islam, Buddhism—were forged in this period. The great philosophies of life, as taught by Plato and Aristotle, Confucius, the Buddha, and other sages, our greatest wisdom traditions, are from this period. The great empires of the age—Assyria, Persia, Greece, Rome, India, China, and later the Ottoman and Mongol empires—competed for glory, beliefs, wealth, and power with an unprecedented level of ambition and energy that continue to amaze and enthrall us today. This period is globalization on the grandest canvas, when the participants themselves felt that they were writing the history of humanity.

We can call this an era of globalization by politics, since the imperial states consciously and deliberately aimed to create global civilizations. The empires used the apparatus of state power to disseminate ideas, spread technologies, introduce new institutions, and build infrastructure on a continental scale, such as the Roman roads, amphitheaters, and aqueducts that still stand throughout Europe, North Africa, the eastern Mediterranean, and western Asia. These were states that acted boldly, sometimes recklessly, and often violently, to spread ideas and to multiply their power and wealth.

These powers could rely on the gains in technology that had been achieved in the past millennia: better ways to grow food, raise farm animals, transport goods, and fight wars. Perhaps their strongest technology was something that is taken for granted today. For the first time, all four major regions of Eurasia—the Mediterranean basin, western Asia, southern Asia, and East Asia—had an alphabet or script that could be read far and wide. For the first time in human history, thousands of books were being written and collected. Great libraries were created, most famously at Alexandria in the Greco-Roman period. Knowledge could now be codified and transferred through books and formal schooling. While other parts of the world continued to tell their histories by word of mouth and myth, governments and independent scholars of the Classical Age empires began to document human history in detail for perpetuity.

Yet with all of this might, knowledge, and ambition, we still find, once again, that geography repeatedly proved decisive in shaping imperial fortunes. The empires we will examine lived by and large within their ecological niches, and climate zones more than generals dictated the imperial maps.

The Axial Age

The twentieth-century German historian and philosopher Karl Jaspers offered a crucial insight into this era with his concept of the Axial Age.[1] Jaspers noted that during a span of roughly five hundred years, between 800 and 300 BCE, there was a simultaneous emergence of profound philosophical and religious insights in four major civilizations of Eurasia: the Greco-Roman world of the Mediterranean Sea, the Persian world of western Asia, the Aryan world of northern India, and the Han Chinese world of East Asia. In all four cases, there occurred remarkable and foundational breakthroughs in thinking about the meaning and purpose of life.

The Greco-Roman world saw the rise of Greek moral philosophy, leading to the profound intellectual breakthroughs of Plato and Aristotle and all that followed. The Persian world gave rise to Zoroastrianism, a vision of the universe as the battleground of good and evil, which in turn was foundational for Judaism and still later for Christianity. The Indian world gave rise to the Upanishads of Hinduism and to the teachings of Buddha about the path to nirvana (eternal happiness) through compassion for all and the renunciation of attachment. The Chinese world gave birth to the teaching of harmonious social order based on ritual piety, the cultivation of virtue, and state law of Confucius and Mencius.

The philosophical and religious breakthroughs of the Axial Age influenced speculative thought from then onward and continue to resonate deeply in today's religious beliefs and philosophical outlooks. Greek philosophy was adopted by the Hellenistic empires and then the Roman Empire, and was also incorporated into Christian theology. Confucianism remained a core doctrine of Chinese dynasties throughout history and until today. Buddhism is not only practiced today by 500 million people in Asia, but its teachings of compassion, mindfulness, and the Middle Path are increasingly adopted in the West as well. Even Zoroastrianism, the state religion of the Achaemenid and Sassanid Persian empires with few adherents today, had profound and lasting influences on the Abrahamic faiths (Judaism, Christianity, and Islam) through its beliefs in monotheism, the battle of good versus evil in the universe, and the free will of individuals to choose good or evil.

Jaspers did not argue that this simultaneous emergence of basic world views reflected the interchange of ideas across Eurasia. He regarded this simultaneity as a puzzle, even an accident, but one that would open a dialogue across civilizations in the two-and-a-half millennia that followed. In all four worlds, the philosophical-religious breakthroughs became the foundational elements of culture in the period after 500 BCE and eventually instruments of state power as well, as philosophical and religious ideas became incorporated into imperial ideologies.

One wonders whether perhaps a common cause was at play. In all four regions, by around 800 BCE, the written scripts of the respective languages had advanced to the stage of enabling the writing of books. In ancient Greece, for example, the tradition of passing down the ancient wisdom, such as Homeric poetry, by bards and the spoken word was being replaced with written manuscripts that used the Greek alphabet. The Greek alphabet, the first in history with letters for vowel sounds, was invented around 800 BCE, adapting the existing Phoenician letters for the consonants and adding letters for vowels. The remarkable outpouring of Greek texts followed. Scripts were similarly being adopted in Persia for the Old Persian language and in northern India for Classical Sanskrit sometime around

500 BCE or later, with ongoing debates about the precise timing. In China, the characters of Classical Chinese were similarly being developed, and Confucian thought was written down in Classical Chinese in the period after 500 BCE. The new scripts, in short, became the means for writing down and transmitting the foundational texts and philosophies of Western, Persian, Indian, and Chinese civilizations.

Thalassocracy and Tellurocracy

As the pace of economic and intellectual development hastened in the eastern Mediterranean and western Asia around 1000 BCE, two kinds of civilizations developed side by side. The first consisted of city-states with economies based on sea-based trading networks, of which the most remarkable were the Phoenicians and the ancient Greeks; the second were the city-states based on agriculture and mining that eventually became the land-based empires of the Classical Age. Ancient Greek offered two wonderful words for these distinct civilizations: *thalassocracy* ("thalatta" meaning sea and "cracy" for power) and *tellurocracy* ("tellus" for land).

The Phoenicians created perhaps the most consequential thalassocracy in history, not only because of the Phoenician accomplishment of creating a network of maritime trade throughout the Mediterranean region, but also by inspiring the Greek and Roman empires that followed. Phoenicia arose in present-day Lebanon, in the ancient coastal cities of Byblos and Tyre, dating back to around 5000 BCE, though the peoples of Phoenicia may have been more recent arrivals from the Red Sea or Persian Gulf region. Starting around 1500 BCE, the Phoenicians began to establish coastal colonies around the Mediterranean, eventually extending westward to the Atlantic. The most important of these in the western Mediterranean was Carthage, founded by the Phoenicians in the ninth century BCE. These coastal cities constituted a remarkable network for Mediterranean-wide trade in diverse products, including timber, glass, wine, and dyes (notably a purple dye from sea snails that might be the root of the word *Phoenicia*, believed by some to derive from the ancient Greek for blood-red).

In addition to creating a thick network of Mediterranean commerce, the Phoenicians created a twenty-two-letter consonantal writing system for their

Semitic language that in turn was adapted by the Greeks in the eighth century BCE and later by the Romans. The Phoenician alphabet itself is assumed to have derived from Egyptian hieroglyphs. The eastern Mediterranean writing systems thus emerged from a great arc of intellectual transmission from Egypt's hieroglyphs to proto-writing in the Levant to the Phoenicians' consonantal writing system and then to the decisive breakthrough of the consonant-plus-vowel-based alphabet of the ancient Greeks.

The Phoenicians displayed legendary trading and financial skills (Plato describes them in his *Republic* as "money-loving" compared with the "wisdom-loving" Greeks) but not military dominance. Thus, the Phoenicians were conquered by the rising tellurocracies of the era. Cyrus the Great of the Achaemenid Persian Empire conquered the Levantine city-states in 539 BCE. Alexander later conquered the region in 322 BCE, and Phoenicia was incorporated into the Ptolemaic and Seleucid empires that followed Alexander's conquests. Carthage lived on as an independent city-state until it, in turn, was destroyed by the Roman Empire in the Punic Wars.

The Emergence of the Classical Land-Based Empires

The emergence of land-based states that spread beyond their home river basins to reach imperial scale dates to around 900 BCE. Ancient Egypt was unified along the Nile River, and the successive empires of Mesopotamia (including the Akkadians, Assyrians, and Babylonians) largely fought among themselves along the Tigris and Euphrates river valleys. Then, the Neo-Assyrian Empire (figure 5.1) gained sufficient military advantage to conquer not only Mesopotamia but also parts of eastern Anatolia, the Levant, and eventually Egypt (671 BCE). Despite these remarkable conquests, the empire collapsed very soon after, the result of civil strife, the loss of territories to local reconquests, and finally the invasion of its capital, Nineveh, by a combined army of Assyria's enemies, in 612 BCE.

The stage was now set, however, for a new age of globalization, one in which large land empires across the lucky latitudes would conquer vast territories, engage in intensive trade and cultural exchanges with the other empires, and wage incessant war. The Mediterranean basin and western Asia, stretching from the Atlantic Ocean to the Indus River, became an

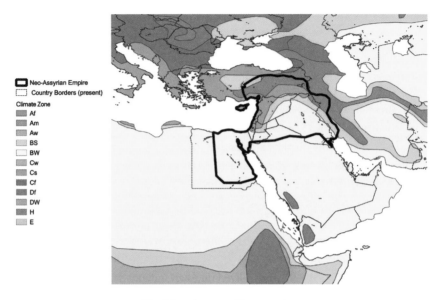

5.1 The Neo-Assyrian Empire, 671 BCE

east-west battleground of contesting empires, with civilizational conflicts that have indeed continued to the present. When the United States goads and provokes Iran today, it does so—mostly unaware, to be sure—in a way that mirrors ancient conflicts and prejudices between the western Mediterranean and Persia that date back 2,500 years.

The first great Persian empire, the Achaemenid Empire, was founded by Cyrus the Great around 559 BCE. The Achaemenid Empire swept away the remnants of the Neo-Assyrian Empire, the Babylonian state, and other powers of Mesopotamia, and went on to conquer Anatolia, the Phoenicians, and Egypt. It was Cyrus who in 539 BCE allowed the Jews to be exiled by Babylonia after the Babylonian conquest of Judea (597 BCE) to return to Jerusalem. According to some scholars, Cyrus also supported the priestly compilation of the Jewish historical and sacred texts that became the Jewish Torah.

The remarkable expansion of the Achaemenid Empire brought Persia to the doorstep of the Greek city-states, setting up the most famous and arguably most decisive east-west clash in history, the war between Persia and Athens. Persia attacked mainland Greece in 490 BCE, yielding three historic results. First, the Athenian victory, which repulsed Persia and led to Persia's ultimate defeat in the Persian-Greek Wars in 449 BCE, marked a decisive victory for the Western civilizations over invasions from the East. Second, the victory of Athens at Marathon, of course, gave us the eponymous twenty-six-mile race. Third, the Persian-Greek Wars marked the invention in the West of the field of historical writing, with Herodotus's magnificent and pathbreaking *Histories*.

There was no rest for the weary in the wake of the Persian-Greek Wars. Just years after the end of those long wars, Athens and Sparta entered into the Peloponnesian Wars, 431–404 BCE, which led to the downfall of the Athenian Republic. Aside from giving us the second great book of Western history, Thucydides' *Peloponnesian Wars*, the defeat of Athens ended decades of Athenian preeminence that would forever after be remembered as the Golden Age of Athens, a period of efflorescence of democratic institutions, scholarship, the arts, and civil participation that has inspired the West ever since.

Yet Athens's decisive role in Western history was far from over, for it was the next century that gave us Plato, Aristotle, and the very foundations of Western philosophy. Socrates' death sentence was carried out in 399 BCE, and his greatest student and follower, Plato, opened his famed Academy in 387 BCE. There Plato put forward many of the core concepts of Western ethics, including the commitment to reason over the passions, the goal of self-knowledge, the pursuit of virtue, the objective of leading a good life, and the notion of politics as the search for the common good, that would be enshrined in Western thought. These ideas were further advanced, and modified, by Plato's greatest student and arguably the greatest thinker in Western history, Aristotle. Aristotle went on to start his own school, the Lyceum, rightly considered to be the world's first university, in 335 BCE. Unlike his teacher Plato, Aristotle was committed not only to philosophical contemplation but also to empirical research. Aristotle's direct study of life forms and ecology marked the birth of the science of biology. Aristotle is also credited with founding many other scientific disciplines, including logic, rhetoric, aesthetics, politics, ethics, and more.

Aristotle is remembered also for his most famous student. In 343 BCE, Aristotle was summoned by Philip of Macedon to tutor his young son Alexander, a task that Aristotle pursued for several years. Alexander became king of Macedonia and, in 334 BCE, embarked on his wars against Persia to the east, a retribution for the Achaemenid invasion of Greece a century-and-a-half earlier. In 332 BCE, Alexander captured Egypt, then a satrapy of Persia.

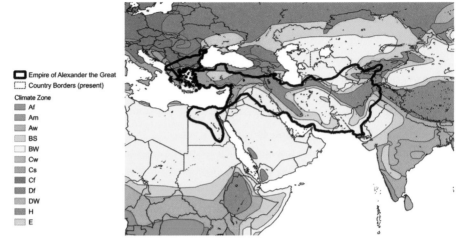

Empire of Alexander the Great
Country Borders (present)
Climate Zone
Af
Am
Aw
BS
BW
Cw
Cs
Cf
Df
DW
H
E

5.2 Empire of Alexander the Great, 323 BCE

He conquered the Persian Empire in 330 BCE with the capture of Persepolis, the capital, and continued his conquests to the east to the Indus River. On his march back toward Macedonia, Alexander died suddenly in Babylonia, of unknown causes, at the age of thirty-three in 323 BCE.

The maximum extent of Alexander's conquests is shown in figure 5.2. We see clearly the decisive east-west axis of Alexander's empire, following the now familiar east-west axis of climate zones and technological diffusion. Alexander conquered the regions to the east of Macedonia where his horse-drawn army could carry him. The Hellenistic empires that followed Alexander's death also remained within the ecological zones that could be governed by the Greeks— temperate zones and dryland alluvial regions characterized by mixed-crop and animal-husbandry agriculture, horse breeding, and the familiar range of infectious diseases—never venturing southward into the tropics. It was not until more than two thousand years later that European conquerors would discover how to survive in malarial regions of tropical Africa.

The Unmatched Legacy of the Greeks

When Alexander died suddenly, his generals and followers launched into a complex series of wars of succession. Parts of the empire were seized by followers, thereby creating several Hellenistic successor states. The most important of these were the Seleucid Empire, including Anatolia, the Levant, Mesopotamia, and Persia (essentially the Hellenistic successor of the Achaemenid Empire defeated by Alexander); the Ptolemaic Kingdom of Egypt; and, after a few decades of strife, the Antigonid Empire of Macedonia. Other Hellenistic kingdoms included Pergamum, the Greco-Bactrian Kingdom, and the Indo-Greek Kingdom, among others.

The result was centuries more of Greek colonization, trade, culture, and philosophy throughout the lands that Alexander had conquered. Greek wisdom continued to guide, train, and inspire a vast region from the eastern Mediterranean to the Indus River. Politics and trade were conducted in Greek as a lingua franca, and Greek texts circulated throughout this vast area. This influence would persist even after Greece itself was conquered by the Romans in 146 BCE, and even after the Ptolemaic Kingdom of Egypt finally succumbed to Rome in the epic battle of Actium, between Augustus and the combined forces of Cleopatra and Marc Anthony, in 31 BCE.

Greek culture was propagated by the establishment of *gymnasia* (schools for young men) that were designed to promote character, athletic ability, and fealty to Greek cultural ideas. The Greek concept of *paideia*, the education of youth to build the excellence of character needed for virtuous citizenship and the good life (*eudaimonia*), as described by Aristotle in the *Nichomachean Ethics*, was promoted throughout the Hellenistic empires. This ideal of the educational program has remained a formative concept throughout Western society up to the present.

The Roman Empire itself, which completed its conquest of Greece in 146 BCE, remained heavily dependent on Greek science, philosophy, and religion. The Eastern Roman Empire remained largely Greek speaking, and Roman elites were often bilingual in Greek and Latin. For a long period, Athens remained a preeminent center of learning, and the great libraries of the Roman Empire, notably in Alexandria and in Pergamum, avidly collected and protected Greek texts and learning. The Roman emperor Trajan's library in Rome had both Latin and Greek sections.

Greek learning became part of both Jewish and Christian thought through the reception of Greek philosophical ideas into religious thought by Jewish theologians such as Philo of Alexandria and early Christian theologians such as Origen, also of Alexandria. When Diocletian divided the Roman Empire into Western and Eastern parts, the Eastern Roman

Empire conducted its affairs in Greek, further reinforcing the fundamental role of Greek ideas in Roman rule. When the Western Roman Empire was conquered by Germanic tribes, the Greek learning largely disappeared from public institutions in the West but was kept alive, at least faintly, in the Christian monasteries.

In the east, with the rise of Islam in the seventh century, ancient Greek learning was given yet another great historical impetus by the Arab caliphs and generations of Islamic philosophers, who methodically studied and translated the ancient Greek volumes into Arabic, a principal route by which the Greek treasures have survived to the present. The Abbasid caliph Abdullah ibn Muhammad al-Mansur moved the capital of the caliphate from Damascus to a new City of Peace (Madinat-al-Salam), today's Baghdad. He attracted scholars to the new city and embarked on a huge mission of translating ancient texts. Throughout the Islamic world, great philosophers, including Ibn Sina (Avicenna) and later Ibn Rushd (Averroes), followed in the path of Philo and Origen by incorporating Aristotelian science and ethics into Islamic thinking and wisdom.

Mansur's grandson and successor as caliph established the Bayt-al-Hikmah (House of Wisdom) as Baghdad's great library and repository of ancient and current knowledge. Fortuitously, a great invention arrived in Baghdad at the same time: papermaking, a Chinese innovation. As described by Violet Moller, the art of making paper from fibrous plants was transferred to the Arab world by two Chinese soldiers captured in battle, leading to the first paper mill in the Muslim world in Samarkand in 751, with the know-how arriving in Baghdad some forty years later.[2]

Ancient Greek wisdom ultimately came full circle, returning to Rome and the West more generally in the Western Middle Ages. Arabic translations of the ancient Greek and Islamic commentaries on the Greek philosophers were translated into Latin and studied by church theologians in the twelfth and thirteenth centuries, most importantly by Thomas Aquinas (1225–1274), whose *Summa Theologica* is a profound meditation on faith and reason using the tools and philosophy of Aristotle combined with Christian theology. Aristotelian philosophy was embraced as the curriculum for Europe's new universities, in Paris (where Aquinas taught), Bologna, Padua, Salamanca, and elsewhere. The Italian Renaissance added a secular impetus with the new Renaissance passion for the ancient world. Another important event gave a further push. When the Ottomans captured

Constantinople in 1453, Greek scholars in Constantinople fled for their lives and brought their classical knowledge and texts to new positions within the European universities.

The Roman Empire

But let us return to the drama of imperial competition in the Classical Age. The Roman Empire, which defeated Macedonia during several wars between 214 and 148 BCE and then went on to conquer the other Hellenistic states (including the Ptolemaic Kingdom of Egypt in 32 BCE), lies along the familiar east-west axis of the lucky latitudes. In figure 5.3, we see that the Roman Empire's maximum extent as of 117 CE under Emperor Trajan closely tracks the Köppen-Geiger Mediterranean climate zone (Cw). The extent of the Roman Empire, like those before it, was largely defined by climate.

It is clear why the Roman emperors stopped at the coastal edge of North Africa. To go further south meant to hit the desert, with its inhospitable and largely uneconomic environment. And to go north of the imperial boundaries, across the Rhine into present-day Germany, meant to enter a difficult region characterized by thick forests, heavy soils, and cold

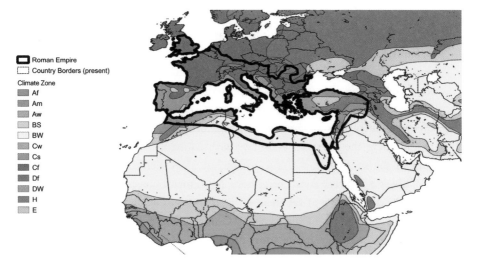

5.3 The Roman Empire, 117 CE

winters. In his study *Germania*, written around 98 CE, the Roman historian Tacitus observed: "Moreover, quite apart from the danger of a rough and unknown sea, who would abandon Asia or Africa or Italy and seek out Germania, with its unlovely landscape and harsh climate, dreary to inhabit and behold, if it were not one's native land?"

The Han Empire

Let us now turn our attention to the eastern edge of Eurasia in the same period as the rise of the Roman Empire. In China, the emperor Qin Shi Huang, famed for his burial in Xi'an with his terracotta army of warriors, horses, and chariots, first united China in 221 BCE. In explaining Qin's military success in unifying China, historian L. Carrington Goodrich notes: "The combination of excellent preparation, constant pressure, and superb mastery of the newest arts of war, especially cavalry, proved too much for his enemies."[3] Fighting on horseback, which had arrived from the western steppes, and many other technologies, including the ox-drawn plow (from the Near East), glassware (from the Mediterranean), and astronomical ideas (from South Asia), flowed into ancient China from the West, spurring China's own great capacity for technological innovation.

Although the Qin Dynasty lasted only from 221 until 206 BCE, it was followed by the Han Dynasty, which lasted for four hundred years, from 206 BCE to 220 CE. The Han Dynasty established boundaries of China that remain the core of the Chinese state today. To understand those boundaries, examine the climate zones of China and its neighbors. Modern-day China is characterized by a warm temperate climate in the east and south of the country, a cold temperate climate in the northeast, a dry steppe region along the northern boundary with Mongolia, the Himalayan plateau in the southwest, and a southern boundary along the tropical zone of China's Southeast Asian neighbors, Myanmar, Laos, and Vietnam. The Han Dynasty, shown at the peak of its area in 73 CE (figure 5.4), included the temperate zones of modern-day China plus a buffer zone of steppe separating the Han Empire from the steppe region of China's northern neighbor, the Xiognu Khanate (today's Mongolia). Then, as now, the tropics to the south were not part of the Han Empire.

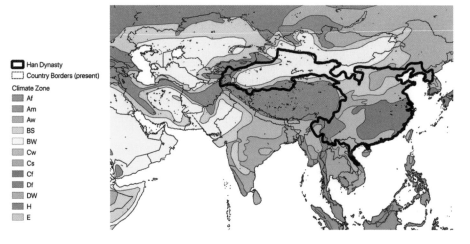

Han Dynasty
Country Borders (present)
Climate Zone
■ Af
■ Am
▨ Aw
▨ BS
□ BW
▨ Cw
□ Cs
■ Cf
■ Df
□ DW
■ H
▨ E

5.4 The Han Dynasty, 73 CE

The Han imperial extent, in other words, was the temperate region of continent East Asia plus a strip of steppe in the north that served as a buffer with the vast northern steppes. The population was centered on the two largest river basins, the Yellow River running west to east through the steppe region in the north and the Yangtze running west to east through the temperate zone in the south. The Yellow River farm system was based on wheat and millet in the cool and dry climate, while the Yangtze basin farmers mainly grew rice.

The Han fought vigorously to extend its rule into Vietnam and directly ruled Vietnam for repeated stretches, but each time, Han rule was reversed by local rebellions. At other times, the rule was indirect, with Vietnamese kingdoms paying tribute to the Chinese empire. While China's cultural influences on Vietnam were deep, China never succeeded in incorporating its southern tropical neighbors. The climate barrier ultimately set the limit of imperial expansion. The scholar Pita Kelekna, writing of the role of the horse in history, puts it this way: "The horse, evolved in semiarid climes, was definitely unsuited to dense rain forests and jungle warfare. The Chinese repeatedly attempted expansion southward, but as we have seen, even the Mongol Yuan could not consolidate conquest in tropical Southeast Asia."[4]

While China had received a flow of crucial technologies from the west in the first millennium BCE, the Han Dynasty is noted for a remarkable flowering of homegrown technologies. A partial list of spectacular break-throughs during the Han Empire includes papermaking, navigation (the rudder), mathematics (negative numbers, solution of equations), flood control (along the Yellow River), the waterwheel, metallurgy (wrought iron), and the seismometer. The empire also invented a model of administration that would last throughout China's history: a centralized national government ruling over a hierarchy of provinces, counties, districts, and villages. Confucianism was codified as the state ideology.

With its internal peace, the high productivity of mixed-grain and animal-husbandry farm systems, and an era of rapid technological break-throughs, the population of the Han Empire around 1 CE reached an estimated 60 million people, and the population of the Roman Empire at the time reached around 45 million. The Han and Roman empires together accounted for roughly one-half of the world's population.

The Developed World as of 100 CE

The Eurasian world in 100 CE (figure 5.5) was comprised of three major empires along the west-east axis of the lucky latitudes: the Roman Empire in the Mediterranean basin; the Parthian Empire of western Asia (today's

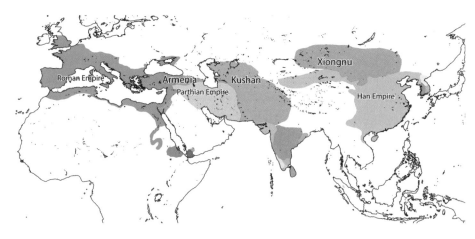

5.5 Major Eurasian Empires as of 100 CE

82

Iraq and Iran), and the Han Empire of China. After the collapse of the vast Mauryan Empire of India in 187 BCE, the Indian subcontinent was divided among a number of ruling states, including the Kushan, Indo-Scythians, Indo-Greeks, and others. To the north of the three great empires lay the heavily forested regions of northern Europe, the west Eurasian steppes north of Parthia, and the east Eurasian steppes north of China. To the south lay the deserts of North Africa and Arabia and the tropical lands of Southeast Asia.

As of 100 CE, the Roman and Han empires each had a population of around 60 million, and the Indian subcontinent had roughly the same or perhaps slightly more. The population of Parthia might be guessed at around 15 million. Combined, these regions were home to perhaps 200 million of the estimated 225 million world population. The populations of sub-Saharan Africa and the Americas were tiny, a few million each, as were the populations of the Eurasian steppes, deserts, and tropical regions. The vast productivity of the mixed-grain and animal-husbandry systems of temperate Eurasia, supported by horse-based trade and governance and the flow of technological advances across a vast east-west axis, meant that the lucky latitudes really were the center of world population, economy, and technology.

It is important to remember that the lucky latitudes contain two major climate zones: the temperate zones of Western Europe and China, at the western and eastern ends of Eurasia, and the vast stretch of semiarid and desert regions that lie in between in West and Central Asia. The Roman Empire and the Han Empire were each temperate-zone empires with high population densities fed by highly fertile grain production (mostly wheat in the Roman Empire and wheat, millet, and rice in the Han Empire), while the Persian Empire and others of West and Central Asia were far more sparsely populated, living on grains, fruits, and vineyards in the irrigated river valleys and the vast grasslands that fed their horses and maintained their cavalries.

The data in table 5.1 are therefore insightful. I use the estimates of the HYDE project on historical demography to estimate the population distribution across climate zones of several major empires: Alexander's empire, the first-century Roman Empire, the first-century Han Empire, and four empires that I discuss below: the eighth-century Umayyad Empire (the first Arab-Islamic empire) and the fifteenth-century Ottoman, Mongol, and Timurid empires. We see that the West Asian and Central Asian empires of Alexander, the Arabs, and Timur were largely dryland empires, while the Roman and Han empires were mainly temperate-zone empires.

Table 5.1 Percent of Population by Climate Zone for Major Empires

	Alexander the Great	Roman Empire	Han Dynasty	Umayyad Empire	Mongol Empire	Ottoman Empire	Timurid Empire
A	–	–	–	–	0.46	–	–
B	50.7	17.1	17.6	54.3	22.3	37.0	60.0
C	26.4	77.2	67.4	25.3	51.2	48.7	8.7
D	–	0.33	12.1	–	18.3	1.5	0.06
H	22.9	5.3	2.8	20.5	7.8	12.9	31.3

Source: Author's calculations using HYDE data. See data appendix for details.

The Ottoman Empire, successor to the Eastern Roman Empire, was a mix—temperate in Anatolia and the Balkans, dryland in western Asia. Ultimately, the larger populations and higher population densities of the Roman and Han empires gave them enormous advantages in scale and technological achievements but did not protect them from conquest by more sparsely set-tled neighbors—the Germanic tribes of northern Europe, the Turkish con-querors of the eastern Mediterranean, and the nomadic tribes of the Central Asian drylands that would raid and conquer China.

Global Trade Within the Lucky Latitudes

The three great empires and the northern kingdoms of the Indian sub-continent engaged in a long-distance exchange of technologies, manufac-tured goods, and ideas. The steppe regions provided the highways along the so-called Silk Road that connected Rome in the west with the Han Empire in the east (figure 5.6). Silks from China flowed into Rome, while glassware from the Mediterranean glassworks flowed into China. The Silk Road carried official embassies, such as one from Roman emperor Marcus Aurelius (r. 161–180 CE) to the Han emperor, as well as philosophers and teachers. The first mention of Buddhism in China, arriving from its home in northern India, occurred in 65 CE.

84

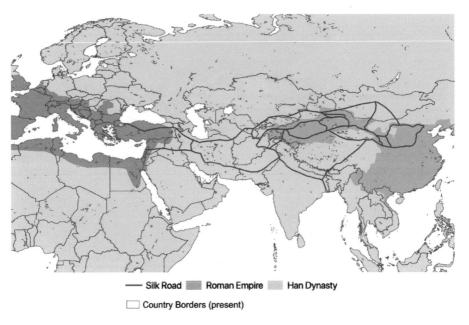

Silk Road ▬ Roman Empire ▨ Han Dynasty
☐ Country Borders (present)

5.6 The Silk Road, First Century CE

The Fall of Rome and the Rise of Islam

Despite Rome's dominance of technology and population, the political stability of the Roman Empire waned over time. In 285 CE, the Roman emperor Diocletian divided the rule of the vast empire between the Eastern Roman Empire ruled from Byzantium, later Constantinople, and the Western Roman Empire ruled from Rome. While the governance of the Roman Empire would go through further cycles of unity and east-west division, Diocletian's decision was never permanently reversed. The Western Roman Empire succumbed to conquest by Germanic tribes from the north, with the final fall of Rome in 476 CE. Meanwhile the Eastern Roman Empire lived on as the Byzantine Empire and still governed most of the Mediterranean basin from Constantinople. The extent of the Byzantine Empire in 555 CE is shown in figure 5.7.

For centuries after, the temperate lands faced a constant menace from the horseback warriors arriving from the Eurasian steppes. The Huns made devastating raids from the Black Sea region into Eastern and Western

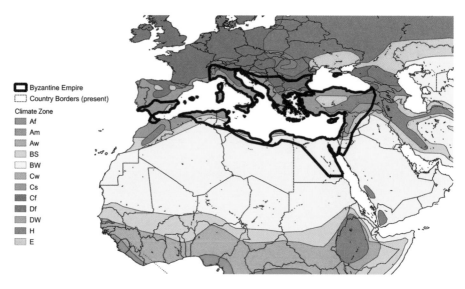

Byzantine Empire
Country Borders (present)
Climate Zone
Af
Am
Aw
BS
BW
Cw
Cs
Cf
Df
DW
H
E

5.7 The Byzantine Empire, 555 CE

Europe in the middle of the fifth century. The Goths, Avars, Magyars, Bulgars, and Xiognu, all originating in the steppes of Central Asia, attacked the temperate-zone civilizations to their south and are remembered for their ferocity and destruction. The military victories of these peoples over vastly more numerous populations is testimony both to the persisting advantage of cavalry in that era and to the decisive edge that military technology can offer to smaller states that are outnumbered and outclassed in other technologies. The even greater land victories of the Mongols, another conqueror from the steppes, would occur a few centuries later.

The great upheavals of the Mediterranean region following the fall of Rome, along with the weakening of the Persian (Sassanid) Empire in the seventh century, opened the way for yet another lightning conquest, this time by Arabs on horseback and camel who emerged from the Arabian desert with a new religion. Islam, and a succession of vast Islamic empires, arose rapidly and at a massive scale. Once again, the geographic logic followed the east-west ecological gradient, this time spreading across the deserts of Arabia into the drylands of North Africa and Spain to the west and into the drylands of West and Central Asia to the east. The Byzantine Empire was quickly shorn of its holdings in North Africa and the Levant.

Within one century, the Islamic realm extended from the Atlantic coast of Iberia across North Africa, the Arabian Peninsula, and the Levant into Persia and beyond to the Indus River. The Umayyad Dynasty was founded in 661 CE by the third caliph, with the capital in Damascus. The Umayyad Caliphate was in turn overthrown by the Abbasid Caliphate in 750 CE.

The Arabs failed in their attempt to extend their direct conquests into the temperate regions of Western Europe. The invading Islamic army was defeated by the Franks in the Battle of Tours (732 CE) in today's France, thereby limiting Islam's conquest in Western Europe to the Iberian Peninsula. In the eastern Mediterranean, the Arab armies battled the Eastern Roman Empire (Byzantium) over several centuries. By and large, the Byzantine Empire was able to repulse the Arab invaders from Anatolia and the Balkans region but lost several islands in the eastern Mediterranean, including Crete, Malta, and Sicily (figure 5.8). Islam, however, extended far beyond the conquests by the Arabs. Arab merchants and seafarers brought Islam to Indian Ocean settlements as early as the late seventh century. Islam subsequently took hold in parts of India, China, and Southeast Asia along major trade routes. Sufi missionaries created syncretic religious

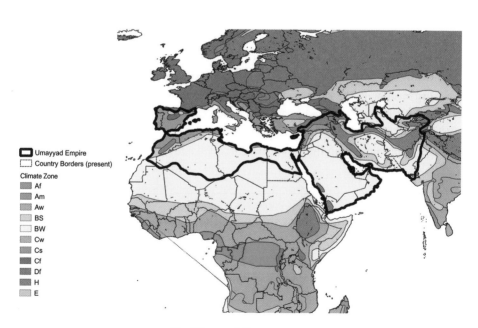

5.8 The Umayyad Empire, 700 CE

practices with local animist communities. And in the fifteenth and six-teenth centuries, rulers in the Indonesia archipelago and Malay peninsula converted to Islam to bolster their political authority.

Roughly four centuries after the rise of the Arab caliphates, the Arab-led empires were themselves confronted with a new and vigorous rival: Turkish tribes that emerged from Central Asia (present-day Turkmenistan and Kazakhstan) and entered the lands of western Asia via Persia. These Turkish tribes, beginning with the Seljuks, were heavily influenced by Per-sian society and converted to Islam around 1000 CE. The Seljuks defeated the Persian Empire and then advanced into Anatolia, wresting Anatolia from the Byzantine Empire step by step, with a key victory in 1071. The arrival of the Seljuks in western Asia and the Levant was the trigger for the First Crusade in 1095, called by Pope Urban II, which in turn launched centuries of competition in the Levant and Balkans between the Christian kingdoms of Europe and Byzantium on one side and the Muslim-Turkish empires of western Asia on the other.

The Seljuks, in turn, were displaced by another Turkish empire, the Ottomans, who eventually conquered the Arab lands of North Africa, the Byzantine capital at Constantinople in 1453, and the Byzantine lands of the Balkans and parts of Central Europe, including Budapest, but were stopped at the gates of Vienna. As we can see by comparing figures 5.7 and 5.9, the Ottomans governed most of the lands of the Byzantine (Eastern Roman) Empire at its maximum extent in 555 CE under Emperor Justinian, with the exceptions of the Italian peninsula and the westernmost regions of Morocco and Spain. Both the Byzantine and Ottoman empires were empires of the Mediterranean basin—the lands of wheat, olive groves, and vineyards—and the desert margins.

The Remarkable Song Dynasty of China

During the same years as the rise of the Seljuks and Ottomans, China was experiencing another golden age, the Song Dynasty, which is dated from 960 to 1279 (figure 5.10). On the eastern border of temperate Eurasia, a newly unified and peaceful China entered a period of stunning techno-logical innovation, population growth, and economic prosperity. China's

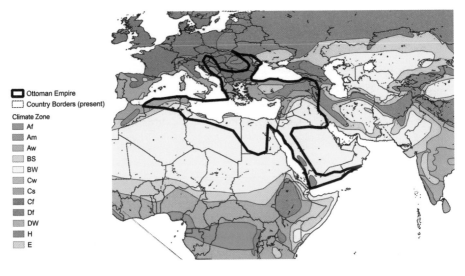

Ottoman Empire
Country Borders (present)
Climate Zone
Af
Am
Aw
BS
BW
Cw
Cs
Cf
Df
DW
H
E

5.9 The Ottoman Empire, 1566 CE

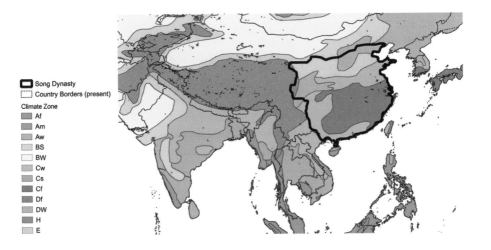

Song Dynasty
Country Borders (present)
Climate Zone
Af
Am
Aw
BS
BW
Cw
Cs
Cf
Df
DW
H
E

5.10 The Song Dynasty, 1200 CE

remarkable successes in technologies (such as the compass and gunpowder) and in governance (such as the issuance of paper currency) would eventually travel west and empower Western Europe in its global ascent after 1400. Yet for several centuries, China was far in the lead in technological innovations and peaceful governance.

At the base of the Song triumphs was the excellence of governance. The Song Dynasty has been termed "The Age of Confucian Rule." Dieter Kuhn explains:

> Between 960 and 1022, the early emperors of the Song and their councilors set high standards of government practice, intellectual activity, and personal conduct that would serve as a model for their successors. . . . Under the leadership of these three men [the first three Song rulers]— all lovers of learning—Song China came closer to the ideal of Confucian rule than any other dynasty in Chinese history. . . . Confucianism rooted in the classics offered an ethic based on humanness, righteousness, appropriateness, filial piety, loyalty, the civil principle over the military, and the performance of rites.[5]

The Song Dynasty might justly be considered the world's first large-scale capitalist economy: land was privately owned, merchant families invested in joint-stock companies, international trade was open, harbors were improved, and Chinese ocean-based trade expanded throughout the Indian Ocean to East Africa and the Red Sea. A navy established in the twelfth century policed the seas. Agricultural productivity rose, supporting a doubling of the Song population, to an astounding peak of around 120 million, and a massive increase of the urban population. The cities of Kaifeng and Hangzhou hosted populations of more than 1 million each. China still faced violence from its northern neighbors, and the Song Dynasty ceded the North China plains, including the Yellow River basin, to the Jurchen horsemen from Manchuria in 1142. The Jin Dynasty, as the Jurchens called their kingdom, would in turn be conquered by the Mongols a century later.

The technological innovations of the Song era, propelled by urbanization, peace, prosperity, and market forces, were astounding—one of the greatest technological flowerings of human history. The Song age brought major advances in navigation, including the nautical compass, the rudder, improved shipbuilding, and other maritime technologies; gunpowder and artillery; the moveable-type printing press, roughly two centuries before Gutenberg; structural engineering; metallurgy; artisanal ware, including fine porcelain and silk textiles; mechanical clocks; paper currency; and institutions of banking, insurance, and joint-stock enterprises. These advances gradually found their way west along the steppes and lucky latitudes to Venice and on to Western Europe.

The Last Hurrahs of the Steppe Conquerors

For more than three thousand years, semi-nomadic horsemen from the steppes settled, invaded, battled, dominated, and retreated from the temperate lands to the south. Regularly outnumbered, they won their victories through superior horsemanship, cavalry charges, careful planning, and valor. Their names—Huns, Alans, Goths, Turks, and Mongols—still inspire fear in Europe. Yet it was during a time of apparent peace and prosperity in the lucky latitudes, during the High Middle Ages in Europe and the Song Dynasty in China, in the thirteenth century, that the final burst of horsepower arrived from the steppes with the Mongols.

Genghis Khan was a Mongol warlord who defeated rival Mongol leaders and declared himself king of all the Mongols in 1206. From that point, he and his successors led the Mongol armies of tens of thousands of horsemen into conquests of China, Central Asia, Russia, the Caucasus, West Asia, and Eastern Europe. When Genghis Khan died in 1227, the empire already extended from the Pacific to the Caspian Sea. He was succeeded by his son Ogedei, who continued to expand the empire until his death in 1241. The Mongols had expanded into China, the Caucuses, and Central Asia and were invading Poland and Hungry when word of Ogedei's death reached the troops. This stopped the imminent invasion of Europe as the princes returned for the funeral and to elect the next Khan.

One intriguing hypothesis as to the extraordinary burst of Mongol military might is a climate period especially suited to livestock. According to a study of tree rings from Central Mongolia over a period of 1,112 years, my Columbia University colleague Neil Pederson and his associates found that the period 1206–27 was "warm and persistently wet." In particular, there

91

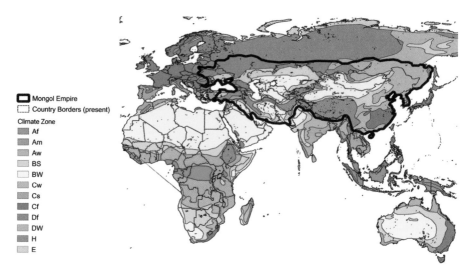

Mongol Empire
Country Borders (present)
Climate Zone
Af
Am
Aw
BS
BW
Cw
Cs
Cf
Df
DW
H
E

5.11 The Mongol Empire at its Maximum Extent, 1259 CE

were fifteen consecutive years of above-average moisture that was "unprecedented over the last 1,112 years." They propose that "these climate conditions promoted high grassland productivity and favored the formation of Mongol political and military power." In essence, exceptionally good rains led to good grasses, which fueled the horsepower to conquer Eurasia.[6]

By 1259, the Mongol Empire had reached the astounding extent shown in figure 5.11, making it the largest contiguous land empire in history. China, the Kievan Rus (the forerunner of Russia), Central Asia, the Caucasus, Persia, and parts of the Balkans and Eastern Europe were under Mongolian rule. Eurasia was at the mercy and control of the Mongols, a result of stunning military organization based on a superior cavalry and their remarkable exploits, including the capacity to cover vast distances in difficult terrain. A postal system united the vast empire, with riders covering up to two hundred kilometers per day.

The conquests were extraordinarily bloody, with millions killed. It was also by way of the Mongolian trading network that the Black Death reached Sicily from the Black Sea in 1347, eventually killing up to a quarter of the European population. Yet the Pax Mongolica that extended over the vast part of Eurasia also ushered in a massive expansion of east-west trade that connected Western Europe and East Asia. Merchants were protected, and trade flourished. It was on the Mongol Silk Road that Marco Polo took his famed journey to Khanbaliq (today's Beijing), Kublai Khan's capital in China.

The Mongol Empire began to unravel in the fourteenth century from internal dissension, disintegrating into a number of separate khanates. Those, in turn, soon collapsed. China was recaptured by Han rulers in 1378, ending a century of Mongol rule and ushering in the Ming Dynasty. Other Mongol khanates lasted longer, but generally were overtaken by local powers.

The Mongol Empire was not, in fact, the last attempt to create an all-encompassing Muslim land empire across Eurasia. The final remarkable attempt was due to an ethnic Turk, born near Samarkand (modern-day Uzbekistan), who took his inspiration from Genghis Khan. Timur, known to the West as Tamerlane (Timur the Lame) because of injuries he had incurred as a youth, was born circa 1330, roughly 170 years after Genghis Khan. While Timur was not a direct descendant of Genghis, and was ethnically Turco-Mongol rather than Mongol, he claimed a common ancestor with Genghis and depicted his conquests as serving to restore the rightful rule of the Mongols. He also declared his conquests to be in the name of Islam.

Timur spent thirty-five years in wars and expeditions, attempting to restore the Mongol Empire and indeed to conquer the known world. At its maximum extent, shown in figure 5.12, the Timurid Empire had swallowed

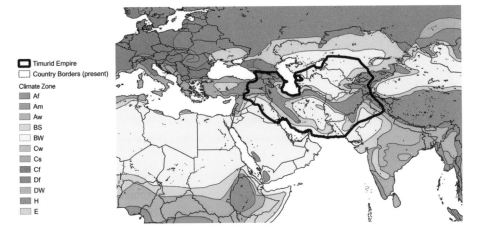

5.12 The Timurid Empire, 1400 AD

Persia, the trans-Caucasus (present-day Georgia, Armenia, and Azerbaijan), and much of Central Asia (present-day Afghanistan and Pakistan), but it was held in check in the Levant, Russia, and China. The empire was contained almost entirely within the BS (desert) and BW (steppe) climate zones, with little success in extending beyond the dryland regions. Timur's empire collapsed soon after his death in 1405, and with that collapse ended the empires of the steppe warriors of Central Asia. The steppe regions would in turn be conquered by others, notably Persia and Russia, in coming centuries.

Some Lessons from the Classical Age

It is easy to be awed by the Classical Age, with its breathtaking scale, dramas, and achievements. Here was civilization-making on a grand scale. Four great civilizations—Greco-Roman, Persian, Islamic, and Chinese—vied for power, while also engaging in long-distance trade and a continuous interchange of ideas and technologies across Eurasia. Of course, these achievements did not include the entire world; I have left out the stories of Africa, the Americas, and Oceania during this era. Yet it is also starkly true that Eurasia was home to 85 percent of humanity from 1000 BCE to 1 CE and 77 percent in 1500 CE.[7] And within Eurasia, the lucky latitudes were home to 67 percent of the Eurasian population in 1000 BCE and 57 percent in 1500 CE. As I've repeatedly emphasized, much of world economic history and technological advances were concentrated in the Eurasian lucky latitudes.

Two thousand years ago, the potential for multinational governance at a vast scale was already achieved. The European Union, one can say, seeks to govern Europe at the scale of the Pax Romana, but without the imperial wars and without the chauvinism of one people dominating the rest. The People's Republic of China similarly aims for the internal peace of the Han Dynasty and the remarkable innovative spirit of the Song Dynasty. Today's Islamic world is fragmented, yet the Golden Age of Islam under the Abbasid Caliphate of Baghdad reminds us of the era when Islamic scholars led the world in knowledge and sought ancient wisdom from all sources in order to create an integrated knowledge and science. That noble effort saved much of the Classical heritage for later generations, including our own.

6

The Ocean Age

(1500–1800)

As of 1500, we arrive at a pivotal moment in human history, when the Old World and the New World were suddenly reunited through ocean-going vessels, and when Europeans first sailed to Asia by circling the Cape of Good Hope at the Southern tip of Africa. For the first time in more than ten thousand years, ever since the land bridge Beringia between Asia and Europe was submerged at the beginning of the Holocene, there resumed an active interchange between the Old World and the Americas. Two voyages of the 1490s—those of Christopher Columbus from the Atlantic coast of Spain to the Caribbean in 1492 and of Vasco de Gama from Lisbon to Calicut, India, in 1498 and back in 1499—decisively changed the direction of world history. Humanity's understanding of the world and our place in it, the organization of the global economy, the centers of global power, and the decisive technologies of society were all upended by the new era of ocean-based globalization. Yet before we can appreciate the vast implications of these two voyages and their aftermath, we should first address a more basic question: Why did Western Europe rather than East Asia come to dominate the seas, and thereby the world?

The Great Chinese Reversal

In the early fifteenth century, China's navigational capacity was second to none in the world. The famed seven voyages of Admiral Zheng He during

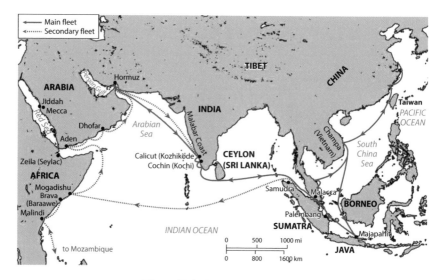

6.1 Zheng He's Fourth Voyage, 1413–1415

the early Ming Dynasty, in the first three decades of the fifteenth century, are justly remembered hundreds of years later as remarkable naval accomplishments of China.[1] These voyages of enormous fleets sailed from China to Southeast Asia, through the South China Sea and the Malacca Pass, around Java and Sumatra, into the Indian Ocean, and all the way to East Africa, Arabia, the coasts of India, and back to China. The route of the fourth voyage, 1413–15, is shown in figure 6.1.

These great voyages were a triumph of naval technology, a remarkable demonstration of China's grandeur, and an act of Chinese statecraft. The first voyage is described as consisting of a fleet of 317 ships with twenty-eight thousand crewmen; the other six voyages were of similar scale. One of the key goals of the Ming emperor was to ensure that all the countries of the Indian Ocean understood clearly the geopolitical ordering of the time. China was the undoubted Middle Kingdom, the one to which all other kingdoms should pay tribute and obeisance. The voyages aimed to establish a system of tributary trade. The visit by the Chinese fleet was to be followed by return visits by representatives of the respective kingdoms to China. In those latter visits, these states would pay tribute to the Middle Kingdom and in return receive reciprocal gifts from China. At the same time, private commercial trade independent of the tributary trade was highly restricted. Indeed, in 1371, the Ming emperor had prohibited purely private trade.

Zheng He's patron and sponsor was the Yongle emperor (r. 1402–24). Upon the emperor's death, his son discontinued the voyages on the grounds that they were unnecessary, expensive, and a violation of Confucian principles. The son died in 1425, and his successor, the Yongle emperor's grandson, ordered Zheng He in 1430 to undertake a seventh voyage. Zheng He apparently died at sea in 1433 or perhaps soon after the completion of the seventh voyage.

At that point, Chinese history took a more decisive anti-trade turn, one whose repercussions are still felt today. At a hinge moment of history, with China dominating the seas, and its naval power and abilities far surpassing anything known by Europeans, the Ming Dynasty largely abandoned the high seas, called off further voyages, and drastically reduced its fleet. Port facilities were scaled back, and the coastal population declined, signaling a decline in overall commercial maritime activity. While historians still debate the extent to which international commercial trade was ended, China surely downplayed the importance of the oceans in its future statecraft. One common argument is that the continuing threat of steppe warriors on the northern border led China to look northward rather than oceanward. Another argument is that Confucian bureaucrats of the Ming Dynasty looked askance at commercial activity.

The ramifications were profound. China largely abandoned the competition for the Indian Ocean at just the moment that two small kingdoms on the Atlantic coast, Portugal and Spain, began to increase their interest in oceangoing navigation and trade. Instead of China circling the Cape of Good Hope en route to Europe, it was European powers that circled the Cape of Good Hope en route to Asia. And within a century of 1433, it was the gunboats of Spain, Portugal, and other European powers that were plying the waters of the Indian Ocean and circumnavigating the Earth. China gradually ceded its technological leadership and fell behind Europe in the sciences, engineering, and mathematics. By the nineteenth century, the gap in technological capacity was so large that China's sovereignty was compromised not by its northern neighbors as in the past, but by North Atlantic European nations that were far less populous than China and halfway around the world.

Writing in 1776, 340 years after the last voyage, Adam Smith described China in this way:

> China has been long one of the richest, that is, one of the most fertile, best cultivated, most industrious, and most populous countries in world. It seems, however, to have been long stationary. Marco Polo, who visited it more than five hundred years ago, describes its cultivation, industry, and populousness, almost in the same terms in which they are described by travellers in the present times. It had perhaps, even long before his time, acquired that full complement of riches which the nature of its laws and institutions permits it to acquire.[2]

That China was "stationary" for this long period was likely due in part to its having abandoned the gains in technological and scientific knowledge that would have accompanied more vigorous ocean-based commercial trade. Only in 1978, 545 years after the end of the seventh voyage, would China again enthusiastically embrace open world trade as a core policy of statecraft.

The North Atlantic Quest for Ocean Navigation

On the other side of Eurasia, a very pioneering king of a small nation, King Henry the Navigator of Portugal, was encouraging naval exploration and advances in navigational technology with Portuguese caravels venturing down the coast of west Africa. Eventually those farsighted efforts would culminate with the Portuguese navigator Bartolomeu Dias reaching the southern tip of Africa, the Cape of Good Hope, in 1488. Then, with the help of Arab or Indian sailors in the Indian Ocean, Vasco da Gama sailed around the southern tip of Africa to the Calicut coast of southern India in 1498.

The main reason that Europeans were searching for a sea route to Asia was the knock-on effect of the fall of the Eastern Roman Empire. In 1453, the Ottoman sultan Mehmed II defeated the Byzantine emperor Constantine XI Palaiologos and occupied Constantinople. With the Ottoman Empire reigning in the newly named Istanbul, the ancient silk routes and sea routes to Asia were at risk. (The sea routes involved Mediterranean trade to a port in Egypt or the Levant, land portage to the Indian Ocean via Suez or the Arabian Peninsula, and then sea-based trade with Arab merchants to India or China.) Navigation in the eastern Mediterranean was under the threat of the Ottoman fleet, and the challenge of finding an alternative sea route to Asia became urgent.

The rulers of Western Europe gained a new and keen interest in ocean-based navigation. Suddenly, the countries of the North Atlantic (Spain, Portugal, Britain, France, and Holland) had the upper hand of geography compared with the previous longtime leaders of east-west trade, Genoa, Venice, and Byzantium. Fittingly, in 1492, the same year that saw the completion of the Christian reconquest of Spain from the long reign of Islamic powers, King Ferdinand and Queen Isabella sponsored the voyage of Christopher Columbus, who proposed to sail west across the Atlantic to find a new sea route to Asia. (The third act of 1492, sadly, was the expulsion of the Jews from Spain.)

The rest, one might say, is history. Rather than reaching India, Columbus stumbled upon the Americas (figure 6.2), though he still believed he had reached India. Vasco da Gama, for his part, sailed from Lisbon and made

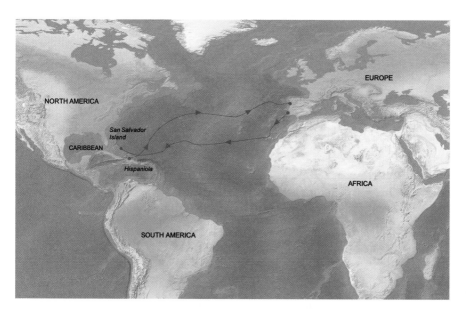

6.2 Columbus's First Voyage, 1492–1493

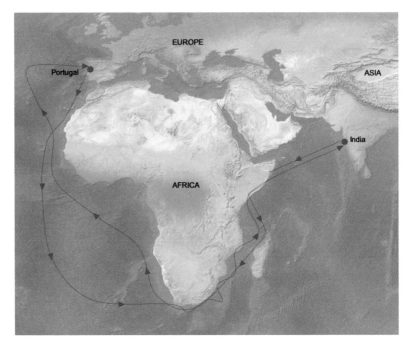

6.3 Vasco da Gama's First Voyage, 1497–1499

it to India and back in 1498–99 (figure 6.3). The race was now on, initially between Portugal and Spain, to earn the spoils from these two historic breakthroughs. More fundamentally, these two voyages reconnected the entire inhabited world for the first time in more than ten thousand years, ever since the rising ocean level at the end of the Pleistocene had submerged the Beringia land bridge between Asia and North America.

The Columbian Exchange

As noted by the great environmental historian Alfred Crosby, Columbus's voyages produced much more than a meeting of Europeans and Native Americans. They created a sudden conduit for the unprecedented two-way exchange of species between the Old World and the New—plants, animals, and disastrously, pathogens. This two-way exchange, which Crosby calls the

Columbian exchange, was biologically unprecedented, with profound consequences that have lasted to the present day.[3]

The most obvious effect was the exchange of crops between the Old World and the New, along with the introduction of many domesticated animals into the Americas for the first time. The Americas offered the Old World such staples as maize, potatoes, and tomatoes. In return, the Old World offered wheat and rice, crops that had never before been cultivated in the Americas. Suddenly, too, there were farm animals: horses in North America for the first time in ten thousand years, along with cattle, sheep, goats, and pigs. Addictive crops also flowed in both directions: tobacco from the Americas to Europe, and sugarcane to the Americas, a crop that would fundamentally transform the Caribbean and the European economies. Other crops in the two-way exchange are shown in figure 6.4.

The arrival of Europeans and their livestock also brought Old World diseases to the Americas, diseases that that the indigenous populations in the Americas had never previously encountered and to which they therefore had no genetic or acquired immunity. The Old World delivered almost all of the pathogens in a one-way exchange to the Americas; few, if any,

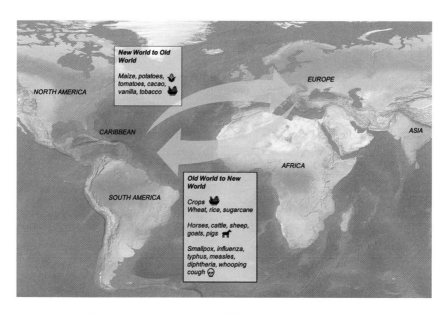

6.4 The Columbian Exchange of Crops, Animals and Pathogens

diseases were transferred from the Americas to the Old World. The reason is that most of the diseases of the Old World began in animal reservoirs, notably in domesticated farm animals, which were not present in the Americas. Since the indigenous Americans had few domesticated farm animals, they had few novel zoonotic (animal-to-human) diseases to transmit to the European arrivals.

The list of newly arrived diseases from Europe was long and deadly including smallpox, influenza, typhus, measles, diphtheria, and whooping cough. Smallpox was the mass killer; it wiped out a shocking proportion of the native populations encountering the newly arrived Europeans. African slaves and slave traders also transmitted two mosquito-borne pathogens, malaria and yellow fever, from Africa to the New World. There is a remaining question as to whether new microbial pathogens were in fact transmitted from the Americas back to Europe. One candidate is syphilis, which had its first outbreak in Europe in 1495. There remains considerable controversy among three possibilities: that syphilis existed in the Old World but was not diagnosed; that syphilis was brought to Europe by Columbus's returning crew; or that European syphilis was a mutated form of the bacterium *Treponema* brought back from the Americas. Recent evidence points toward the New World origin of the disease.[4]

There is also a continuing debate about the demographic impact of the Columbian exchange because there is substantial uncertainty about the size of the native populations in the Americas prior to European arrival. Estimates of the population of the Americas on the eve of Columbus's arrival have varied enormously, from a few million to 100 million or even more. A recent very careful assessment by Alexander Koch and colleagues has produced the estimates shown in table 6.1. According to these estimates, the indigenous population in 1500 stood at 60.5 million. By 1600, the population had declined by 90 percent, to just 6.1 million.[5]

One result of this catastrophic decline in population was a commensurate decline in the land in the Americas used for farming. With land use per capita around one hectare, the fall in population resulted in a reduction in land use of some 55 million hectares. Much of this land returned to forest or other vegetative cover, leading to a biological drawdown and storage of atmospheric carbon, which the authors estimate to have been on the order of 7.4 billion tons of carbon (GtC) between 1500 and 1600, or a drawdown of roughly 3.5 parts per million of CO_2 in the atmosphere. This reduction

Table 6.1 Estimates of Population and Land Use in the Americas,
1500 and 1600

	1500	1600
Population (millions)	60.5	6.1 (–90%)
Land use per capita (hectares)	1.04	1.0
Land use (millions of hectares)	61.9	6.1 (–90%)
Net carbon uptake (GtC)	–	7.4 (from 1500 to 1600)

Source: Data from Alexander Koch, Chris Brierley, Mark M. Maslin, and Simon L. Lewis, "Earth System Impacts of the Europrean Arrival and Great Dying in the Americas after 1492." *Science Direct* 207 (March 2019): 13–36

of atmospheric CO_2, in turn, likely played a role in the observed cooling of the Earth's temperature in the sixteenth century, which is estimated to have been around 0.15 degrees Celsius. This slight cooling has sometimes been termed the Little Ice Age in Europe in the 1500s.

Whatever the case with climate, the decline in native populations was undoubtedly tragic and catastrophic. Disease was the major initiating factor, but war, plunder, conquest, and subjugation of indigenous communities and destruction of their cultures also no doubt contributed. Even today, the Americas remain sparsely populated relative to Europe and Asia. The population densities of the continents (population per km²) as of 2018 are estimated as follows: Asia, 95; Europe, 73; Africa, 34; North America, 22; South America, 22; Australia, 3.

The Gunpowder Age and the High Seas

The strategic situation for the European nations was different in the Indian Ocean. There, the Europeans faced populous and long-established societies with sophisticated military capacities and, unlike in the Americas, a shared pool of pathogens with the arriving Europeans. Yet the Europeans were still able to gain a foothold to establish both a commercial and a military presence. Over time, they came to dominate the Indian Ocean sea-lanes despite being interlopers from thousands of miles away. Their advantage lay heavily with military technologies that had originally arrived from China but were now turned to Europe's advantage: gunpowder and well-protected fortresses.

Gunpowder was first developed in China in the Song Dynasty, and the earliest guns were developed there as well. Yet it was in Europe that these technologies were pushed forward. Gunpowder and early guns may have been brought to Europe by the Mongols, who had adopted the technology from the Chinese. The European powers, heavily engaged in wars within Europe, quickly innovated cannons of increasing power and accuracy and placed them on oceangoing galleons and other ships.

These cannon-laden ships gave the European nations the military advantage to establish new colonies, trading posts, and fortresses throughout the Indian Ocean. While China and other Asian countries rather quickly emulated the new artillery arriving from Europe, the early military advantage of the European naval powers was enough to establish beachheads in several strategic outposts. The gains in trade that resulted for Europe were matched by losses in the authority, prestige, and trading income of China. China's tributary system largely collapsed, both because of China's self-imposed withdrawal from the Indian Ocean and because of the rising military strength of the European powers in the Indian Ocean.

The New European Age of Inquiry

The fall of Constantinople and the discovery of the sea routes to the Americas and Asia did more than reroute global trade. These events also rerouted the European mind. The discovery of new lands based on new technologies radically altered the European worldview. The Americas were not mentioned in the Bible, nor were the species of plants and animals that the Europeans discovered there. Here truly was something new under the sun.

Three other currents of the time contributed to a radical change in the European worldview regarding empiricism, science, and technology. The first was the flood of Greek scholars to Europe after the fall of Constantinople to the Turks. A great concentration of philosophical learning, with roots back to ancient Greece, suddenly showed up in Western Europe, with Greek scholars arriving to the Italian universities at Bologna, Naples, Padua, and Siena.

This flood of scholarship was a prime factor in the second great tide of the times, the arrival of the Renaissance in Western Europe. The rediscovery of the arts, philosophy, and great learning of ancient Greece and Rome was already under way in the first half of the fifteenth century but was given an added spur by the fall of the Eastern Roman Empire. The Renaissance had its roots as well in the growing commerce and urbanization occurring throughout Western Europe, but notably in northern Italy, the Netherlands, and southern Germany. Florence, with its burgeoning trade and industry in woolens, was a center of the new Renaissance learning and arts.

The third great event of the age was the invention (or, in part, the reception from China) of printing with movable type, led by Johannes Gutenberg around 1439 in Mainz. This invention dramatically reduced the cost of books and quickly led to the establishment of more than a hundred printshops in Europe by 1480. An estimated 20 million book copies were printed by 1500, and the numbers would soar in the coming century. The age of learning was spurred immeasurably by the rapid dissemination of knowledge through low-cost printing.

The cumulative impact of these trends was an era of revolutionary thought, as dogma and accepted wisdom flew by the wayside. The 1510s are certainly among the most remarkable years of human thought in modern history. In 1511, the humanist scholar Desiderius Erasmus of Rotterdam published his satirical critique of the church, *In Praise of Folly*. In 1513, Nicola Machiavelli of Florence published *The Prince*, his handbook of power for European princes. In 1514, Nicolaus Copernicus, in Krakow, circulated an early draft of his heliocentric theory, *Commentariolus*, which was formally published three decades later. In the following year, 1515, Sir Thomas More published *Utopia*, focusing European minds on the possibilities of political and social reform. And in 1517, Martin Luther posted his Ninety-Five Theses on the church door in Wittenberg, setting off the explosion of the Reformation.

While these remarkable events did not point to any single intellectual outcome, they represented an unleashing of intellectual ferment across Europe and led to remarkable advancements of knowledge. (The Reformation also led to spasms of violence between Catholics and Protestants that would rage for centuries.) The intellectual ferment gathered into Europe's scientific revolution, with Galileo's discoveries at the end of the sixteenth century in turn leading the way to Newton's physics in the mid-seventeenth century. These historic breakthroughs were accompanied by a surge in experimentation and an intense interest in engineering and new technical devices, in part to address military challenges. At the start of the seventeenth century, Francis Bacon enunciated, in *Novum Organum*, the new scientific method of experimentation and the age's emerging belief that directed scientific research would improve the world, or perhaps conquer it. In 1660, Britain's greatest minds, following the path set by Bacon, launched a new Royal Society of London for Improving Natural Knowledge, and in 1666, King Louis XIV of France launched the French Academy of Sciences, creating important new institutions to promote the new scientific outlook.

Europe's universities and scientific academies offered an astoundingly fruitful knowledge network unmatched in scale and depth by any other part of the world. Some of the new European sciences disseminated globally through the remarkable work of the Jesuit order of the Catholic Church.⁶ The order was founded with the approval of Pope Paul III in 1540 by ten graduates of the University of Paris led by Ignatius de Loyola. Jesuit missionaries promptly set forth across the oceans to Portuguese and Spanish settlements to establish new centers of missionizing and learning, some of which would become Jesuit colleges and universities. The Jesuits may plausibly be credited with creating the first global network of higher learning, with Jesuit schools and printing houses quickly established across Europe, and Jesuit missionary and teaching activities established overseas in South America, India, Japan, China, the Philippines, and Portuguese colonies of Africa.

These far-flung Jesuit missions collated new global knowledge of botany and geography, and during the sixteenth and seventeenth centuries, brought many advances of European science and mathematics to the Mughal court in India, the Ming Dynasty in China, early Tokugawa Japan, and elsewhere. The Jesuits also displayed remarkable moral valor in defending the rights of native populations against the depredations of the Portuguese and Spanish colonists, often at extreme danger and duress to the Jesuit missionaries themselves at the hands of the colonial authorities and slave traders.

The Birth of Global Capitalism

Europe's new global-scale trade with the Americas and with Asia also marked the birth of global capitalism, a new system of global-scale economic organization. The new economic system was marked by four distinctive features:

(1) Imperial power extended across oceans and ecological zones. The temperate-zone nations of Western Europe colonized tropical-zone regions in the Americas and Asia to produce tropical products such as tobacco, sugarcane, cotton, rubber, or minerals.

(2) Production systems were globalized, with plantations and mines established in the colonized countries exporting primary commodities to the home country for industrial processing, notably in the case of cotton.

(3) Profit-oriented, privately owned corporations were chartered by European governments to carry out these global activities. The most important of these new chartered companies were the British East India Company, chartered in 1600, and the Dutch East India Company, chartered in 1602.

(4) These private companies maintained their own military operations and foreign policies under the protection of their founding charters and their states' navies.

The European powers faced different challenges in the Americas and in Asia. In the Americas, the main goal was to exploit the natural resources of the New World, most importantly gold and silver, and over time, to produce high-value crops for the European market. These included crops found in the Americas, such as cacao, cotton, rubber, and tobacco, and crops brought by the Europeans from Africa and Asia to plant in the Americas, notably sugar, coffee, and rice.

In Asia, the first aim was to gain control over parts of Asian trade, including spices from the Indonesia archipelago, cotton fabrics from India, and silks and porcelains from China. Before 1500, trade in these commodities was largely in the hands of Arab, Turkish, and Venetian intermediaries, meaning high prices in European markets. The Atlantic powers aimed to cut out the middlemen and profit directly from European-Asian trade. Later, as European countries and private companies extended their military sway over parts of coastal Asia, they aimed to control local production as well as trade and to repress the export of Asian finished goods to Europe (e.g., Indian textiles sold in European markets) in order to protect nascent industries in Europe.

The powers of trade and production were vested in private companies that became the forerunners of today's multinational corporations. The British East India Company and the Dutch East India Company were given monopolies by their respective governments to trade in the East Indies, with the goal of wresting control of the trade away from Portugal and Spain, which in turn had taken it from the Arabs and others. Britain and Holland, as late arrivals to Indian Ocean trade, would have to fight wars with Portugal and Spain to win their place in global trade. The British East India Company not only vanquished its rivals, but in time vanquished India as well.[7]

Europe's Scramble for Global Empire

Europe's discovery of new lands in the Atlantic Ocean and the Americas set off a brutal battle for global empire, one that continues today. The first new colonies after 1450 were in the Atlantic Ocean islands and the Americas, and then in Asia and Africa. The seafaring countries of the North Atlantic would take the lead: Portugal, Spain, Holland, and Britain, with France, Russia, Germany, and Italy entering the race for overseas colonies later.

Henry the Navigator's expeditions around West Africa set off the scramble with the discovery of the Cape Verde islands in 1456. Portugal colonized these uninhabited tropical islands six years later, in 1462, making Cape Verde the first tropical colony of a European country. When the Spanish reconquest was completed in 1492, enabling Spain's Christian monarchs Ferdinand and Isabella to turn their attention to oceanic trade, they backed Columbus's attempt to find a western sea route to Asia in order to counter Portugal's attempts to find a southern sea route around Africa. Columbus's discovery of the Caribbean islands set up a scramble for colonial possessions between the two Iberian powers.

Portugal asserted that it had the rights to all "southern lands" based on its earlier discoveries. Spain's monarchs turned to the Spanish pope

Alexander VI, the second pope of the House of Borgia, whom they knew would be sympathetic to the Spanish cause. In 1493, the pope recognized the Spanish claims to the newly discovered lands and then, in 1494, brokered an agreement between Portugal and Spain to divide the world. According to the Treaty of Tordesillas (Spain), Portugal would own all newly discovered possessions east of a longitude line set in the middle of the Atlantic Ocean, 370 leagues west of Cape Verde. Spain would own all newly discovered lands west of that meridian. (The precise meridian would be in heated dispute thereafter because of differences in estimates about the size of the Earth.)

Initially the dividing line referred just to the Atlantic Ocean, but with the voyages to Asia and Magellan's circumnavigation in 1519, it became necessary to divide the world in Asia as well. The Treaty of Zaragoza in 1529 ostensibly drew the dividing line at the anti-meridian of the Tordesillas line (the completion of a great circle, 180 degrees opposite) in the Indian Ocean. Spain would have the lands west of this meridian, including the Philippines, while Portugal would have the lands east of the line, including the coveted spice islands in the Indonesian archipelago, the source of the highly popular and lucrative nutmeg.

The world's newly discovered lands were thus to be divided between two Catholic nations, Portugal and Spain. Yet other newcomers had quite different ideas. From the early sixteenth century onward, two other rising Atlantic powers, Britain and Holland, both part of the Reformation that rejected papal authority, aggressively contested the papal treaties. Eventually Britain would triumph, winning the greatest global empire by the nineteenth century. In its early naval forays, Britain chose to explore a northwest passage to Asia, one that would not directly confront Portugal and Spain in the tropics. Hence came the British discoveries along the northern coast of North America, today's New England and Canadian coasts.

But Britain's voyages failed to find a northwest passage to India. As a result, Britain resorted first to piracy and then to outright military confrontation to challenge the Portuguese and Spanish claims. Britain's naval heroes, such as Sir Francis Drake, were simply pirates or terrorists from Spain's point of view. As the sixteenth century progressed, Britain gained mastery over naval design, building fast and maneuverable galleons that could threaten Spain's warships. The decisive showdown came in 1588, when the Spanish monarch decided to invade Britain to put down the upstart nation. The effort failed disastrously, with Britain's defeat of the Spanish armada, a signal event in military history that put Britain on the path to global power and Spain on the path of imperial decline.

With its growing naval power, Britain entered the imperial fray with Portugal and Spain in the East Indies as well as in the Caribbean. In 1600, Queen Elizabeth chartered the British East India Company and granted it a monopoly of trade in the East Indies. This was quickly followed by the Dutch East India Company (VOC), chartered in 1602; the French East India Company following several decades later in 1664. From the start, trade, warfare, and colonization were inextricably linked.

Spain and Portugal were the first European nations to establish global empires in the sixteenth century, with Britain and Holland scrambling to catch up in the seventeenth century. The Spanish and Portuguese empires around 1580 are shown in figure 6.5, with the effects of the Treaties of Tordesillas and Zaragoza evident. Spain controlled, or at least claimed to

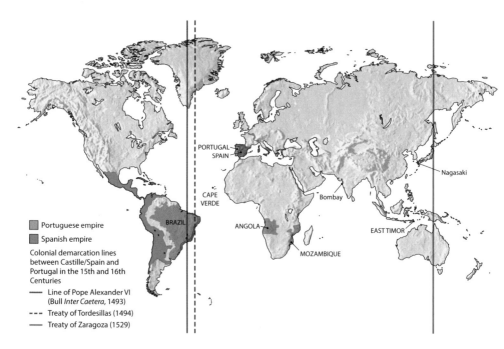

6.5 Spanish Portuguese Overseas Empires, With Papal Lines of Demarcation

control, the lands of the Americas other than Brazil and eastern North America (mainly claimed by Britain and Holland), as well as the Philippines and other islands in the western Pacific. Spain also had coastal possessions around Africa. Portugal's empire included Brazil, Atlantic islands, coastal settlements around Africa, and settlements throughout the Indian Ocean.

By 1700, the world's division of power was as shown in figure 6.6. The great land powers of Asia included the Qing Dynasty in China, the Mughal Empire in India, the Safavid Empire in Persia, and the Ottoman Empire in West Asia. The New World was now divided among four European powers: Portugal, Spain, Britain, and France. The Dutch Republic had been knocked out of the running by Britain's victories in three British-Dutch wars of the seventeenth century. Dutch New Amsterdam became British New York as of 1664, with a temporary reversion to the Dutch in 1673 that was then reversed in 1674.

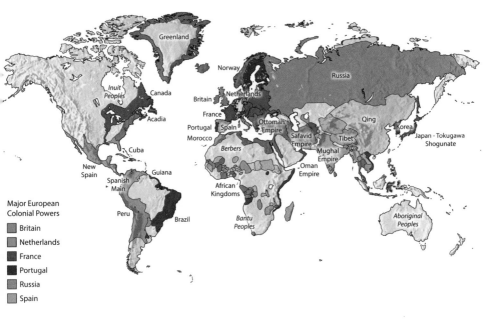

6.6 World Empires and Selected Nations, 1700.

Map by Network Graphics

Over time, the British Empire would come to achieve global naval dominance. The great naval historian of the late nineteenth century, Alfred Thayer Mahan, attributed Britain's long-term economic and imperial success and the long-term declines of France, Holland, Portugal, and Spain, to Britain's naval superiority over its rivals. In Mahan's 1890 book, *The Influence of Sea Power Upon History, 1660–1783*, he explained that national wealth depended on long-distance trade, long-distance trade depended on overseas colonies, and the security of overseas colonies depended on naval preeminence.[8] In Mahan's telling, Spain's decline (and Portugal's, under the shared crown) was inevitable after the British defeat of the Spanish armada in 1588. Holland's relative decline in the seventeenth century followed the decline of Holland's naval power and Holland's subsequent reliance on the British navy. France's loss of empire, in Mahan's view, was determined by its naval defeats by the British in the Seven Years' War of 1756–63.

Russia's Land Empire of the North

While Europe's Atlantic states were vying for transoceanic empires, Russia emerged in the eighteenth century as Eurasia's vast land empire of the north, seen in figure 6.6. As the inheritor of the Mongol and Timurid empires, Russia became history's second largest contiguous empire by size, 22 million km² at its peak in 1895, second only to the Mongol empire's 23 million km² at its maximum extent in 1270. Only the British Empire was larger, with a land area across the globe summing to 35 million km² at its maximum extent in 1920.[9]

The Russian Empire is geographically distinct: an empire of the northern climate. Taking the region of the Commonwealth of the Independent States (CIS) as our reference point, the region is approximately 70 percent in the D (cold) climate, 7 percent in E (polar) climate, and 19 percent in the B (dry climate), with essentially no land area in the tropical or temperate climates, as we see in table 6.2. Whereas Europe west of Russia is largely temperate (around 71 percent by area), and Asia is a mix of tropical, dry, and temperate regions (with A, B, and C climates totaling 76 percent by area), Russia is cold, polar, or dry.

Russia's climate had three overwhelming implications throughout the history of Russia until the twentieth century. First, grain yields were very

Table 6.2 CIS, EU, and Asia by Climate Zone and Population Density

Climate zone	Area (%) CIS	EU	Asia	Population density (pop/km²), 1400 CIS	EU	Asia	Population density (pop/km²), 2015 CIS	EU	Asia
A	0.0	0.0	17.7	–	–	11	–	20	243
B	18.7	1.0	40.4	1	10	4	19	91	83
C	0.5	70.7	17.7	3	12	21	80	128	348
D	70.0	22.9	8.0	0	3	8	11	48	153
E	6.6	2.3	0.0	0	0	–	0	0	–
H	4.2	3.1	16.2	2	10	2	43	115	40
Total	–	–	–	1	10	8	13	106	157

Source: Author's calculations using HYDE and CIESIN data. See data appendix for details.

low in the short growing seasons of the far north and the steppe regions in the south of the empire. Second, as a result, populations remained small and the population densities were far lower than in Europe and Asia. In 1400, for example, the CIS lands had a population density of fewer than one person per km², less than one-tenth the population density of Europe and Asia. Third, as farm families struggled to feed themselves in the harsh environment, much less provide any surplus for the market or for taxation, the Russian population remained overwhelming rural until the twentieth century. The HYDE 3.1 estimates put the Russian urbanization rate at just 2 percent as late as 1800, roughly one-tenth the urbanization rate of Western Europe.[10]

Russia's peasant farmers were not only impoverished and sparsely settled but also mostly enserfed until their liberation from serfdom in 1861 by imperial decree. Thus, the long legacy of Russia's unique geography was a sparse, illiterate, and overwhelmingly unfree rural population that formed the sociological crucible of the Bolshevik Revolution of 1917. Under Soviet communism in the twentieth century, the lands of the Russian Empire were industrialized and urbanized via a brutal top-down one-party state that claimed tens of millions of lives in the course of forced industrialization and the collectivization of farmlands—a "second serfdom"—that was carried out by Joseph Stalin's regime in the late 1920s and 1930s.

Insatiable Greed of the Empire Builders

The remarkable scramble by the European powers for riches, glory, and colonies in the New World and Asia, and the privatization of wealth-seeking via the new joint-stock companies, ushered in a new ethos of greed. It was one thing to exploit the native populations and grab their land; it was another to create an ethos that justified such actions. The Christian virtues of temperance and charity had long preached self-control over the passions for wealth and glory. A new morality was needed to justify the remarkable efforts toward conquest and the subjugation of whole populations. Over time, the justification was the idea that conquest was a God-given right, even a responsibility, to bring civilization to the heathens. Success, moreover, was a sign of God's favor and providence. There were demurrals, to be sure. The Spanish monarchy, for instance, eventually outlawed the enslavement of native populations in the Americas in the New Laws of 1542. Yet those demurrals were limited, to say the least. The age of global empire was also an age of monumental cruelty, with ruthless greed built into the emerging capitalist order.

By the eighteenth century, a new ideology was taking form, especially in Britain, that "greed is good" (to use a recent summary formulation), because greed spurs a society's efforts and inventiveness. By giving vent to greed, the logic goes, societies can best harness the insatiable ambitions, great energies and ingenuity of their citizens. While greed by itself might be unappetizing and seem to be antisocial, the unleashing of greed could in fact lead to the common good. Thus was born the idea that Adam Smith would crystalize as the "invisible hand"—the idea that the pursuit of self-interest by each person promotes the common interest of society as a whole as if by an invisible hand. Smith himself was a moralist and a believer in personal virtues, self-restraint, and justice. Yet Smith's concept of the invisible hand quickly became an argument to let market forces play out as they might, no matter the distributional consequences.

The first statement of this counterintuitive idea came not from Smith but from a London-based pamphleteer and poet at the start of the eighteenth century, Bernard Mandeville, in an ingenious poem called "The Fable of the Bees." In the poem, greedy and self-interested bees create such energy that the beehive becomes the marvel of the bee kingdom. Vice produces virtues. With wit, Mandeville put it this way:

Thus every Part was full of Vice,
Yet the whole Mass a Paradice;
Flatter'd in Peace, and fear'd in Wars
They were th'Esteem of Foreigners,
And lavish of their Wealth and Lives,
The Ballance of all other Hives.
Such were the Blessings of that State;
Their Crimes conspired to make 'em Great;
And Vertue, who from Politicks
Had learn'd a Thousand cunning Tricks,
Was, by their happy Influence,
Made Friends with Vice: And ever since
The worst of all the Multitude
Did something for the common Good.

The worst of the multitude, Mandeville claims, creates the common good. It's a view, alas, that would not have been shared by the conquered peoples on the receiving end of European imperialism.

The Intertwining of State and Capital

In the theory of free trade, government is to stay clear of market forces, letting supply and demand play out as they may. This doctrine, I have emphasized, fails to address the distributional consequences of market forces that can leave multitudes impoverished. It also fails to describe capitalism as it is, and as it was from the start. Not only have capitalist enterprises often been extraordinarily ruthless in their pursuit of profit; they have often, even typically, had the power of the state at their disposal to magnify their profits and shift losses to others, sometimes to fellow citizens but more often to the weak and vulnerable of other societies.

Consider Britain's entry into global markets in its competition with Spain and Portugal. Queen Elizabeth was a personal investor in 1577 in Francis Drake's plan to circumnavigate the globe on his vessel the *Golden Hind*. Yet in addition to exploration, the real plan was piracy: to loot the Spanish fleet bringing bullion and other treasures back from South America. In 1578, Drake captured a Spanish galleon with a phenomenal haul of gold, silver, jewels, porcelain, and other treasure. On Drake's return, the pirated gains were shared with the queen, who used them to pay off the national debt. Drake became a national hero, and went on to serve as vice admiral in the defeat of the Spanish armada in 1588.

In 1600, the launch of the East India Company marked an even more decisive breakthrough to modern capitalism. Here was a joint-stock company formed specifically to engage in multinational trade. Once again, the private investors could count on the power and beneficence of the state. Queen Elizabeth charted the East India Company as a monopoly to engage in all trade east of the Cape of Good Hope and west of the Straits of Magellan. From the start, the company paid bribes and gifts to the court and to leading politicians while acting as a state within a state in its dealings in India, complete with private army, the powers of bribery, and the protections of limited liability.

Indigenous Populations and African Slaves in the New World

The history of the New World quickly became the drama of three distinct groups of humanity. The first were the indigenous peoples of the Americas, struck hard by Old World diseases and conquest but continuing to fight for physical, cultural, and political survival. The second were the European conquerors and settlers. The third were the African slaves brought by the millions to work the mines and plantations of the New World. The cauldron of conquest and stratification has shaped the Americas to this day as a region of sky-high inequality and conflict, yet one that would try over the centuries to forge an avowedly multiethnic and multiracial society.

The European conquerors came for glory and wealth, but grappled from the start with the fundamental question of who was going to produce that wealth. The hope, of course, was for easy riches—Eldorado, the city of gold, based on imagined vast and easy riches. The Spanish found gold and silver mines that they ruthlessly exploited in the sixteenth century, flooding Europe with precious metals, but even the mines needed workers for the backbreaking, life-threatening labor. The plantations were also brutal, requiring harsh physical labor in tropical conditions, causing heat stress, extreme vulnerability to a host of tropical diseases, and very often early death. Enticing European settlers to the tropical lands was a difficult task from the start, especially as news got back to Europe about the grim realities in the New World.

The indigenous populations survived in large numbers mainly in the less accessible mountain regions of Mesoamerica (Mexico and Central America) and the Andes (today's Bolivia, Colombia, Ecuador and Peru). Native American nations also survived in the sparsely settled regions of North America. Yet deaths were rampant in the Caribbean, along the Brazilian coast, and wherever the Europeans launched intensive mining and plantation operations. Initially, the Spanish conquerors gave grants of land and authority, so-called *encomiendas*, to leading figures, the *encomenderos* (those receiving the grants), empowering them to enslave the natives living in their lands. A heated debate quickly ensued among the Spanish elites, including the church and the monarchy, concerning the rights of the indigenous populations. The famed Franciscan friar Bartolome de las Casas argued that the Indians had souls and as such could not be enslaved or mistreated by the *encomenderos*. Remarkably, the monarchy agreed and in 1542 issued the Leyes Nuevos (New Laws), outlawing the enslavement of indigenous Americans. This act must be regarded as a powerful case of moral reasoning triumphing over power and greed, all too rare in human history.

Yet the net outcome was hardly satisfactory. Not only did brutal treatment of the native population continue, but the labor shortages that resulted from the New Laws and the decline of indigenous populations quickly gave way to decisions to import slaves in vast numbers from Africa. Brazil under Portuguese and Spanish rule became the main destination for the slave trade for the next two centuries. The British, for their part, did not hesitate to join the slave trade with enthusiasm, turning the Caribbean into slave colonies for hundreds of years.

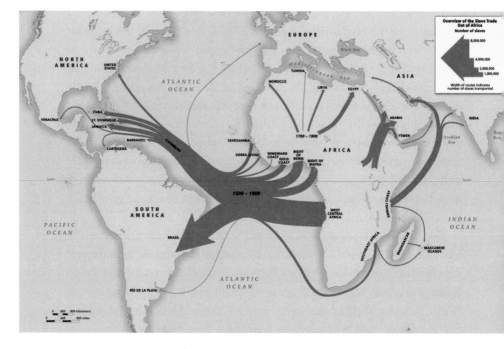

6.7 The Slave Trade from Africa, 1500-1900

Source: Eltis & Richardson, ATLAS OF THE TRANSATLANTIC SLAVE TRADE
(2010), Map 1 from accompanying web site, Overview of Slave Trade out of Africa, 1500–1900.
Reproduced with the permission of Yale University Press.

Figure 6.7 illustrates quantitatively the massive movement of slaves
from Africa to the Americas in the course of an estimated thirty-six thousand voyages between 1514 and 1866, as well as smaller transport of slaves
to North Africa, the Arabian Peninsula, and other destinations in the
Arabian Sea. The map is based in part on a painstaking calculation of the
number of Africans transported in the brutal "middle passage" from Africa
to the Americas. Most African slaves brought to the New World came
from the Gulf of Guinea and farther south along the Atlantic coast of
Africa, especially present-day Angola, and were sent in largest quantities
to Brazil and the Caribbean. Some were sent to North America, where
slave labor would take hold as the basis of the cotton empire in the colonies that would become the southern United States after the American
War of Independence.

African slaves powered the new plantation and mining economies of the Spanish, Portuguese, and British colonies, especially in the tropical regions. The most important plantation commodity was sugar, grown in northeast Brazil and the Caribbean, which together accounted for the vast preponderance of slave arrivals to the Americas, and also the Peruvian coast. Slaves were also directed to the mines of Mexico and the Andes, to the coffee plantations of Brazil and Mesoamerica, and to tobacco and cotton plantations in the southern United States. Slaveholding was mainly a tropical matter; free laborers from Europe would not accept the deadly conditions of farmwork in the neotropics, especially after falciparum malaria became prevalent following its introduction into the Americas from Africa by the slave trade itself. While some slavery existed in the temperate zones of the Americas, slavery never took hold in large numbers and was abolished far earlier in the temperate zones than in the tropics. The northern U.S. states abolished or began to phase out slavery by the early 1800s, while slavery in the southern states ended only with the Confederacy's defeat in 1865 in the U.S. Civil War. Slavery ended in Spanish Cuba only in 1886, and in Brazil in 1888.

With the slave plantations in the Americas arose the infamous three-way trade pattern commonly known as the "triangular trade." The slave colonies of the Americas imported slaves and exported slave-made products—sugar, cotton, and tobacco—to Europe. Europe imported the commodities and exported manufactured goods, including textiles, weapons, and metals, to Africa. And African chieftains exported slaves to European slave traders in return for Europe's manufactured goods.

The colonization of the Americas and the expanded trade with Asia also unleashed a new frenzy of consumerism in Europe, marked by soaring demand for spices from Asia and Africa. The most sought after products were tea, silks, and porcelain from China; fine textiles from India; coffee from Yemen; and a trio of addictive products from America's new colonial plantations—sugar, coffee, and tobacco. Portugal and Spain brought sugarcane cultivation from Iberia to Brazil and the Caribbean. The Dutch first brought coffee cultivation to their Caribbean colony, Martinique, from plantations on Java. Tobacco, native to the Americas and smoked by Native Americans, was introduced to the European colonizers, who then established tobacco plantations in the Caribbean and on the North American mainland, especially around Virginia.

Sugar, coffee, and tobacco all set off a surge of demand in Europe and, in turn, soaring profitability of plantations in the Americas. All three crops, however, were arduous to grow in the unhealthy tropical and subtropical climates of the Caribbean, Brazil, and the southern parts of North America. The demand for African slaves, therefore, soared as well. Around half of all African slaves brought to the Americas worked in the sugar plantations, mostly in the Caribbean, which overtook Brazil in sugarcane production by the eighteenth century. The overriding demographic reality of the sugar plantations was the shockingly high mortality rate, with up to a third of the newly arrived slaves dying within their first year.

In total, an estimated 14 million Africans were carried as slaves during this period. This was truly a grim and horrific stage of global capitalism. The cruelty that accompanied the development of the modern world economy must not be forgotten, because that cruelty shows up in other ways today; human trafficking is one of the greatest examples, which also continues in the form of bonded labor and child labor as part of global supply chains. Humanity is not done with the horrific abuse of others in pursuit of greed and profit.

Feeding Europe's Factories: Cotton

The British and Dutch East India companies may rightly be considered the first corporations of modern capitalism. As profit-driven and greed-based joint-stock companies, they set the tone and behavior for what was to come. As described by historian Sven Beckert in his book *Empire of Cotton: A Global History*, much of their early business in the 1600s was trade in cotton fabrics, purchased in India for sale in Africa to slave traders and in Europe to the growing urban population. Then, in the eighteenth century, as Britain protected its domestic textile manufacturers against Indian imports, British manufacturers increasingly demanded a supply of raw cotton. The demand multiplied with the mechanization of spinning and weaving, and then with the introduction of steam power into the textile mills.

As Beckert observes, this made Britain's cotton manufacturing "the first major industry in human history that lacked locally procured raw materials."[11] Thus began a new episode of global capitalism, with British businesses frantically seeking to secure increased access to raw cotton supplies for Britain's booming textile industry. The "salvation," of course, came in the form of slaves, growing the "white gold" in the plantations of the Caribbean and Brazil. Yet even then, upheaval hit the industry with the slave rebellion in Saint-Domingue in 1791, giving birth to an independent Haiti. Britain's raw material inputs were suddenly in jeopardy.

Once again, a solution arose, seemingly providentially from the industry's point of view. The U.S. South would provide the land and the slave labor to feed Britain's mills. Beckert explains the essence of this solution:

> What distinguished the United States from virtually every other cotton-growing area in the world was planters' command of nearly unlimited suppliers of land, labor, and capital, and their unparalleled political power. In the Ottoman Empire and India, as we know, powerful indigenous rulers controlled the land, and deeply entrenched social groups struggled over its use. In the West Indies and Brazil, sugar planters competed for land, labor, and power. The United States, and its plentiful land, faced no such encumbrances.[12]

This alliance of British industry and capital with U.S. slavery was to last from the 1790s until the Civil War. Far from slavery being an outmoded system alien to modern capitalism, slavery was at the very cutting edge of global capitalism, creating vast wealth on the foundations of untold misery. The brutality of the Anglo-American system is underscored by the fact that the United States was essentially the only country in the world where it took a civil war to end slavery. Even tsarist Russia ended serfdom peacefully, with Tsar Alexander's Emancipation Decree of 1861, just as the United States, ostensibly the land of freedom, was sliding into civil war.

Global Empire and Global War

Europe's global empires, spanning oceans and continents for the first time, unleashed another new phenomenon, global war, also spanning oceans and continents. From the late seventeenth century on, major conflicts among the European powers involved battles on several continents. The implications were dire. More and more of the world would be swept into Europe's wars, so that eventually the two world wars of the twentieth century each claimed tens of millions of lives across the globe.

The Nine Years' War of 1688–97 might be considered the first global war, as it was fought simultaneously in the Americas, Europe, and Asia. The main European combatants were France under Louis XIV facing a coalition of Britain, Holland, and the Holy Roman Empire. The main theaters of the war were in Europe, along France's borders, following the attempts by Louis XIV to expand France's influence into neighboring countries. Early in the war with France, Holland's monarch William of Orange successfully invaded Britain and took the throne from King James II, an invasion subsequently known as the Glorious Revolution of 1688. The war became global when news of the conflict reached the Americas and Asia. In North America, the war, known as King William's War, mainly involved British colonialists and their Native American allies against French colonialists and their Native American allies. It would be the start of several wars between France and Britain fought in North America. In Asia, the fighting was between the French and Anglo-Dutch forces in southeast India, notably Pondicherry. While the battles in the Americas and India were not decisive, they set the pattern for the coming centuries of European wars spilling over to the Americas, Asia, and eventually Africa as well.

The next global war was the Seven Years' War between 1756 and 1763. This one was a five-continent conflict—Europe, North America, South America, Africa, and Asia—between two European grand coalitions, one led by Britain, with Portugal, Prussia, and other German principalities, and the other led by France, with the Austrian (Holy Roman) Empire, Spain, and Sweden. This war, like the Nine Years' War, began in Europe as a contest between Austria and Prussia for control over Silesia, but it quickly spread worldwide. In the Americas, it was preceded by skirmishes between British and French colonists but after 1756 led to a broad contest for territories throughout the Americas and the Caribbean. The main result of the war in the Americas was France's loss of territories to Britain and Spain. In Africa, the British navy conquered France's colony in Senegal, and much of the colony was transferred to Britain by treaty at the conclusion of the war. In southern India, France's holdings were reduced by British victories.

France quickly got even with its rival Great Britain during the U.S. War of Independence, beginning in 1776. France's active intervention on the side of the breakaway British colonies was decisive for the Americans' victory in their war of independence. Yet in the escalating contest between France and Britain, each victory contained the seeds of a future reversal. France's heavy financial outlays in support of American independence contributed to France's financial crisis of the 1780s that in turn fomented the unrest leading to the 1789 French Revolution. The French Revolution, in turn, unleashed a new round of bloody European wars from 1793 to 1815. The latter part of the French Revolutionary Wars became known as the Napoleonic Wars with the rise of Napoleon to First Consul of France in 1799 and then to Emperor of France in 1804.

The Napoleonic Wars, the bloodiest yet, cost millions of civilian and military casualties and was again fought in theaters across several continents, including Europe, North America, South America, Africa (Egypt), the Caucasus, and the Indian Ocean. These were "total wars," with a mass mobilization of the population, mass conscription, and massive civilian casualties. The main geopolitical results of Napoleon's defeat in 1815 were the rise of Britain to European supremacy over the oceans and the nearly fatal weakening of the Portuguese and Spanish empires, both of which had been conquered by Napoleon. Within a few years of the end of the Napoleonic Wars, both Portugal and Spain would lose most of their colonial possessions in the Americas to wars of independence.

As of 1830, Europe's empires were as shown in figure 6.8. The Americas were now mostly independent nations, with Britain maintaining colonial possessions in Canada and the Caribbean and other European countries maintaining some island colonies in the Caribbean. Africa was as yet colonized only on the coasts, other than the British and Dutch settlements in the hinterlands of South Africa. The rest of Africa succumbed to European imperialism only toward the end of the nineteenth century, for reasons described in the next chapter. In Asia, Britain now dominated much of India and Malaya, as well as Australia, while Holland maintained its colonies in the Indonesian archipelago. Spain and Portugal each held some Asian colonies as well, including the Philippines under Spain and eastern Timor under Portugal.

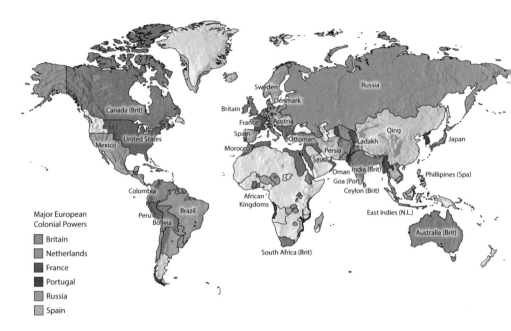

6.8 World Empires and Selected Nations, 1830

Much of the ensuing drama of nineteenth-century economic development would take place on the mainland of Europe, which pioneered the
new age of industrial globalization.

Adam Smith's Summation of the Age of Global Empire

Adam Smith, the great inventor of modern economic thought, living in
Scotland in the eighteenth century, published his magnum opus, *The Wealth
of Nations*, in 1776. As a great humanist, he observed the consequences of
globalization with a globalist perspective rather than British partiality.
(In his own work on moral sympathy, Smith spoke about the "impartial
spectator" as the vantage point for moral reasoning.) This is what Smith
had to say about this remarkable fourth age of globalization. I quote him
at length because it is wonderful to listen carefully to a great mind like

124

Smith's reflecting on such pivotal events. His words inspire us to think hard and with sympathy about our own times.

The discovery of America, and that of a passage to the East Indies by the Cape of Good Hope, are the two greatest and most important events recorded in the history of mankind. Their consequences have already been very great; but, in the short period of between two and three centuries which has elapsed since these discoveries were made, it is impossible that the whole extent of their consequences can have been seen. What benefits or what misfortunes to mankind may hereafter result from those great events, no human wisdom can foresee. By uniting, in some measure, the most distant parts of the world, by enabling them to relieve one another's wants, to increase one another's enjoyments, and to encourage one another's industry, their general tendency would seem to be beneficial. To the natives however, both of the East and West Indies, all the commercial benefits which can have resulted from those events have been sunk and lost in the dreadful misfortunes which they have occasioned. These misfortunes, however, seem to have arisen rather from accident than from anything in the nature of those events themselves. At the particular time when these discoveries were made, the superiority of force happened to be so great on the side of the Europeans that they were enabled to commit with impunity every sort of injustice in those remote countries. Hereafter, perhaps, the natives of those countries may grow stronger, or those of Europe may grow weaker, and the inhabitants of all the different quarters of the world may arrive at that equality of courage and force which, by inspiring mutual fear, can alone overawe the injustice of independent nations into some sort of respect for the rights of one another. But nothing seems more likely to establish this equality of force than that mutual communication of knowledge and of all sorts of improvements which an extensive commerce from all countries to all countries naturally, or rather necessarily, carries along with it.[13]

This wonderful statement is filled with humanity and relevance for us. Smith is saying that the events leading to the fourth age of globalization—the discovery of the sea routes linking Europe with the Americas and with Asia—are the most significant events of human history because they united, "in some measure, the most distant parts of the world." But while this might have brought benefits for all of humanity through mutually beneficial trade (enabling the various parts of the world "to relieve one another's wants"), in fact they had as of Smith's time brought benefits to one part of humanity—namely, Western Europe—while bringing misery to the inhabitants of both the East and West Indies, who suffered from Europe's overwhelming power. After all, the Europeans came not merely to trade but also to plunder and conquer.

Smith, remarkably, looks forward to a fairer and more balanced world, one in which the inhabitants of the East and West Indies "may grow stronger, or those of Europe may grow weaker," in order to arrive at "an equality of courage and force" that will enable "a mutual fear," and thereby a mutual respect. How will that come about, asks Smith? Through global trade itself. As Smith puts it, commerce will necessarily bring about the equality of force through the "mutual communication of knowledge and of all sorts of improvements." In short, trade will cause the spread of knowledge and eventually cause the rebalancing of power. Smith is speaking about British colonialism here, but he could just as easily be speaking about our time, when China and other former colonies are achieving great advances in technological capacity and military strength through their participation in the global economy. Smith foretold a time when such a rebalancing would lead to "some sort of respect for the rights of one another." That indeed should be the hope for our own time.

Some Lessons from the Ocean Age

The Ocean Age gave birth to global capitalism. For the first time in history, privately chartered for-profit companies engaged in complex, global-scale production and trading networks. Private businesses, drunk with greed, hired private armies, enslaved millions, bribed their way to privileged political status at home and abroad, and generally acted with impunity. But even beyond the private greed, it was an age of conquest and unchecked competition among Europe's powers. The world beyond the oceans was up for grabs, and little would hold back the rapaciousness that was unleashed as a result.

Adam Smith's masterwork, *The Wealth of Nations*, provided a template for riches: global trade as the spur for specialization and rising productivity. Smith's recipe worked beyond his wildest imagination. As we shall see in the next phase of globalization, productivity began to rise rapidly and persistently as new inventions expanded the market and thereby the incentives for even more inventions. The process of self-feeding growth was under way. The result would create a new kind of political power—a global superpower—that would come to be known as the hegemonic power, a global dominance achieved by Great Britain that outpaced even the scale of power and accomplishment of the Roman Empire. But, as we shall see, the gains for Britain and other major powers would often be reflected in the misery of those under their whip in the Industrial Age.

7

The Industrial Age

(1800–2000)

W e have arrived at the sixth age of globalization, the Industrial Age, the one that created the modern world. For convenience I date this from 1800 to 2000, lasting two centuries. I could perhaps have put the starting date a bit earlier, say 1750, when industrialization began to gather force in Britain, or I might have put it at 1820, after the Napoleonic Wars, when the new peace in Europe would enable a continental-scale transformation more rapid than any other in history. But no matter the details, we can be certain of the overriding point: the sixth age is a period of decisive transformation that was faster, deeper, and more extensive than ever before in history. During just two centuries, everything changed about how and where we live and how we govern ourselves.

At the start of the sixth age of globalization, around 1820, the world was still overwhelmingly poor and rural. Perhaps 85 percent of the world's population sustained itself through farming, almost all of it at a level at or near subsistence. Around 93 percent of the world lived in rural areas. Most people never ventured far from their birthplace, often because they were enslaved, enserfed, or bonded to the land and landowner in some way. Extreme poverty was pervasive and life expectancy was short, mainly because infant and child mortality rates were extremely high. By 2000, however, all had changed. The world had become almost half urban (46.7 percent); average incomes had soared; average life expectancy had

Table 7.1 Population and Urbanization

World	Around 1800	Around 2000
Population	1 billion	6 billion
Rate of urbanization	7.3%	46.8%
Average GDP per person, PPP-adjusted (2018 prices)	$1,200 (1820)	$10,500
Extreme poverty rate	84% (1820)	25%
Life expectancy at birth	29	66

Sources: François Bourguignon and Christian Morrisson. "Inequality among World Citizens: 1820–1992." American economic review 92, no. 4 (2002): 727–44; James C Riley. "Estimates of regional and global life expectancy, 1800–2001." Population and development review 31, no. 3 (2005): 537–43; Kees Klein Goldewijk, Arthur Beusen, and Peter Janssen. "Long-Term Dynamic Modeling of Global Population and Built-up Area in a Spatially Explicit Way: Hyde 3.1." The Holocene 20, no. 4 (2010): 565–73; Angus Maddison. "Statistics on World Population, GDP and Per Capita GDP, 1-2008 AD." Historical Statistics 3 (2010): 1–36.

reached sixty-seven years (for 2000–2005).[1] These remarkable changes are summarized in table 7.1.

The texture of life also changed beyond recognition. From the quiet life of villages, most of humanity now lived in the tumult of cities. From the relative isolation of villages, humanity was now interconnected in a worldwide web of nonstop data. From the slow pace of technological change throughout most of human history, we arrived to a world of nonstop technological upheavals. And we arrived also to a world of ever-present existential worries, where human survival is threatened by our own creations, whether nuclear weapons or global-scale environmental threats.

Certain key aspects of this remarkable sixth age of globalization are coming to an end—most notably, the two hundred years of Anglo-American dominance of the world economy and technology. And digital technologies, discussed in the next chapter, are once again upending our patterns of production and indeed our patterns of daily life. But to understand our current era and the choices before us, we must understand the Industrial Age, and how it created the modern economy.

A good year to start our investigation of industrialization is 1776. Four remarkable events that year capture the essence of the story of the Industrial Age. The first, as you might guess, is the birth of the United States with its Declaration of Independence from Britain. That was indeed a notable event in history, as it unleashed the forces that would create America as a global power by the second half of the twentieth century. The second event is one I have already mentioned many times: the publication of Adam Smith's *Wealth of Nations*. Here was a new guide to a modern economy based on global reach and the global division of labor. The third is another publication: Edward Gibbon's *Decline and Fall of the Roman Empire*. Like Smith, Gibbon epitomizes the wisdom and humanity of the eighteenth-century British Enlightenment. Gibbon's masterwork reminds us that world-dominant powers such as Rome decline, as occurred with the British Empire in the twentieth century and is happening in its own way with the United States in the early twenty-first century.

Yet in historical significance, the fourth event of 1776 is probably the most significant. This is the year when the inventor James Watt successfully commercialized his new steam engine. We have discussed many pivotal inventions throughout history: agriculture, animal domestication, the alphabet, gunpowder, the printing press, ocean navigation, and others. Yet with the possible exception of Gutenberg's printing press, it is very hard to think of an invention by a single inventor as consequential as Watt's steam engine (figure 7.1). The steam engine gave birth to the Industrial Age and the modern economy. While the steam engine is not solely responsible for economic modernity, without the steam engine most of the other technological breakthroughs of the past two centuries would not have been possible.[2]

Newton had declared "If I have seen further it is by standing on the shoulders of giants." Watt too made his great breakthroughs by building on the innovations of worthy predecessors. Thomas Savery invented the first modern steam engine in 1699, using steam created by burning coal to pump water. The aim was to use the steam engine to pump water from coal mines to raise the productivity of the mine. Savery's breakthrough idea was then advanced by Thomas Newcomen, who added the idea of moving a piston with steam power. Savery's pump worked by creating a temporary vacuum that forced water through the pump. Newcomen's 1712 steam engine used the steam to move a piston to pump the water. The coal mined with the help of these steam engines was used mainly for heating homes in Britain's winter months. Later on, of course, the coal would be mined for the steam engines themselves, which became the source of power for

7.1 James Watt's Steam Engine, c. 1776

Source: Wikimedia Commons contributors, "File:Maquina vapor Watt ETSIIM.jpg," Wikimedia Commons, the free media repository, https://commons.wikimedia.org/w/index .php?title=File:Maquina_vapor_Watt_ETSIIM.jpg&oldid=362051513

Britain's railroads, steamships, and industrial factories, and notably for use in massively scaled-up steel production.

Newcomen's engine was deployed to pump water out of coal mines, but it was not very efficient. It required an enormous input of energy and was not economical to use for other applications. In the 1760s, James Watt, employed in a workshop at the University of Glasgow in Scotland making scientific instruments, began thinking about how to make Newcomen's steam engine more efficient. Brilliantly, Watt made two great innovations to Newcomen's engine. One involved the translation of the steam energy into motion. Rather than the alternating beam that Newcomen had used, Watt introduced rotary motion into a steam engine. Watt's second change was even more revolutionary: the addition of a separate condenser. Newcomen's steam engine involved heating and then cooling the boiler to create the alternation of hot and cold temperatures to create and condense steam. This wasted a tremendous amount of heat energy, meaning that Newcomen's engine required a tremendous amount of coal, at high expense, to operate. By introducing a condenser separate from the boiler, Watt made the steam engine vastly more efficient, and hence much more economical. He turned the steam engine from a high-cost device for pumping water from mines to a low-cost device that could be deployed in literally thousands of uses in the future. The world economy was transformed by that single insight.

From the Organic Economy to the Energy-Rich Economy

With the invention of the steam engine, Britain entered the Industrial Age. From 1700 to 1820, British output per person rose 0.26 percent per year. During 1820–1850, the growth rate increased to 1.04 percent per year; during 1850–1900, it increased again to 1.32 percent per year. The time period needed to double output per person fell from 270 years at the growth rate of the period 1700–1820 to sixty-seven years at the growth rate during 1820–1850 to just fifty-three years at the growth rate during 1850–1900.[3]

The British economic historian E. A. Wrigley has characterized the breakthrough as the transition from the "organic economy" to the "energy-rich economy."[4] By organic economy, Wrigley means an economy in which "all industrial production depended on vegetable or animal raw materials." The energy used in the production of raw materials and the industrial transformation of those materials into final products came overwhelmingly from human labor and draft animals, types of organic inputs. Windmills and waterwheels provided some energy, but only a small fraction of the organic inputs. Then came coal, the first of the three fossil fuels (coal, petroleum, and natural gas) that would be deployed on a large scale after 1800. With the liberation from scarce organic-based energy, and ultimately the foodstuffs and feed grains grown to sustain the human and animal populations, the economy could take off.

Wrigley's estimates of energy consumption in England and Wales by type of input, shown in table 7.2, are highly instructive. Total energy consumption rose by 37 percent in the first half of the eighteenth century, by 124 percent in the second half of the century, and by 255 percent in the

Table 7.2 Energy Consumption (petajoules)

	1700–1709	1750–1759	1800–1809	1850–1859
Draught animals	32.8	33.6	34.3	50.1
Population	27.3	29.7	41.8	67.8
Firewood	22.5	22.6	18.5	2.2
Wind	1.4	2.8	12.7	24.4
Water	1.0	1.3	1.1	1.7
Coal	84.0	140.8	408.7	1689.1
Total	168.9	230.9	517.1	1835.5
Coal as % of total	49.7	61.0	79.0	92.0

Source: E. A. Wrigley, *Energy and the English Industrial Revolution* (Cambridge University Press, 2010), 27, table 2.1.

first half of the nineteenth century. Note the high use of coal already in 1700–1709, before the steam engine. Most of this coal was likely used for home heating and cooking.

Watt's steam engine had applications across the economy. It was, in modern parlance, a general-purpose technology (GPT)—the kind of technology that finds applications across many sectors of the economy.[5] With the steam engine, equipment of all kinds could be mechanized. Major applications came quickly in textiles production, with the mechanization of spinning and weaving and the introduction of large-scale factory production using steam power. Metallurgy soared as well, with tremendous advances in steam-powered blast furnaces for steel making. Fundamental breakthroughs were also quickly achieved in transport, with the steam-powered railroad, steam-powered river barges, and steam-powered ocean-going vessels.

As steam power drastically reduced the costs of transport, coal production, steel making, textile production, and other industrial processes, new possibilities soared across the economy. One of the most important cost reductions came in agriculture. With steam-powered ocean shipping, it became economical to ship organic fertilizers from South America, namely, the nitrate deposits from bird and bat guano off the coasts of Peru and Chile. Railroads allowed the commercial opening of new agricultural regions, such as the Argentine Pampas, with much of the new production destined for transoceanic exports. During the nineteenth century, the world's capacity to grow food soared, bolstered by scientific breakthroughs in agronomy and the increased mechanization of agriculture.

With increased food production came rising populations. More food meant more survival and higher fertility rates. The shift from the organic economy to the energy-rich economy thus enabled a vast increase in the global population. The world's population grew from around 600 million in 1700 to 900 million in 1800 and then to 1.6 billion by 1900. The age-old constraint on the size of the global population, limited by food production in the organic economy, was ended.

The unprecedented increases in world population and output per capita with the advent of the Industrial Age appear vividly in figures 1.1 and 1.3. The turning point around 1820 is clear enough. The long history of nearly unchanged output per person ended with the onset of industrialization. Between 1000 CE and 1820, the world average output per capita increased at the nearly imperceptible rate of 0.05 percent per annum. During the period from 1820 to 1900, the growth rate was ten times higher, reaching 0.5 percent per annum. Similarly, the global population, which grew at a miniscule 0.1 percent per year between 1000 and 1700, accelerated to 0.5 percent per year between 1700 and 1820 and then to 0.6 percent per annum between 1820 and 1920. The world economy had, in short, made the breakthrough to modern economic growth, and the global population soared along with rising incomes.

Why Did Industrialization Start in Britain?

What made Watt's invention possible? Why did Britain industrialize first and soar to the lead? Britain certainly was not the only home of scientists. Italy has to have pride of place, I would say, with Leonardo da Vinci and Galileo as prime movers of the European scientific revolution. One could cite Poland's Copernicus early in the sixteenth century as providing one of the key insights, the heliocentric universe, that got Galileo and then Newton thinking about a new physics. And one could cite the huge advances in governance and commerce in Holland as precursors of Britain's own commercial revolution. After all, it was the invasion of the Dutch monarch, William of Orange, in 1688 that gave Britain its Glorious Revolution and the clear path to modern capitalist institutions.

What Britain offered was an extraordinary *combination* of favorable conditions that, taken together, made Watt's invention and its subsequent rapid adoption possible. The industrial revolution was not a commonplace affair. Several conditions had to align to achieve the takeoff to self-sustaining industrialization and ongoing economic growth. Britain's uniqueness lies in putting all of the necessary pieces together for the first time. Perhaps the Song Dynasty in China, roughly one millennium earlier, offered similarly propitious circumstances, but lacked the spark to set industrialization in motion.

The first condition in Britain was the intellectual milieu, in which science and empiricism were deeply respected, even revered. It was in Britain that theologian and philosopher Roger Bacon in the thirteenth century preached a philosophy of empirical knowledge of nature, and where his namesake and perhaps distant relation Francis Bacon in the early seventeenth century put forward the modern idea of human progress through science and technology, with science based on the experimental method. This empirical approach underpinned the new physics that arrived with Galileo and Isaac Newton in the next century.

As poet Alexander Pope wrote of Newton, "Nature and Nature's laws lay hid in night: / God said, Let Newton be! and all was light." Newton explained the cosmos with his new physics and made possible many of the scientific breakthroughs that were to come. Newton did his work at the University of Cambridge, an institution that continues to be a pioneer in the basic sciences today. Britain's universities were crucial for industrialization. The very fact of an instruments laboratory at Glasgow University where Watt could do his pathbreaking work speaks volumes about the intellectual basis for technological advances. And Watt was highly respected for his breakthroughs, winning membership in the Royal Society of Edinburgh and the French Academy, among other institutions.

The intellectual milieu and support were not sufficient. Italy too had a glorious scientific tradition and a great university network. Additional factors were at play in Britain. Another key point is that Watt sought to develop his technology not only as a technological concept but also as a business venture. He aimed to make money, and indeed succeeded in doing so. Britain offered an environment where market institutions were well developed and where the ownership of intellectual property in the form of patent rights had long existed. On that basis, Watt was able to attract private capital, notably from his business partner and leading manufacturer Richard Boulton. Watt and Boulton needed to defend their patent rights against infringements by others, and the courts indeed recognized their claims.

Scientific inquiry, universities, and market institutions were not sufficient either. One might say, indeed, that Holland had arrived at that combination before Britain. But Britain had something that Holland lacked: coal. Easily accessible coal was the key—and not just coal, but a coal industry. Britain had long used coal for home heating and cooking and was therefore highly experienced in mining, shipping, and marketing coal. This was an extraordinary advantage. An economist, speaking in hypotheticals, might claim, "Well, if it wasn't coal, it would have been something else, perhaps oil or gas." But coal had to come first in order to make the other fossil fuels possible. The far more complex internal combustion engine and gas turbine both built on the steam engine, and neither could have emerged without the decades of advances in mining, metallurgy, machine-making, and engine technologies made possible first with the coal-based steam engine.

Yet even empiricism and a scientific outlook, the universities and market institutions, and the accessibility of and experience with coal are still not the full story. The steam engine proved so profitable because Britain was part of a global trading system, backed by multinational companies (exemplified by the East India Company) that could transport commodities such as cotton for processing into textiles in Britain's new steam-driven factories. In other words, Watt had an enormous potential market, not just an idea and access to a patent and to coal.

Self-sustaining industrialization took off just once in human history, in Britain in the eighteenth and early nineteenth centuries. All other industrialization since then are descendants of the technologies, corporate laws, and financial mechanisms of Britain's breakthrough. Before Britain's industrial revolution, other places had developed industry—textiles, iron-making, machinery—but none had broken free of the organic economy. Perhaps

China in the Song Dynasty or the Ming Dynasty was the best placed to do so before Britain. China, too, had markets, trade, scientific and technological knowledge, and coal, albeit less accessible coal. There is perhaps no fundamental reason why Britain beat China to industrialization. Human history, like natural evolution, is subject to accidents and randomness.

A useful analogy, perhaps, is the beginning of life itself on Earth. Scientists suspect that life emerged from a unique confluence of circumstances: organic materials (notably self-replicating RNA), an energy source (perhaps the thermal vents in the deep ocean), and the self-organizing properties of the components of a first living cell (such as a lipid membrane and a self-replicating strand of RNA). Somehow the pieces of the puzzle self-assembled. It must not have been a likely process. Since all of life today apparently shares a common ancestry with the same DNA chemistry, the emergence of self-replicating life may have occurred just once.

The same seems to be true about self-sustaining economic growth. Several conditions were needed simultaneously in Britain to set off the Industrial Revolution. And all subsequent industrialization, in the U.S., Western Europe, Russia, Japan, China, and now Africa, can trace their own industrial lineage to a single common ancestor: Watt and his steam engine in Glasgow in 1776.

Endogenous Growth and Kondratiev Waves

The steam engine was so decisive, unleashing advances in factory production, precision manufacturing, and countless applications of the new steam power, that it set off a chain reaction of further discoveries. Professor Martin Weitzman of Harvard University noted that innovations can be built upon current technologies through the "hybridization of ideas"—that is, by combining existing technologies into new patterns that in turn can be combined into still more innovative designs.[6]

Let me offer a very simple illustration based on his thoughts. Suppose that there are ten distinct technologies. There are then forty-five two-way combinations of the ten technologies (1/2 × 10 × 9). Suppose that 20 percent of those pairwise combinations yield a useful new technology. We would have nine additional technologies. The nine new technologies could then hybridize (combine) with each other or with the original technologies, to produce yet more innovations. Weizmann called this ongoing process "recombinant growth."

The basic idea is that innovations beget innovations. We can view this dynamic from a related perspective, the opportunity to make profits. Suppose that each technological breakthrough causes the economy to grow. To stay with simple numbers, suppose that each fundamental technological breakthrough doubles the size of the economy. If we set Britain's GDP to 100 units before Watt, then we might say the steam engine raised GDP to 200. With a larger GDP, the incentive to invent is also greater. Each invention is likely to earn more revenues and thereby cover the costs of R&D and the early implementation of new ideas. With GDP equal to 200, more potential Watt-like inventions are explored, and eventually another one is developed that boosts the GDP to 400, causing still more R&D and further innovation. Economists label this self-sustaining process (innovation → larger market size → innovation → larger market size) as "endogenous growth." The economist Paul Romer provided a rigorous mathematical account of endogenous growth in the 1980s and received the Nobel Prize in Economics for his achievement.

The steam engine and the breakthrough to an energy-rich economy set off such a process of endogenous growth that it has so far lasted for more than two centuries. Global GDP per capita, which hardly budged for centuries before the age of industrialization, has been rising rapidly and fairly consistently since 1820. The fuel for that long-term growth has been a continuing wave of technological advances, many building on previous technologies through hybridization and others introducing fundamentally new ideas and approaches.

These waves of technology are often bundled into distinct phases, much like bundling the ages of globalization. The earliest theory of technology waves came from the Russian economist Nikolai Kondratiev, writing in the 1920s. He identified major waves of technology arriving roughly every fifty to sixty years. Each wave generates a new era of business investments that boost the economy and continues the path of economic growth. One rendition of such "Kondratiev waves" is shown in figure 7.2, due to Wilenius and Kurki.[7] In this depiction, the steam engine gives rise to the first wave, 1780–1830. This is followed by a second wave of investments in railways and steel, 1830–1880, both depending on the steam engine, as well as

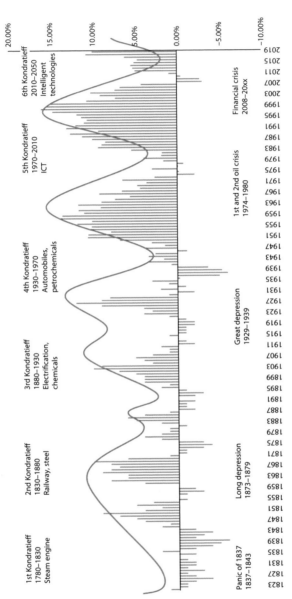

7.2 Kondratieff Waves, 1823–2019

Source: Rolling 10-year return on the S&P 500 from Jan. 1814 to June 2019 (in % per year). Data from Datastream, Bloomberg, Helsinki Capital partners (illustration), Markku Wilenius.

other new technologies. The third wave is the era of electrification (building on Faraday's discoveries of electromagnetic induction) and modern chemistry, 1880–1930. The fourth wave builds on the automobile (and the internal combustion engine) and petrochemicals, the age of oil, one might say, 1930–1970. This is followed by a fifth wave, based on information and communications technologies (ICTs), to around 2010. Finally, Wilenius and Kurki identify a sixth wave of "intelligent technologies," including robotics and artificial intelligence, for the years 2010–2050. The columns in red measure the ten-year annual return on equities using the S&P 500. The argument is that each technological wave gives rise to an increase in stock market prices, signaling future profitability and incentive to invest. At the end of the technology cycle, the returns fall back to zero, awaiting a new technological innovation to set off the next investment cycle. Another recent usage identifies four rather than six stages of industrialization: (1) water and steam power; (2) electricity and the internal combustion engine; (3) information and communications technologies; and (4) the fusion of technologies, combining ICTs, biological technologies such as genomics, and new materials (e.g., nanotechnologies).[8]

The Diffusion of Industrialization in Europe

British industrialization started in the mid-1700s with Newcomen's steam engine and other innovations in textiles and metallurgy. Yet full-fledged industrialization only took off with the end of the Napoleonic Wars. As of 1820, Britain and Holland were in the lead of Europe in per capita GDP (measured at a consistent set of international prices, according to data developed by historian Angus Maddison), but the gap was modest. Table 7.3 summarizes the story over the nineteenth century. Each country's income per person is shown relative to Britain's, which is given an index value of 100. A value of 70, therefore, signifies a per capita income that is 70 percent of Britain's. As of 1820, Britain led the rest of Europe, with the exception of the Netherlands, which stood at 108. Between 1820 and 1850, Britain and countries close to Britain (such as France and the Netherlands) generally grew more rapidly than countries more distant from Britain (such as Spain, Italy, Greece, and Finland). By 1900, there was a rather clear

Table 7.3 GDP per Capita, PPP adjusted, Selected Countries and Years (UK = 100)

	1820	1850	1870	1900
United Kingdom	100	100	100	100
France	67	69	59	64
Netherlands	108	102	86	76
Spain	59	46	38	40
Western Europe	70	67	61	64
China	35	26	17	12
India	31	23	17	13
Japan	39	29	23	26
United States	74	77	77	91
Africa	25	–	16	13
Latin America	41	–	21	25

Source: Angus Maddison. "Statistics on World Population, GDP and Per Capita GDP, 1-2008 AD." *Historical Statistics* 3 (2010): 1–36.

distance gradient. On average, the closer a country was to Britain (measured as direct distance between national capitals), the higher was its per capita income in 1900.

What we are observing is a geographical diffusion process. Industrialization started in Britain and then gradually over time moved to the rest of Europe, with those regions farthest away generally industrializing at a later date. It's a bit like dropping a stone in water. The ripples go outward in concentric circles, so the impact is felt earliest near where the stone hits the water and only later at greater distances.

What is the reason for this gradual diffusion? Remember that Britain's industrialization had several foundations, including a market for industrial products, access to coal, access to transport, industrial skills, and technological know-how. These were the prerequisites as well for the later arrivals to industrialization. They needed a market for their output. Britain often provided that market. They needed access to coal, which might come from their own mines or from shipments from Britain or other mining sites. They needed transport, which tended to be higher in cost over land routes in Central and Eastern Europe than the sea routes of coastal economies. And they needed industrial skills (beginning with literacy and numeracy) and technological know-how. For every one of these prerequisites, proximity to Britain, the home of big industry, was helpful. The result was a spreading wave of industrialization, starting with Britain's near neighbors, including Belgium, the Netherlands, and France in the years 1820–1850, extending to more distant countries (Scandinavia, Germany, Italy, Spain) in the second half of the century, and finally reaching Eastern Europe and Russia late in the nineteenth century.

Of course, national specificities mattered as well. Some countries had coal; others did not. A country like Switzerland could tap into hydroelectric power once the technology became known. Some had national markets from the start (France, the Netherlands) while others (Italy, Germany) were not yet unified nations until around 1870. And some parts of Europe, particularly in Eastern Europe, still had pre-capitalist institutions of serfdom that had to be eliminated before market-based industrialization could get underway. Yet for all these countries, Britain set the pace and served as the role model. It provided the technologies, financial capital, know-how, and marketplace to boost the incomes of the laggard nations.

The Great Global Divergence

The age of industrial globalization dramatically increased the gap between the North Atlantic—Western Europe and the United States—and the rest of the world in terms of incomes, industrial production, and military power. Since 1500, Western Europe had made important advances on many fronts, including military power, global conquests, scale of industry, and multinational production and trade in many sectors, including cotton, sugar, tobacco, and others. By 1820, according to Maddison's estimates, a significant gap in production per person had already opened between Western Europe and Asia. China, India, and Japan each had incomes per capita of around $600 (in 1990 international dollars) compared with Western

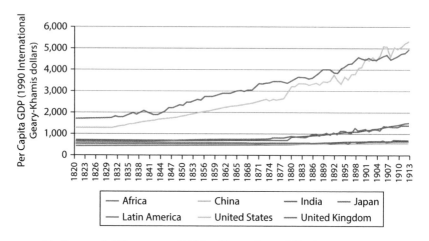

7.3 Economic Divergence of Major Countries and Regions, 1820–1913

Source: Angus Maddison. "Statistics on World Population, GDP and Per Capita GDP, 1–2008 AD." *Historical Statistics* 3 (2010): 1–36.

Europe's average of around $1,200 and Britain's global lead at around $1,700. With the industrialization that followed, that gap widened dramatically in the nineteenth century.

Figure 7.3 summarizes the dramatic story by comparing the two most dynamic industrializing nations—the United Kingdom and the United States—with several other world regions. We see three groups of outcomes. The UK and the United States held the global lead, with soaring economies that reached a per capita income of roughly $5,000 by 1913. Latin America and Japan constituted a middle group, with much more limited economic growth beginning in the second half of the nineteenth century and incomes rising to around $1,400 by 1913. The laggard group included Africa, China, and India, which experienced essentially no rise in output per person, each with a GDP per capita of around $600 in 1913. Thus, by 1913, the two leading nations had roughly eight times the per capita income of Africa, China, and India! The United States alone, with around 100 million inhabitants, has greater production than China and India combined, with roughly 750 million inhabitants.

The story of the great divergence between Europe and Asia is the great drama of the nineteenth-century world economy. This is the period when the world fell into the hands of the North Atlantic powers, first Britain and the other European empires, and then in the twentieth century the United States, especially after World War II. Only with the rapid growth of China and India toward the end of the twentieth century would Asia begin to narrow the huge gaps in relative income and power that opened in the nineteenth century.

One of the factors in determining the global patterns of industrialization was the presence or absence of coal, and then in the twentieth century, the presence or absence of petroleum and natural gas. Places close to coal deposits tended to industrialize earlier, while regions far from coal tended to industrialize much later. As seen in figure 7.4, the world regions that are best endowed with coal include Western Europe, the United States, Australia, Russia, China, India, Indonesia, South Africa, the Andes, and southeastern Brazil, while most of tropical Africa and much of tropical America are bereft of coal deposits. The first phase of coal-based industrialization began in Western Europe in the first half of the nineteenth century, following Britain's early lead. Coal mining and coal-based industrialization followed some decades later in the United States, Australia, Japan, and Russia in the second half of the nineteenth century, and eventually spread

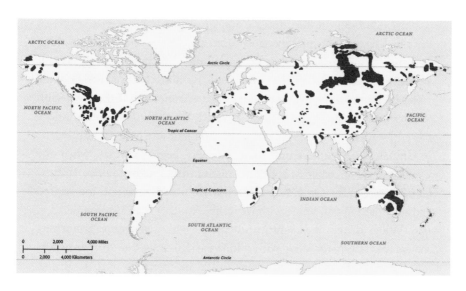

7.4 Major Geological Deposits of Coal, 2017

Source: "World Coal Deposits Map," mapsofworld.com. Reproduced with permission.

to other coal regions in the twentieth century. In the twentieth century, following the inventions of the internal combustion engine and the gas turbine, the presence of hydrocarbons became advantageous not only for oil and gas production but also for the development of petrochemical industries and other energy-intensive sectors.

The Asian Drama: China, India, and Japan

The story of Asia in the face of European and U.S. industrialization is vital to understand because it made the world that we inherited, one that is now being rapidly reordered. China, a proud empire with an astounding 37 percent of the world's population in 1820, found itself humbled by countries less than a tenth its size. While China avoided direct colonization during the nineteenth century, it did not avoid chaos, military defeat, or European imperial encroachments on its sovereignty. India, with 20 percent of the world's population, fared even worse. From the mid-1700s onward, India was absorbed step by step by the East India Company, and in 1858, it fell entirely into the clutches of the British Empire, which formally took over the job of colonial rule from the East India Company. Japan was the relative success story in Asia, not only preserving its sovereignty but successfully embarking on a path of industrialization at the end of the nineteenth century, albeit at an income level far below that of Europe. By dint of its industrialization, Japan became Asia's military powerhouse from the end of the nineteenth century until Japan's defeat in World War II. Accounting for these distinctive pathways is one of the great tasks of economic and political history.

China's nineteenth-century story actually begins in 1793, when the Chinese emperor rebuffed a British mission that sought to open British-Chinese trade. The Qing emperor could see no advantage in the request and sent the mission home without result. Another such mission failed in 1816. When Britain next returned, it did so with a vengeance, launching the infamous Opium Wars with China in 1839. This time Britain would not accept no for an answer. China would be forced to open to British trade—not just normal trade, but also opium from India peddled by British merchants. When the Chinese authorities refused and tried to confiscate the opium brought into Chinese waters, the British responded with war.

A British expeditionary force launched several assaults on coastal cities and ports, culminating in the Nanjing Treaty of 1842, which opened four ports, including Shanghai, to trade and transferred Hong Kong Island to Britain "in perpetuity." When Britain increased its demands in the 1850s, the Second Opium War (1856–60) broke out; this time, Anglo-French forces entered Beijing and burned the Summer Palace.

The incursion of the European imperialists put China into an economic tailspin from which it would not recover for more than a century. With the Qing Dynasty humiliated and weakened by the losses of the First Opium War, an internal rebellion broke out between 1850 and 1864. Known as the Taiping Rebellion, it pitted the Qing Dynasty against the followers of a self-declared brother of Jesus. The rebellion eventually turned into a total war with the staggering death toll of many tens of millions of people. China would try to recover from the mass bloodletting and adopted reforms in the later part of the nineteenth century as part of a "self-strengthening movement" to resist the Europeans, but the Qing Dynasty was never able to formulate a coherent reform program nor to resist the ever-growing demands of the European imperialists. Yet another rebellion broke out in 1899 against concessions to the Europeans, and this so-called Boxer Rebellion led once more to a massive show of force by the European powers. The Boxer Treaty, imposed by the European powers in 1901, allowed the foreign powers to station troops in Beijing and called on Beijing to pay reparations to the Europeans.

The authority of the Qing Dynasty finally collapsed in 1912, and Sun Yat-Sen declared the Republic of China, but once again the chance for order, reform, and economic development gave way to internal disorder within a few years. The Chinese state fragmented, and warlords competed for territory and power. In 1927, the Nationalist government launched attacks on the Chinese Communist Party, igniting a civil war that would last until 1949. Japan invaded China in 1931, brutally occupying parts of China until Japan's defeat in 1945 at the end of the Second World War. The Communist forces under Mao Zedong defeated the Nationalist forces under Chiang Kai-shek in 1949 and proclaimed the People's Republic of China.

Even then, China's turmoil did not end. The new state embarked on a Soviet-style centrally planned economy in the 1950s, but Mao became impatient with the results by the end of the 1950s and launched the Great Leap Forward to accelerate industrialization. The result was chaos and starvation, as farmers were required to leave the fields and devote their meager resources and physical labor to Mao's illusion of building a nation with backyard steel mills. As many as 45 million people may have starved. Yet Mao was not finished with upheaval, as he then launched the Cultural Revolution, which created another decade of chaos from 1966 to his death in 1976. Only in 1978—130 years after the First Opium War—did China finally embark on market-based economic reforms and transformation. By then, China was an impoverished rural economy with a per capita income well below one-tenth of Western Europe's.

India's saga is also one of long-term decline. In the seventeenth century, India was a unified state under Mughal rule. It was home to around one-fourth of the world's population and produced roughly one-fourth of the world's output. India was by far the largest manufacturing nation in the world, with textiles widely admired and sought after by European consumers. Yet from that lofty position, India, like China, experienced a catastrophic and continuous decline in per capita income relative to the industrial nations and in India's share of the world economy until the beginnings of recovery in the second half of the twentieth century.

India's decline began with multiple challenges to Mughal rule in the late seventeenth century. In western India, Mughal rule was challenged by several powers, including Persia, a Sikh confederacy in the Punjab, and the rising Maratha Empire in the Deccan Plateau. The Maratha defeated the Mughals in several wars and extended their control over much of India. In Bengal, to the east, the British East India Company, with its own private army, defeated the ruling state in the Battle of Plassey in 1757, which gave the company effective control and tax authority over Bengal. The company also successfully defeated France in battles along the southeastern coast as part of the global Seven Years' War. Mughal rule was effectively at an end.

From the Battle of Plassey to the Indian Rebellion of 1857, the British East India Company fought countless wars of conquest, including three wars with the Maratha Empire between 1775 and 1818, to take control over all of India. British rule was harsh and profoundly disruptive, marked by famines and administrative ruthlessness that contributed to the deaths of millions. The gaudy corruption of company officials led the British government to assert partial control over company affairs and policies toward the end of the eighteenth century, so that British rule in India in the first half of the 1800s was under the mixed authority of the company and the Crown.

In 1857, an Indian rebellion against British rule was decisively defeated, and the British government took over direct control of India, creating the British Raj that was to rule India until its independence from colonial rule in 1947.

British economic policies decisively weakened the economy and society. As told vividly by historian Prasannan Parthasarathi, trade protectionism by Britain throughout the eighteenth century kept India's famed textiles out of the British market, eventually driving millions of spinners and weavers to penury in the nineteenth century. Far from a victory of the free market, Britain defeated the Indian textile industry in the eighteenth century through a series of measures including progressively tighter bans on imports of Indian textiles. Parthasarathi summarizes the sequence of policies as follows:

> From the late seventeenth century, British cotton manufacturing expanded in tandem with state policies of protection. The ban on imports of Indian painted and printed cloth in 1700 gave a great boost to a British cloth-printing industry, which was given the exclusive right to supply the home market. The ban on imports of Indian white calico in 1721 led British manufacturers to search for and develop a locally made substitute for what had formerly been imported from the sub-continent. This search was successful in the 1770s with the invention of Arkwright's water frame and then Crompton's mule. But the era of protection was not over. Tariffs on Indian muslin imports in the 1780s helped British muslin manufacturers to expand and improve their manufacturing capabilities. Trade policies were integral to the development of the British cotton industry.[9]

From 1858 until India's independence, British policy aimed to turn India into a supplier of raw materials for the British market rather than a competitor of British industry producing finished textiles. Britain ruthlessly governed the countryside, standing idle in the face of multiple famines that reflected the combination of nature and Britain's neglect of Indian lives. Basic services of health, education, and food relief were shirked, leaving a vast population of impoverished and largely illiterate peasants. While there were pockets of industrialization, such as in steel, in the first half of the twentieth century, India's industrialization and development had to await its political independence. Around the time of independence, India's illiteracy rate stood at 80-85 percent, and its life expectancy during 1950-55 average 37 years.[10]

Industrialization occurred in only one place in Asia in the nineteenth century: Japan. Japan alone was able to avoid subjugation to European rule and to undertake internal reform measures to propel an early industrialization. Japan's success reflected a combination of its history, geography, and effective reforms in the face of imperialist threats from Europe and the United States. Japan's early modern history can be dated to 1603, when one clan ruler, Tokugawa Ieyasu, was able to unite Japan under his feudal rule. The Tokugawa Shogunate ruled from 1603 until 1868. The shogun, or military ruler, governed from Edo (today's Tokyo), while the emperor ruled symbolically in Kyoto. In 1635, Japan sharply curtailed international contacts and trade to stop the rising influence of Christianity and Western powers on Japanese politics and society. Trade was limited to a few ports and to inbound ships only from China, Korea, and the Netherlands.

The Tokugawa era was a period of internal peace and extraordinary development of culture, basic education, agricultural intensification, urbanization, and proto-industry, albeit highly labor-intensive industry. According to Maddison's estimates, Japan's population rose from 18.5 million in 1600 to 34.4 million in 1870. By the late Tokugawa era, an estimated 40–50 percent of men and 15–20 percent of women were literate, a remarkably high rate for the time. As early as 1750, Edo (Tokyo) had a population of some 1.2 million, and four other cities (Osaka, Kyoto, Nagoya, and Kanazawa) each had populations above one hundred thousand.

The developments that ensued after 1853, when U.S. naval vessels under Commodore Perry entered Edo Bay, are among the most striking in history. Perry was demanding trade rights for the United States in the same way that the European powers had demanded access to the markets of China and India. Japan, like China and India, faced the decisive threat of Western imperial rule, but only Japan was able to respond internally with the speed and coherence that enabled it to keep the outsiders mostly at bay, protect Japan's sovereignty, and embark on a period of successful industrialization.

Geography played a role in Japan's success. As an island archipelago, Japan was better able to defend itself from invasion. Agricultural productivity ensured food sufficiency. Locally available coal provided the basis for early industrialization. And as a densely settled, partially urbanized society, Japan was able to institute economic, political, and social reforms far more decisively and effectively than either China or India. By dint of good luck and good strategy, Japan maintained a united front vis-à-vis the European and U.S. threats during the second half of the nineteenth century, and by the early twentieth century had successfully reformed and modernized.

The decisive event occurred in 1868, when a group of clans under the Tokugawa feudal system successfully revolted in the name of the emperor against the ruling Tokugawa clan. The Meiji Restoration, as it is known, sought to respond to the Western challenge by modernizing Japan. The feudal structure was ended and the feudal lands (daimyo) were converted into prefectures under the control of a new centralized government. The four-class structure of the feudal society was ended, including elimination of the warrior (samurai) class. A most remarkable diplomatic initiative, known as the Iwakura Mission, was launched. Senior Japanese diplomats voyaged around the world to establish new diplomatic relations with Europe and the United States and to study best practices abroad as the basis for Japanese reforms in many key areas, including the structure of government, central banking, the military, higher education, and industrialization.

The result was a successful transformation, almost entirely peaceful (save for one short-lived uprising, the Satsuma Rebellion in 1877). The result might be called a "capitalist revolution" against the feudalism of the Tokugawa era. Industry began to grow, infrastructure was established, foreign experts brought to Japan the new machine technologies, imperial universities were created, and by the 1890s, Japan had become Asia's industrial powerhouse. Between 1870 and 1890, Japan's GDP per capita grew at an annual rate of 1.6 percent. The results in terms of military strength were demonstrated by Japan's defeat of China in the First Sino-Japanese War of 1894–95, which established Japan's imperial control over Taiwan. Japan next defeated Russia in the Russo-Japanese War of 1904–5 and established imperial rule over Korea in 1905. While Japan still lagged far behind Europe and the United States in per capita income, by 1913 Japan's per capita income was roughly 2.5 times that of China.

Europe Swallows Africa

Though Africa was the poorest and least industrialized part of the world, and though Europeans had been enslaving Africans for centuries, Africa was the last continent to face the full onslaught of European colonial domination. Until the end of the nineteenth century, Europe's imperial foothold in Africa consisted of colonies in the north and south of Africa and a few trading outposts and forts along the coasts of East and West Africa. The interior of Africa was largely beyond European control or even knowledge. The most important reason was the biogeography of disease.

With a tropical climate and countless animal reservoirs of disease, tropical Africa was home to many fatal and debilitating diseases both for humans and farm animals, including horses. Falciparum malaria, transmitted by the human-biting mosquito *Anopheles gambiae*, created a disease barrier to European conquest. African trypanosomiasis, otherwise known as sleeping sickness, transmitted by the tsetse fly, struck down horses and cattle throughout central Africa. It was only with the discovery of a prevention and cure for malaria in particular that Africa fell prey to Europe's ravenous imperial competition.

That cure for malaria was discovered in Peru. Indigenous Peruvians drank a *mate*, or tea infusion, of the bark of the cinchona tree as a cure for fever. The British learned of this *mate*, stole the seeds of the cinchona tree, and began to cultivate it in England. The active antimalarial agent in the *mate* was quinine, a bitter substance with the capacity to prevent and cure malaria. Even better, quinine could be combined with gin for the perfect beverage on the colonial veranda. Gin and tonic not only soothed the European palate but smoothed the way for Europe's conquest of the interior of tropical Africa beginning in the 1880s. That and improved guns, including the newly developed machine gun, enabled the rapid dismemberment and conquest of Africa by the European powers.[11]

By the 1880s, European imperialism was highly developed, even refined. In order to divide up Africa without instigating clashes among the European powers, the Conference of Berlin in 1885 gathered diplomats to divide up Africa among the competitor empires. Depictions of the conference show a roundtable of European diplomats, a map of Africa on the wall, but no Africans in sight. Imperialism was a one-way affair. By 1913, all of Africa, with the notable exceptions of Ethiopia in the Horn of Africa and Liberia in the west, was under European imperial control, as seen in figure 7.5.

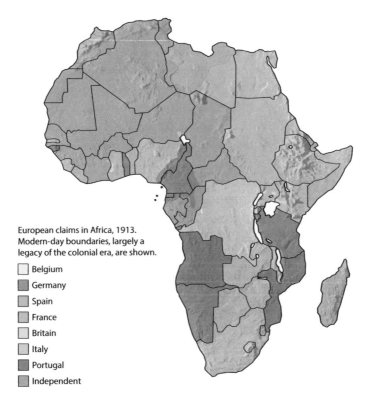

European claims in Africa, 1913.
Modern-day boundaries, largely a
legacy of the colonial era, are shown.

- ☐ Belgium
- ■ Germany
- ☐ Spain
- ☐ France
- ☐ Britain
- ☐ Italy
- ■ Portugal
- ■ Independent

7.5 Africa Divided Among European Empires, 1913

Source: Wikimedia Commons, https://commons.wikimedia.org/w/index
.php?title=File:Colonial_Africa_1913_map.svg&oldid=367487165 (accessed October 27, 2019).

Anglo-American Hegemony

By the end of the nineteenth century, Britain was first among the imperial
powers, with Queen Victoria reigning over the British Isles, India, Burma,
Ceylon (Sri Lanka), Malaya, much of Africa ("Cape to Cairo"), New Guinea,
and dozens of islands and smaller possessions around the world. Many of
these served as fueling stations for the Royal Navy, which had unrivaled
dominance over the oceans. The British navy, by far the most powerful

in the world, policed the sea lanes of the Indian Ocean that connected Britain and India through the Suez Canal (which opened in 1871). Britain maintained de facto control of Egypt after 1882 in large part to ensure the sea routes to India. Interestingly, China's GDP remained the largest in the world until 1888, when it was finally overtaken by the United States, but China was impoverished. In 1870, with a population around 358 million, China's per capita income was just $530 (Maddison data, 1990 international prices); the UK, with 31 million people, had a per capita income of $3,100, roughly six times that of China.[12]

Britain, of course, also gave rise to the major English-speaking offshoots, most importantly the United States, as well as Canada, Australia, and New Zealand. The last three remained subordinate to the British Crown until the Westminster Act of 1931. The United States soared in economic development, overtaking Britain in total GDP around 1872, and in GDP per person around 1905, according to Maddison's estimates.

Let's consider the size of the combined Anglo-American economy as a share of the world (figure 7.6), adding together the British Empire and the United States. For this purpose, I define the British Empire to mean Britain and sixteen colonial possessions for which Maddison provides estimates of GDP during the nineteenth century. The largest of the colonial possessions were Ireland until 1922, Canada and Australia

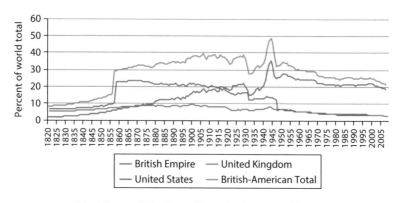

7.6 The Rise and Decline of British-American Economic Dominance, 1820–2008

Source: Angus Maddison. "Statistics on World Population, GDP and Per Capita GDP, 1–2008 AD." *Historical Statistics* 3 (2010): 1–36.

until 1931, and India until 1947. As of 1820, the British Empire accounted for around 6 percent of the world's output. By 1870, by dint of Britain's own industrialization and its expanded imperial holdings, the British Empire accounted for around 23 percent of the world economy, of which the United Kingdom itself was around 9 percent. The British Empire remained around 20 percent of the world economy until 1918, then began to decline with the independence of various colonial possessions, beginning with Ireland in 1922.

During the nineteenth century, the United States became the world's largest economy, with the U.S. share of world output rising from 2 percent in 1820 to 9 percent in 1870, 16 percent in 1900, and 19 percent in 1918. At the end of World War I, therefore, the United States and the British Empire were about the same size. From that point, the U.S. share continued to rise, reaching more than 25 percent at the end of World War II, while the British imperial share continued to decline, falling below 10 percent of the world economy by 1950, following India's independence in 1947. If we consider the British-American world combined, this English-speaking hegemonic duo accounted for around 40 percent of world production as of 1900, and sustained that remarkable share until World War II, after which India and other British colonies gained their independence. By 1980, the British Empire was basically gone, and the UK itself accounted for less than 4 percent of world output.

Until World War I, Britain was undoubtedly the conductor of the Anglo-American orchestra. Britain was an industrial powerhouse, the City of London was the indisputable financial center of the world, and the pound sterling reigned supreme over the world's currencies. The British navy ruled the seas. As late as 1913, one could hardly imagine a twentieth-century world in which Britain would not be the dominant power, or at least a coequal with the United States. Of course, France had its long-standing empire, and Germany too had acquired imperial possessions in Africa. The United States was the single biggest country in the world, but a latecomer to overseas empire building.

On the eve of World War I, the world was linked together by trade, empire, and the Pax Britannica. Britain can rightly be considered the world's first hegemonic power. Though Spain had acquired the first global empire, it never commanded the oceans as did Britain. In his post–World War I masterwork, *The Economic Consequences of the Peace*, John Maynard

Keynes vividly described this interconnected prewar world from the vantage point of London just before the onset of World War I.

> The inhabitant of London could order by telephone, sipping his morning tea in bed, the various products of the whole earth, in such quantity as he might see fit, and reasonably expect their early delivery upon his doorstep; he could at the same moment and by the same means adventure his wealth in the natural resources and new enterprises of any quarter of the world, and share, without exertion or even trouble, in their prospective fruits and advantages; or he could decide to couple the security of his fortunes with the good faith of the townspeople of any substantial municipality in any continent that fancy or information might recommend. He could secure forthwith, if he wished it, cheap and comfortable means of transit to any country or climate without passport or other formality, could despatch his servant to the neighboring office of a bank for such supply of the precious metals as might seem convenient, and could then proceed abroad to foreign quarters, without knowledge of their religion, language, or customs, bearing coined wealth upon his person, and would consider himself greatly aggrieved and much surprised at the least interference.[13]

Yet stunningly, the world soon crashed upon Europe and the British Empire. As Rome was defeated by the German tribes, the Byzantines by the Ottomans, the Chinese by the Mongols, and Asia by Europe, so too Europe experienced a decisive shock as of 1914 that again changed the world and dethroned Europe's empires from the apex of global power.

The Thirty-Year European Bloodletting

One must account the thirty-year period from 1914 to 1945 as one of the greatest disasters ever to afflict humanity. It was Europe's second Thirty Years' War. The first, from 1618 to 1648, was a war within the Holy Roman Empire, mainly between different branches of Christianity. The second Thirty Years' War was a prolonged struggle between the German-speaking nations, notably Germany and Austria, with the rest of Europe, including Britain, France, and Russia.

The war from 1914 to 1945 was a war among the mightiest industrial powers of the world. And it was a war that had no fundamental purpose. The world had never been so prosperous for the very countries that ended up nearly destroying themselves and killing tens of millions of people. At the core, the two European bloodlettings show the madness of violence and self-destruction, not wars as means to any rational ends.

The second Thirty Years' War began with World War I. At the end of World War I, the Treaty of Versailles was supposed to be the peace to end all wars. To later historians, it has become known as the peace to end all peace. The agreements reached in Versailles were so cynical and destabilizing that Europe failed to recover its economic vitality, and the political, diplomatic, and economic conflicts within Europe remained intense. The resulting instability was a major cause of the Great Depression, an economic collapse so devastating and destabilizing that it brought to power the most villainous and heinous regime of modern history, perhaps of all history: the Nazi regime of Hitler's Germany. Germany's aggression, in turn, led to the Second World War, which devastated much of the world and lasted until Germany's defeat in 1945.

We are now more than a full century past the onset of World War I, yet there is still no real explanation of this war. There is a chronology, to be sure, but no explanation. The reason is this: World War I was a war without any real purpose. It was a war that surely could have been avoided.

We know, of course, the basic chronology. In July 1914, the archduke of the Habsburg Empire was killed by a nineteen year-old separatist, Gavrilo Princep, in a terrorist act in Sarajevo, a city of the Habsburg Austro-Hungarian Empire. In response to the attack, Germany prodded the Habsburg Empire to make impossible demands on Serbia, which was viewed as the main state harboring anti-Habsburg terrorists. When Serbia predictably rejected those extreme demands, the Habsburg Empire declared war. Russia, as a protector of Serbia and a fellow Slavic nation, mobilized to protect Serbia against the oncoming clash with the Habsburgs. Germany, antagonistic to Russia and defending Austria, launched the war. This, in turn, brought in Russia's allies, Britain and France. Many historians argue that the German military command actively sought the war as a preemptive strike against Russia, out of fear that Russia was gaining too much economic and military power in the early years of the twentieth century, and would soon overshadow Germany unless Germany attacked Russia first.

Europe was suddenly engulfed in war, and not just war but the first fully industrial war, with aerial bombings, machine guns, tanks, and submarines—the full miracle of industrialization put to the nightmarish destruction of human beings. Some 20 million people perished in the war.

In the third year of the war, the United States got pulled in as well, through the coaxing of President Woodrow Wilson. Wilson naively believed that he would make this "the war to end all wars." Wilson's vision proved to be a failure in practice. With America's entry into the war, what might have been a stalemate within Europe, and thereby possibly a return to long-term peace, ended up as the complete defeat of Germany by the United States and its allies. With that defeat came the overthrow of the Prussian monarchy, the overly harsh terms imposed on Germany in the Versailles peace settlement, and the profound destabilization of Germany in the 1920s, leading to Hitler's rise to power in early 1933.

In fact, World War I broke so much pottery you could say that it had destroyed the basis for a return to normal life not only in Europe but also in Russia and the Middle East. Western and Central Europe saw the collapse of the Habsburg and Prussian empires. Russia experienced the overthrow of the Romanov Empire by the Bolsheviks and the launch of seventy-five years of brutal Soviet rule. The Ottoman Empire was defeated and dismantled, opening the way to new European imperialism in the Middle East and North Africa led cynically by Britain and France.

The war, in short, achieved nothing except the dislocation of the political organization of Europe, the former Ottoman lands, the Middle East, and Russia. Trade within Europe and the gold standard of prewar Europe never recovered. Instead, Europe experienced a decade of profound monetary instability in the 1920s followed by economic depression in the 1930s.

John Maynard Keynes, the greatest economist of the twentieth century, served as a young expert on Britain's negotiating team at the Versailles peace conference. He was profoundly disheartened by the narrowness of the perspective of the major powers and the punitive nature of the settlement imposed on Germany. In a remarkable piece of analysis and protest, Keynes's *Economic Consequences of the Peace*, written at the end of the negotiations in 1919, warned that the harshness of the settlement, and especially the heavy reparations payments levied on Germany, would lead to economic disarray in Europe and the likelihood of another disaster to follow. His words were stark, and prophetic:

If we aim deliberately at the impoverishment of Central Europe, vengeance, I dare predict, will not limp. Nothing can then delay for very long that final civil war between the forces of Reaction and the despairing convulsions of Revolution, before which the horrors of the late German war will fade into nothing, and which will destroy, whoever is victor, the civilization and the progress of our generation.[14]

At the end of January 1933, in the midst of the global Great Depression and with Germany suffering 25 percent unemployment and unpayable foreign debts, the aged German president Hindenburg appointed a new chancellor, Adolph Hitler. Hitler remilitarized Germany and set out to conquer the lands to the east, while ridding Germany of its Jews. World War II broke out on September 1, 1939, with the invasion of Poland by both Germany and the Soviet Union. The full onslaught of war ensued, including the Holocaust of the Jews and others groups. At the same time, Japan's fascist regime, an ally of Nazi Germany, waged war on the United States and throughout Asia. The world was in flames.

In one of the most notable statements of modern history, the remarkable UK prime minister Winston Churchill called for the New World, "with all its power and might," to step forth "to the rescue and the liberation of the old." Franklin Roosevelt, arguably the greatest president in American history, heeded that call. The industrial power of the United States came to the rescue. While the Soviet Union was fighting and suffering millions of deaths on the battlefield, America's industrial might soared and provided the munitions for victory. By the end of the war, the United States was by far the world's dominant economy. America was spared any attacks on the homeland after the one-day attack on the Pearl Harbor naval base in Hawaii on December 7, 1941. The industrial sector thrived, growing some 60 percent between 1940 and 1945. As of 1950, the United States accounted for around 27 percent of global output.

The American Century

We have arrived at the moment of America's global hegemonic leadership. In 1941, the publisher of *Time* magazine, Henry Luce, declared the

American Century. He correctly intuited that when the war ended, America would be the world's dominant economic, technological, and geopolitical power. Not only did the United States possess by far the world's largest economy, but that economy had benefited from, and would continue to benefit from, the massive advances in technology developed in the course of the war. The wartime effort contributed to fundamental technological advances in many sectors: aviation, computers, cybernetics (human-machine interactions), public health, electronics (including semiconductors), radar, communications, and of course nuclear power and nuclear weapons. Just as important, the experience of the war contributed to the idea of science-led economic growth. In 1944, Roosevelt asked his science adviser Vannevar Bush for a plan to transfer the wartime advances in technology to peacetime use. Bush's 1945 response, *Science: The Endless Frontier*, brilliantly laid out a strategy for mobilizing science for social and economic development.

The pace and scale of America's economic rise from the early nineteenth century to Luce's declaration of the American Century were unprecedented in economic history to that point. Total output rose from $12.5 billion in 1820 to $929 billion in 1940, a rate of 3.7 percent per annum (in international 1990 dollars). The population rose from 10 million in 1820 to 133 million in 1940, an annual increase of 2.2 percent, while output per person rose from $1,257 to $7,000, an annual increase of 1.4 percent. Most importantly, the United States became a continental-scale industrial power, the only one on the planet. (The Soviet Union tried to emulate the industrial scale of the United States, but consistently lagged far behind.). In 1820, there were twenty-three states, all but one (Louisiana) east of the Mississippi River. By 1940, there were forty-eight states linked coast to coast by a rail network, which spanned the continent after 1869, and by enormous enterprises that also operated at the continental scale. The continent was fabulously rich in natural resources: vast midwestern plains with fertile soils, minerals, coal and oil, timber, navigable rivers and waterways, and a mostly temperate climate. The European settlers and their descendants were prepared to take any steps to clear the way for settlements, profits, and industry, including mass slavery until the Civil War, the war with Mexico in 1846–48, and the genocidal wars against the Native American populations throughout the nineteenth century. Protected by two oceans, the United States built its industry during two world wars while other industrial nations suffered horrendous losses of productive capital.

U.S. dynamism was exemplified from the start by infrastructure development—the building of canals, railroads, and roads—and by the rapid uptake and development of new technologies, including the frequent stealing and copying of superior British technologies. In the first half of the nineteenth century, American inventors improved the steam engine, modified the railroad, improved the cotton gin, developed the steamboat, invented the telegraph, and much more. Up until the Civil War of 1861–65, the U.S. economy as a whole remained mostly rural and agricultural, and based heavily on slave labor in Southern cotton production. The United States was around 20 percent urban as of 1860. Following the Civil War, industrialization soared; by 1910, the country was 46 percent urban, reaching 57 percent by 1940. U.S. GDP surpassed that of the UK in 1872 and China in 1898, and U.S. per capita income overtook that of the UK around 1905.

The United States used its post–World War II geopolitical leadership and economic weight to establish a set of institutions to help govern the postwar order. Most consequential was the new United Nations, established in 1945 as a bulwark for peace and economic development, a successor to the failed League of Nations that had been created after World War I. Two new economic institutions, the International Monetary Fund and the World Bank (formally called the International Bank for Reconstruction and Development), were established under the UN umbrella to foster financial stability and to finance postwar reconstruction and development. A new set of trade rules, the General Agreement on Tariffs and Trade (GATT), aimed to reestablish market-based trade after its collapse during the Great Depression and World War II. Other institutions, such as the Food and Agricultural Organization (1945) and the World Health Organization (1948), were added to the "UN family" to help provide critical global public goods such as food security and disease control.

While the United States stood unequaled in economic might and technological prowess, it faced security challenges, most importantly the struggle with the Soviet Union over the postwar order. The Soviet economy was only a small fraction of America's, perhaps around one-third, but the Soviet Union was a vast country, with nuclear weapons after 1949, an enormous army in Central Europe, and a commitment to one-party state socialism and central planning. The two countries faced off in Europe, almost coming to blows several times over the future of Germany, and also competed internationally for allies, resources, and military advantage. Worst of all, the two countries launched into a massive nuclear arms race, amassing enough nuclear armaments to destroy all human life on the planet many times over. By dint of various accidents, missteps, and misunderstandings, the two countries came to the brink of global nuclear annihilation in October 1962, and at least close to the brink on several other occasions.

The U.S. geopolitical leadership has shown two faces to the world. One was the U.S. interest in building law-based multilateral institutions, including the global institutions of the UN system and regional institutions such as the European Community (and later European Union), of which the United States was a champion from the start. The other was the cynical exercise of power for narrow U.S. interests. While the United States did not directly colonize countries after World War II, it used its vast military power and economic leverage repeatedly and often brutally to put into power governments that would favor U.S. business and security interests and to remove from power governments that opposed U.S. prerogatives. "Regime change" operations, meaning U.S.-led invasions, coups, and subterfuges to bring down foreign governments that U.S. officials deemed hostile to U.S. interests, became a mainstay of U.S. foreign policy. In the 1960s, the United States fought wars in Vietnam, Cambodia, and Laos aimed at installing noncommunist governments. In the 1960s and 1970s, the United States supported military coups throughout Latin America to bring down democracies deemed by U.S. strategists to be too far to the left. In the 1980s, the United States funded wars against left-wing governments in Central America and the Caribbean. From the 1990s to the 2010s, it fought several wars in Central Asia, the Middle East, and North Africa against Russian allies or other governments it disfavored (e.g., Iraq, Syria and Libya).

Most remarkably, the United States created a network of military installations and bases around the world that was in scale unrivaled in history. It is estimated that the United States has military bases in around seventy countries and military personnel in well over 100 countries. Because of the secrecy in which they are shrouded, the precise number of U.S. overseas bases is not known, but expert sleuthing by scholar David Vine and investigative reporter Nick Turse has been a huge help in uncovering the remarkable extent of the bases.[14] Data compiled by the Defense Manpower Data Center list more than sixty countries worldwide with twenty or more active duty U.S. military personnel as of March 2019, as shown in figure 7.7.[16]

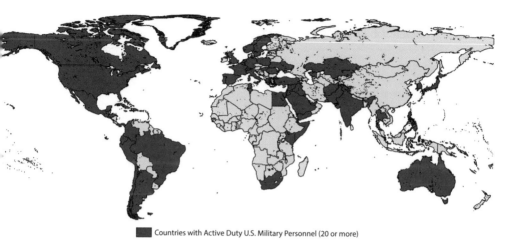

Countries with Active Duty U.S. Military Personnel (20 or more)

7.7 Countries with Active Duty U.S. Military Personnel (20 or more)

Source: Map created using data from: Defense Manpower Data Center, "DoD Personnel, Workforce Reports & Publications," DMDC.osd.mil: USA.gov, 2019.

Decolonization and the Onset of Global Convergence

World War II sounded the death knell of European empires. A process of European colonization that began in the early 1500s rapidly unraveled after 1945. The European powers were exhausted by war, heavily indebted, and without the legitimacy in the colonies to maintain their rule. Local independence movements either convinced the imperial power to withdraw peacefully, as in India in 1947, or eventually forced that outcome through wars of liberation, as in Indonesia, Algeria, Vietnam, Angola, and elsewhere. As newly independent countries joined the world stage, UN membership rose rapidly. An initial UN membership of fifty-one at its founding in 1945 rose to 117 by 1965, 159 by 1985, and 193 by 2015.

The end of the colonial era led to a fundamental change in the process of industrialization. Suddenly, independent countries could pursue their own destinies, promoting industrialization rather than serving merely as a source of primary commodities for the imperial nations. Moreover, and crucially, they could invest in their own people by introducing programs of mass literacy, public schooling, and public health. While poor countries were constrained by meager budgets in pursuing their ambitions to scale up

Table 7.4 Illiteracy and Life Expectancy in 1950, Selected Countries

	Illiteracy (%)	Life expectancy (years)
High-Income Countries		
United Kingdom	1–2	69.4
United States	3–4	68.7
France	3–4	67.1
Former Colonies		
Kenya	75–80	42.3
Indonesia	80–85	43.5
India	80–85	36.6

Source: UNESCO, *World Illiteracy at Mid-Century: A Statistical Study* (Paris: UNESCO, 1957), https://unesdoc.unesco.org/ark:/48223/pf0000002930; World Population Prospects: The 2019 Revision | United Nations Population Division, http://data.un.org/Data.aspx?d=PopDiv&f=variableID%3A68#PopDiv.

education and health care, the intentions were clear. The newly independent countries around the world wanted to make up for lost time, by building the human capital and infrastructure needed to create new industries and to attract domestic and multinational capital.

They had a lot of catching up to do. The European imperial powers had left most of their African and Asian colonies in a desperate condition of very high illiteracy and dreadfully low life expectancy. Table 7.4 shows the conditions of selected countries in 1950: three industrialized countries and three countries long under colonial rule (Kenya and India, UK; Indonesia, the Netherlands). As of 1950, illiteracy had been almost eliminated in the high-income countries and life expectancy was around sixty-eight years, but in the long-time colonies, illiteracy was around 80 percent and life expectancy was around forty years.

By and large, with decolonization the development process began to work, though unevenly. Newly independent countries that opened to global trade and investment, maintained peace, and carried out public investments in health, education, and infrastructure were able to begin a process of convergent growth, that is, growth per capita faster than in the high-income countries. Illiteracy fell sharply and life expectancy rose as education and health care were scaled up. By 2000, illiteracy fell to 18 percent in Kenya and just 10 percent in Indonesia. Life expectancy rose to fifty-three years in Kenya, sixty-three years in India, and sixty-six years in Indonesia—still far behind the rich countries, but with a smaller gap.

The greatest development success stories by far were in East Asia, where the "four tigers" of early postwar industrialization—Hong Kong, South Korea, Singapore, and Taiwan—achieved spectacular growth rates and dramatic declines of poverty. China followed a generation later, with a takeoff to industrialization and rapid growth beginning in 1978. India began an era of rapid growth even later, in 1991, after shaking off lackluster economic development strategies of the early decades of independence.

One of the ramifications of convergent growth is that overall global growth accelerated after World War II. In the first half of the twentieth century, worldwide growth, according to Maddison's estimates, amounted to around 2 percent per year. In the second half of the twentieth century, from 1950 to 2000, aggregate global growth was on the order of 4.6 percent per year, more than doubling the rate of the first half-century.

Broadly speaking, the world shifted from a long era of divergence, in which the early industrializers—Europe, the United States, Canada, Australia, Japan, and a few others—pulled ahead of the rest of the world, to an era of convergence, in which the laggard countries, notably in Asia but also in other parts of the developing world, began to narrow the proportionate income and technology gaps with the early industrializers.

Decolonization accelerated convergence on a global scale. During the period from 1820 to 1950, the rich North Atlantic countries grew faster than the poorer rest of the world. The gap between rich and poor countries widened, and an increasing share of world output and income originated in Europe and North America. Starting with decolonization after World War II, the newly independent countries began to catch up. The share of world income produced in Asia, Africa, and Latin America began to increase (figure 7.8). The relative low point of those countries was the year 1950, when Latin America, Asia, and Africa together constituted just 30 percent of world output but 70 percent of the world's population.

Since 1950, the world has been on an unprecedented path of technological and economic convergence, and the gains have been much broader than income alone. Throughout the developing world, life expectancy has been rising, years of schooling have increased, rates of extreme poverty have been falling, and employment has been shifting away from manual labor

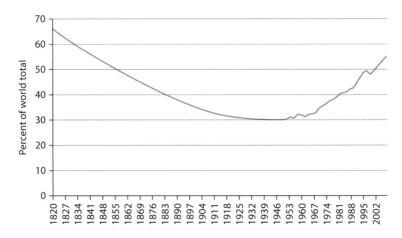

7.8 The Share of World Output Beyond the North Atlantic (Asia, Latin America, and Africa), 1820–2008

Source: Jutta Bolt, Robert Inklaar, Herman de Jong, and Jan Luiten van Zanden. "Rebasing 'Maddison': New Income Comparisons and the Shape of Long-Run Economic Development." *GGDC Research Memorandum* 174 (2018).

to more remunerative, higher skilled, and less arduous work than the traditional jobs in smallholder subsistence agriculture and mining. The task of development is by no means complete: there are still around 700 million people trapped in extreme poverty, and hundreds of millions more who are just one step ahead of destitution. Nonetheless, the progress against poverty is real and substantial.[17]

There is more convergence to come, as the benefits of technological advance are increased by the digital revolution. If well harnessed by developing countries, the new wave of technologies—artificial intelligence, smart systems, robotics, high-speed wireless broadband—are likely to spur further convergent economic growth. And with convergence has come a rising geopolitical weight of the developing countries in global affairs.

The United States, as the global leader between 1950 and 2000, had a complex and ambiguous attitude toward decolonization, convergence, and the rising voice of developing countries in world affairs. In the early post–World War II period, the United States championed decolonization. This fit well with the U.S. aim of replacing Britain and France at the helm of global affairs. During the 1960s and 1970s, the United States continued generally to champion the economic interests of the developing countries—in part to lure them into the U.S. alliance against the Soviet Union—but as the developing countries gained economic strength and political voice, the U.S. position began to change. When developing countries at the United Nations called for a "New International Economic Order" in the 1970s, with the aim of rebalancing global power and wealth between the developed and the developing countries, the U.S. attitude turned hostile, insisting that the developing world get in line behind U.S. leadership—or else. With the presidency of Donald Trump, the U.S. position had become "America First," a stark declaration of U.S. self-interest over internationalist objectives. Many American strategists began to see convergence, especially China's convergence, as a direct threat to U.S. interests rather than an objective of U.S. policy.

Some Lessons from the Industrial Age

The Industrial Age marks a distinct and remarkable phase in the history of globalization. For the first time in history, technological progress was rapid enough and broad enough to create sustained and rapid increases in material living standards. For the first 150 years of the new age, the economic gains went overwhelmingly to a small part of humanity: Western Europe, the United States, and a few other industrializing countries. Much of the world fell into deeper misery, with unabated poverty combined with political subservience to the industrial empires.

Britain, the first mover of the industrial era, also became the world's first superpower—indeed, the world's first hegemonic power. Yet as we have learned at every phase of history, even seemingly impregnable power can quickly dissipate. In the case of Britain, this rapid loss of power occurred as the result of tragedy: two world wars and an intervening Great Depression. The great lasting legacies of British leadership include the spread of parliamentary democracy to many of the former colonies, the shared institutions of global commerce, and perhaps most consequentially, the use of English as a lingua franca of global business, government, tourism, and science. No other language rivals English as a global second language—that is, as a language spoken in addition to one's mother tongue. It is estimated that around 1 billion people today speak English, of which around 500 million speak English as their second language, and English has become the global language of science, finance, and diplomacy.

After World War II, the United States claimed the mantle of global hegemon, but the U.S. position too now looks increasingly tenuous as power spreads more widely in the world. The end of European imperial rule in Africa and Asia set loose a process of sustained growth in the former colonies—growth that has not been even, to be sure, but rapid enough to bring significant increases in output per person, reductions in extreme poverty, rapid urbanization, and structural shifts away from arduous physical labor, with more opportunities for schooling and leisure. The most remarkable case of convergent growth is China. Over the course of roughly forty years, from the beginning of market reforms in 1978 until now, China has eliminated extreme poverty and created a technologically dynamic economy. Geopolitical power and technological prowess are no longer the privileged preserve of the North Atlantic.

Thus we have arrived at the seventh age of globalization, in which digital technologies are reshaping global economics and geopolitics. Every sector of the economy will be affected by the digital technologies, and global power relations are once again shifting as well. The new complex global scene is made even more complicated by the ecological crisis that has accompanied global economic growth. From a global perspective, the world's main challenges are clear: to continue the process of economic convergence while addressing rising inequalities within nations, shifting geopolitics, and increasingly dire environmental threats. This is the drama to which we now turn.

8

The Digital Age

It is estimated that in 2020 the world will create and transmit roughly 44 zettabytes of data per day.[1] In numbers, that is 44,000,000,000,000,000,000,000 bytes, each byte carrying the information of one letter or number. Yet soon enough, these staggering numbers will be superseded by even more remarkable numbers. The ubiquity and scale of data processing and transmission are utterly mind-boggling. Here are some other estimates as of 2019:

- 1.6 billion Facebook log-ons each day
- 3.5 billion Google searches each day
- 5 billion YouTube videos watched each day
- 4.4 billion Internet users (as of June 30, 2019), of which 829 million are in China, 560 million in India, and 293 million in the United States
- $5 trillion cross-border settlements daily through the SWIFT banking system[2]

In the twenty-first century, the world has arrived at ubiquitous connectivity. And there is more connectivity to come with advances in the coverage and capabilities of the Internet and related digital systems such as 5G. The digital revolution is so deep that we can rightly consider our era to be a new seventh age of globalization.

This new age of globalization, like the past ages, will create new patterns of global economic activity, jobs, lifestyles, and geopolitics. This new age arrives together with another fundamental development: a human-caused ecological crisis hitting the planet. The dramatic successes of globalization during the past two centuries have sown the seeds of ecological crisis as well, as human activities—especially fossil-fuel use, farming, transport, and industrial production—have created new and profound challenges of human-induced climate change, the mass destruction of biodiversity, and the dire pollution of the air, soils, freshwater, and oceans. Another set of challenges will arise from further rapid changes in demographics, including the size of the world population, its age structure, its distribution by region, and the share of the world living in urban versus rural areas.

In this century, therefore, we will see the unfolding of several powerful trends: the continued economic rise of China and India, the relative decline of the United States in world output and global power, the rapid population and economic growth of Africa, and a further steep rise in urbanization, along with the ubiquity of digital technologies and their uses. Our social and political systems will be under great stress given the dramatic changes ahead. As the great evolutionary biologist E. O. Wilson has summarized it in his book *The Social Conquest of Earth*, we exist with a bizarre combination of "Stone Age emotions, medieval institutions, and godlike technology."

The Digital Revolution

The uptake of digital technologies is the fastest technological change in history. Facebook, Google, and Amazon came out of nowhere to become, in a few short years, among the most powerful companies in the world. Smartphones are only a decade old, but they have already upended how we live. How did this revolution come about?

The roots of the digital revolution can be traced to a remarkable paper by British genius Alan Turing, writing in 1936. Turing envisioned a new conceptual device, a universal computing machine—a Turing machine, as it became known—that could read an endless tape of 0s and 1s in order to calculate anything that could be calculated. Turing had conceptualized a general-purpose programmable computer before one had been invented. His ideas would fundamentally shape the digital revolution to come. Turing also made legendary contributions to the Allied war effort by showing how to use mathematical cryptography and an early electronic device to decipher the Nazi military secret code. (For all his genius and his contributions, a towering figure in the entire history of mathematics, Turing was hounded by British authorities after World War II for his homosexuality, and possibly driven to suicide, as the cause of his death remains disputed.)

The next step in the digital revolution came out of another remarkable mind, that of John von Neumann, who conceptualized in 1945 the basic architecture of the modern computer, with a processing unit, control unit, working memory, input and output devices, and external mass storage. Von Neumann's computer architecture became the design of the first computers, devices using vacuum tubes to implement the computer's logical circuitry. MIT engineer and mathematician Claude Shannon provided the mathematics of the logical gates and processing systems to implement Turing's programs of 0s and 1s on von Neumann's computer architecture.

The next piece of the puzzle was solved in 1947, with the invention of the modern transistor at Bell Laboratories, which built on advances in understanding of semiconductors gained during the radar work of World War II. The transistor replaced the vacuum tube in Shannon's logical circuitry and enabled the development of microprocessing units with first thousands, then millions, and then billions of transistors. In the early 1950s, the individual transistors were soldered onto motherboards. From 1958 to 1961, two pioneers, Robert Noyce and Jack Kilby, developed ways to etch transistors and other electronic components directly onto silicon wafers, inventing the integrated circuit. With the integrated circuit, it became possible to put larger and larger numbers of transistors, and therefore faster and more powerful microprocessors, onto a silicon chip. This miniaturization enabled the exponential increases in computing speed, memory, and data transmission that underpin the digital revolution.

As computers began to penetrate scientific, military, and business work, the U.S. Department of Defense asked a basic question: How can computers communicate with each other, and do so in a resilient way that would survive the disruption of networks in a war? The answer was a method for sending data packets (bits of 0s and 1s) between computers according to flexible routing, a method known as "packet switching," that became the basis for a new Internet. Initially a U.S. government project, the Internet was later made available to a group of participating U.S. universities before it was opened for commercial use in 1987.

In 1965, Gordon Moore, then the head of Intel, an early manufacturer of integrated circuitry that would become the global pacesetter, noticed that the transistor count etched into a microchip of silicon was doubling roughly every one to two years. Moreover, he predicted that the trend would continue for the coming decade. That was a half-century ago, and Moore's observation and prediction proved to be prescient. The doubling time for various attributes of microprocessing (speed, transistor count, and cost, among others) continued the pattern of rapid geometric growth until the 2010s, with a modest recent slowdown compensated by gains in other dimensions of computation. Intel's 4004 microprocessor in 1971 had 2,300 transistors. Intel's Xeon Platinum microprocessor in 2017 had 8 billion transistors. This is roughly a two-year doubling time over forty-six years, or twenty-three doublings. Moore's law is shown in figure 8.1, illustrated by the development of Intel's microprocessors.

Computer capacities soared, and so too did connectivity. The development of fiber-optic cables enabled a vast increase in the speed, accuracy, and scale of data transmission. Microwave transmission enabled a revolution in wireless connectivity, so that mobile devices could connect to the

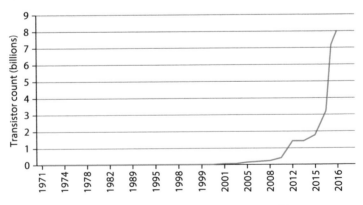

8.1 Moore's Law in Action: Transistor Count on Intel Chips, 1971–2016

Source: Wikipedia contributors; Transistor count Wikipedia, https://en.wikipedia.org/w/index .php?title=Transistor_count&oldid=923570554.

Internet. At the same time, massive advances were made in the ability to digitize materials—text, images, and video—along with countless advances in scientific probes and measurements, such as satellite imagery, gene sequencing, and sensors collecting vast amounts of real-time information from devices.

The uptake of mobile phones parallels the Internet in speed of the dissemination of a breakthrough digital technology. The mobile phone was invented at Bell Labs in 1973. From a few thousand phone subscribers in the early 1980s, mobile subscriptions reached 7.8 billion in 2017 (figure 8.2).

The third dimension of the digital revolution is the intelligence of the computers. Once again, Turing took the lead, asking the pivotal question: Can machines have intelligence, and if so, how would we know? In 1950, he posed the famous Turing test of machine intelligence: An intelligent machine (computer-based system) would be able to interact with humans in a way that the humans would not be able to distinguish whether they were interacting with a machine or a human being. For example, the human subject could carry on a conversation with a machine or a person located in another room, passing messages to and receiving messages from that room, without knowing whether the counterpart was a person or an intelligent machine.

Whether or not machines will reach a form of generalized intelligence, there is no doubt that machines are increasingly able to learn and carry

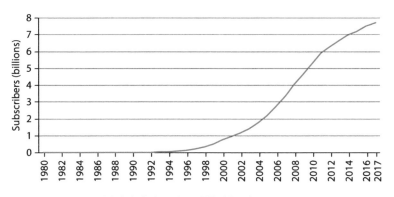

8.2 Mobile Subscribers Worldwide, 1990–2017

Source: "Mobile Phone Market Forecast - 2019." areppim: information, pure and simple, 2019, https://stats.areppim.com/stats/stats_mobilex2019.htm.

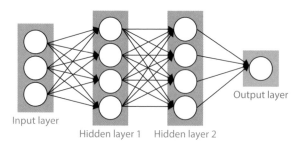

Input layer

Hidden layer 1   Hidden layer 2

Output layer

8.3 The Basic Structure of Neural Networks for Artificial Intelligence

out sophisticated tasks once regarded as the unique purview of highly intelligent human beings. Smart machines now routinely translate texts, identify objects in pictures, drive cars, and play games requiring highly sophisticated skills. Marvelous breakthroughs have been achieved in the past decade through applications of artificial neural networks, currently the mainstay of artificial intelligence.

Artificial neural networks process digital inputs and generate digital outputs based on processing of the inputs through a sequence of layers of artificial neurons. As shown in figure 8.3, digital data from the input level are processed one layer at the time until the signals culminate at the output layer, which then selects an action. The input layer may, for example, code the pixels of a digital image such as an X-ray, or code the board position of a game of chess, or code digitally a natural-language text. The output level would then code the machine's diagnosis of the X-ray, or its chess move, or the computer translation of text into a designated natural language.

The key to the "intelligence" of the artificial neural network is the mathematical weighting that each artificial neuron attaches to incoming signals that it receives from the lower layer of neurons, which determine the signal that the neuron sends onward to the neurons in the next higher level. These weights may be analogized to the strength of synapses connecting neurons in the human brain. They define the network of artificial neurons that translate the digital signals of the input layer into the digital signals produced by the output layer.

The mathematical weights are adjusted by "training" the machine using sophisticated algorithms that update the weights assigned to each neuron based on the performance of the machine in a given test run.

The weights are adjusted in order to improve the performance of the computer, for example in correctly identifying images, or winning chess games, or translating text. The mathematical process of refining the weights in order to generate high-quality output actions is called "machine learning." For example, if the machine is being trained to identify tumors in a digital X-ray, the mathematical weights connecting the artificial neurons are adjusted depending on whether the machine's diagnosis is correct or incorrect on each test image. With enough "supervised learning" of this sort, and using sophisticated mathematical techniques for updating the weights of the artificial neural network, machine learning results in artificial intelligence systems with remarkable skills.

With the vast increases in computational capacity and speed of computers represented by Moore's law, artificial intelligence systems are now being built with hundreds of layers of digital neurons and very high-dimensional digital inputs and outputs. With sufficiently large "training sets" of data or ingenious designs of self-play described below, neural networks are achieving superhuman skills on a rapidly expanding array of challenges, from board games like Chess and Go, to interpersonal games such as poker, to sophisticated language operations such as real-time translation, and to professional medical skills such as complex diagnostics.

The rapidity of advancement has been breathtaking. In 1997, former world chess champion Garry Kasparov played IBM's Deep Blue computer. To Kasparov's amazement and consternation, he was beaten by the computer. In that early case, Deep Blue had been programmed in expert play using a vast library of historic games and board positions. Today, a "self-taught" AI chess system can learn chess from scratch in a few hours, with no library of games or any other expert inputs on chess strategy, and trounce not only the current world chess champion but all past computer champions such as Deep Blue.

In 2011, another IBM system, named Watson, learned to play the TV game show *Jeopardy*, with all of the puns and quips of popular culture and natural language, and beat world-class *Jeopardy* champions live on television. This too was a startling achievement, edging yet closer to passing the Turing test. After the *Jeopardy* championship, Watson went on to the field of medicine, working with doctors to hone expert diagnostic systems.

More recently, we have seen stunning breakthroughs in deep neural networks, that is neural networks with hundreds of layers of artificial neurons.

In 2016, an AI system, AlphaGo from the company Deep Mind, took on the world's eighteen-time world Go champion, Lee Sedol. Go is a board game of such sophistication and subtlety that it was widely believed that machines would be unable to compete with human experts for years or decades to come. Sedol, like Kasparov before him, believed that he would triumph easily over AlphaGo. In the event, he was decisively defeated by the system. Then, to make matters even more dramatic, AlphaGo was decisively defeated by a next-generation AI system that learned Go from scratch in self-play over a few hours. Once again, hundreds of years of expert study and competition could be surpassed in a few hours of learning through self-play.

The advent of learning through self-play, sometimes called "tabula rasa" or blank-slate learning, is mind-boggling. In tabula-rasa learning, the AI system is trained to play against itself, for example in millions of games of chess, with the weights of the neural networks updated depending on the wins and losses in self-play. Starting from no information whatsoever other than the rules of chess, the AI system plays against itself in millions of chess games and uses the results to update the neural-network weights in order to learn chess-playing skills. Remarkably, in just four hours of self-play, an advanced computer AI system developed by the company Deep-Mind learned all of the skills needed to handily defeat the world's best human chess players as well as the previous AI world-champion chess player![3] A few hours of blank-slate learning bested 600 years of learning of chess play by all of the chess experts in history.

Technological Advances and the End of Poverty

In 2006, I published a book titled *The End of Poverty* in which I suggested that the end of extreme poverty was within the reach of our generation, indeed by 2025, if we made increased global efforts to help the poor.[4] I had in mind special efforts to bolster health, education, and infrastructure for the world's poorest people, notably in sub-Saharan African and South Asia, home to most of the world's extreme poverty. Since the end of the last century, remarkable progress has indeed been achieved. The World Bank data for the period 1990 to 2015 are shown in figure 8.4. In 1990, an estimated 1.9 billion people lived in extreme poverty, equal to 35.9 percent of the world's population. By 2015, the number had dropped to 736 million, or just 10 percent of the world's population.[5]

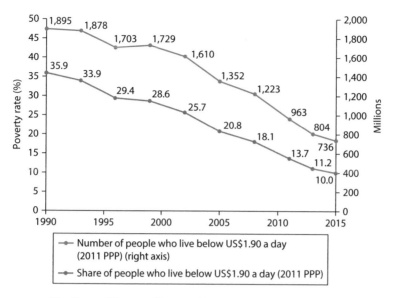

8.4 The Rate of Extreme Poverty (Rate and Headcount), 1990–2015

The most important single reason for this progress was certainly the rapid advances in technologies that enabled major achievements in disease control, access to knowledge, financial inclusion (such as the ability to secure loans), and rise in incomes and decent work conditions in even the poorest parts of the world. The digital revolution is speeding the uptake not only of digitally related technologies but of other technologies as well, through the rapid dissemination of knowledge, skills, and technical systems facilitated through digital connectivity. The greatest advances in poverty reduction were certainly those achieved by China, where rates of extreme poverty plummeted from an estimated 66 percent of the Chinese population in 1990 to essentially zero by 2020, an economic miracle by any standard![6]

Even faster global poverty reduction could have been achieved by now, and can still be achieved in the future, if the global community makes a greater targeted effort. When aid has been targeted to specific challenges of very poor communities—such as disease control, school attendance, and access to infrastructure—progress has been much faster than when progress depends on the general forces of economic growth alone. Still, the progress to date gave the UN member states the confidence to set 2030 as the target date for ending extreme poverty when they adopted the Sustainable Development Goals in 2015. Achieving SDG 1, ending extreme poverty by 2030, is a huge ambition and is indeed out of reach with business as usual, but it could be accomplished if the rich countries took their responsibilities and commitments towards the poor countries more seriously.

Convergent Growth and China's Surge to the Forefront

The second half of the twentieth century was marked by the shift from overall global economic divergence to overall global convergence. The first 150 years of industrialization widened the gap between the rich and poor countries, and indeed left much of the developing world under the imperial yoke of Europe's industrial nations. Yet after World War II, the poor regions of the world were able to increase their rate of growth after they achieved independence from colonial rule. Political sovereignty gave the newly independent nations the freedom of maneuver to increase public investments in health, education, and infrastructure. Not all managed well. Some fell into debt, others into high inflation, but many succeeded in building systems of public health and education, and raising the human capital needed for economic growth. On average, the developing countries grew more rapidly in GDP per capita than the high-income nations, so that the relative gap in incomes began to shrink.

This pattern has continued into the twenty-first century, as shown by the International Monetary Fund data in figure 8.5. The growth rate of GDP per capita of the developing countries has generally outpaced that of the developed countries by 1–5 percentage points per year, though by a diminished margin in the 2010s. The faster growth in GDP per capita, combined with a higher rate of population growth, has meant that the share of global output produced by the developing countries has also been rising—the same pattern that we observed in the previous chapter for the period between 1950 and 2008. The shifting proportions of global output of the developed and developing countries are shown in figure 8.6. Whereas the developed countries accounted for 57 percent of world output in 2000, their share declined to around 41 percent of world output as of 2018 according

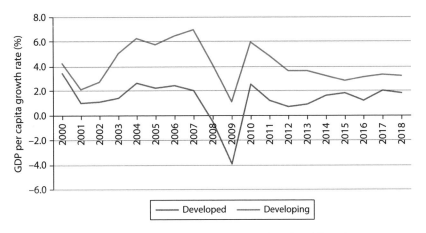

8.5 Growth Rate of GDP Per Capita, Developed and Developing Countries, 2000–2018

Source: IMF World Economic Outlook. Developed countries are the "Advanced Economies," and developing countries are the "Emerging market and developing countries." Data are for GDP per capita at 2011 international dollars.

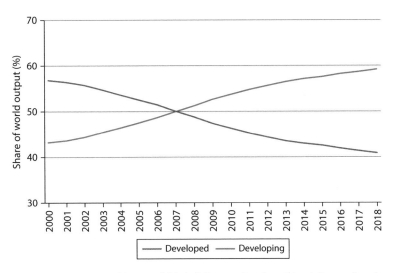

8.6 Trading Places: Shares of Global Output Produced by Advanced and Developing Countries, 2000–2018

Source: International Monetary Fund, World Economic Outlook Database, October 2019.

to the IMF estimates. Of course the developing country share rose from 43 percent to 59 percent. Within nineteen years, the two regions had traded places in their global shares of output.

The most dramatic single change in recent times has been the surge in economic development, and therefore the global role, of China. After nearly 140 years of economic and social strife, marked by foreign incursions, domestic rebellions, civil wars, and internal policy blunders of historic dimensions, China settled down after 1978 to stable, open, market-based production and trade, relying on the catch-up strategy that it had observed to be so successful in its near-neighborhood. Japan had pioneered the strategy back at the time of the Meiji Restoration in 1868 and the years that followed, and had applied it again in Japan's post–World War II recovery. Then the four "Asian tigers"—South Korea, Taiwan, Hong Kong, and Singapore—had demonstrated the success of export-led, labor-intensive manufacturing. China embarked on that path decisively with the rise to power of the brilliant pragmatic reformer Deng Xiaoping in 1978.

Following Deng's sage advice on pragmatic market opening and his famed nonideological approach ("It doesn't matter whether a cat is black or white so long as it catches mice"), China achieved around 10 percent per year GDP growth for nearly thirty-five years, roughly from 1980 to 2015. Growth at 10 percent per year results in a doubling every seven years. Over thirty-five years, that means five doublings, or a cumulative growth of $2 \times 2 \times 2 \times 2 \times 2 = 32$ times. In fact, according to IMF data, China grew just under 10 percent per year (9.8 percent), so that cumulative growth came to an increase of twenty-six times, an extraordinary result.[7]

The result is shown in figure 8.7. Measured at purchasing-power-adjusted prices, China is now the world's largest economy, surpassing the United States (on the IMF's measure) in the year 2013, with the gap in favor of China continuing in recent years. China's growth has been roughly 3–4 percentage points per year higher than that of the United States (6 percent per annum in China compared with 3 percent in the United States most recently). Note that China's overtaking of the United States is in aggregate terms. China's per capita GDP is still only around one-third that of the United States in purchasing-power-parity terms, and roughly one-fifth the U.S. level at market exchange rates and prices. Because China's per capita income is still far lower than that of the US and other high-income countries, China still has the opportunity for rapid "catching-up"

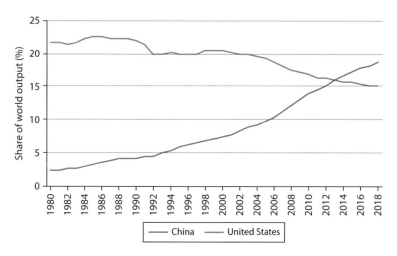

8.7 Changing Places: Chinese and U.S. Shares of World
Output, 1980–2018

Source: International Monetary Fund. "China: Gross domestic product based on purchasing-
power-parity (PPP) share of world total (Percent)", World Economic Outlook (April 2019).

growth, albeit at a pace that is slower than during 1978–2015. As China continues to narrow the relative gap in GDP per capita with the US, China's
economy will become significantly larger than the US economy in absolute
size, given that China's population is roughly four times larger.

One of the key reasons we should expect China's continued vitality and
rapid economic growth is that China has moved from being an importer of
technologies from the United States and Europe to becoming a major technology innovator and exporter in its own right. An example of China's new
technological prowess is in high-speed wireless technology, notably 5G systems. It is the Chinese company Huawei, not a U.S. or European firm, that is
leading the rollout of 5G. The United States has expressed alarm at Huawei's
success and has tried to block its access to world markets, accusing Huawei
of being a security threat. Yet one cannot help feeling that such claims are
merely geopolitics at play. The U.S. government seems to be alarmed mainly
by Huawei's success in a cutting-edge digital technology rather than by any
specific security risk. Indeed, the U.S. government has provided no evidence
of specific risks in its public campaign against the company.

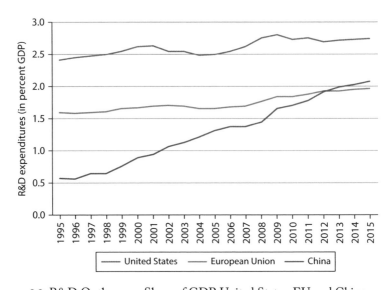

8.8 R&D Outlays as a Share of GDP, United States, EU and China

Source: National Science Board. In *Science and Engineering Indicators 2018* Alexandria, VA: National Science Foundation, 2018.

More generally, China's efforts at innovation are soaring. Based on key metrics of research and development—including R&D expenditures, the training and employment of technical workers, the number of new patents, and the sales of high-tech goods—China has rapidly become a high-tech world power. Figure 8.8 shows R&D outlays as a share of GDP for the United States, the European Union, and China. It is clear that China's R&D investments are rising rapidly, overtaking the EU on this measure. It is also clear that venture capital (VC) funds are moving into Chinese companies at a greatly increased rate, with VC investments in China overtaking VC investments in the European Union, as shown in figure 8.9.

The results are paying off in patents. According to the World Intellectual Property Organization, as of 2017 China became the second largest source of patent applications under the Patent Cooperation Treaty (PCT). In 2017, the United States filed 56,624 PCT applications, followed by China at 48,882, Japan at 48,208, Germany at 18,982, and South Korea at 15,763.[8] If we think regionally rather than nationally, we can say that there are now three centers of endogenous growth in the world economy: the

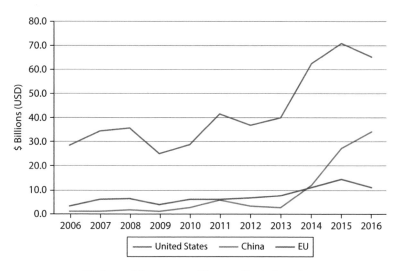

8.9 Early- and Later-stage Venture Capitalism Investments

Source: National Science Board. In *Science and Engineering Indicators 2018* Alexandria, VA: National Science Foundation, 2018.

United States; the European Union; and northeast Asia, including three R&D powerhouses: China, Japan, and South Korea. For the first time since the industrial revolution, innovation is not centered in the North Atlantic region alone. As during the long stretch of globalization before 1500 CE, we are again likely to see key technologies of the future in a two-way flow between east and west.

The Challenges of Sustainable Development

With convergent growth and falling poverty, the world economy might seem to be out of the woods. Technological advances have put the end of poverty within reach, along with a rebalancing of the international order that is much fairer to the countries outside of the North Atlantic region. Yet complacency would be misplaced, and the rising anxiety levels seen around the world reflect deep reasons for worry. This Digital Age poses at least three great risks.

The first global risk is a dramatic and destabilizing increase in economic inequality at the very time when technology properly harnessed holds the promise of ending poverty. The gains from economic growth are not being evenly shared. Within many countries, including both the United States and China, inequality has soared alongside economic growth. While the earnings of some workers are soaring, especially those with advanced degrees, the earnings of workers whose jobs are being replaced by robots and artificial intelligence are stagnant or falling. While those enjoying a boost in income could, in principle, compensate those falling behind, in fact, there is far too little income redistribution taking place in the United States and many other countries.

The second global risk is a devastating global environmental crisis. Two hundred years of rapid economic growth have unleashed several interconnected global environmental shocks. The first is human-induced global warming resulting from the massive emission of heat-absorbing greenhouse gases into the atmosphere. The biggest culprit is carbon dioxide (CO_2) emitted by burning fossil fuels. The second is the massive loss of biodiversity, with an estimated 1 million species under threat of extinction according to a major recent analysis.[9] The main culprit in biodiversity loss is the massive conversion of land agricultural production, with so much habitat taken from other species that they are being pushed to the edge of extinction. The third is the mega-pollution of the air, soils, freshwater, and oceans. We are assaulting the environment with industrial chemicals, plastics, and other waste flows that are not properly recycled or reduced in production and consumption.

The third global risk is war, in a world armed to the teeth. War at this moment among the major countries might seem unimaginable, so terrible and devastating would be the consequences. Yet the same was said about the possibility of major war in 1910, on the eve of the First World War. It is widely supposed today, as it was supposed in 1910, that the lack of war between the major powers would be sustained indefinitely into the future. Yet history proves otherwise. Each new age of globalization, accompanied by deep shifts in geopolitical power, have typically been accompanied by war. We will have to make extraordinary peacebuilding efforts in the coming years to avoid the self-defeating patterns of conflict that have been so prevalent throughout history.

These challenges—inequality, environmental crisis, and the fragility of peace—are the key reasons that many scientists, moral leaders, and statesmen have urged the world to adopt the precepts of sustainable development. The concept itself stands for a holistic approach to globalization, one that combines economic growth with social inclusion, environmental sustainability, and peaceful societies. The theory of sustainable development and the history of globalization suggest that market-based growth can never be enough. Since the start of capitalist globalization in the 1500s, the global economic system has been a ruthless, violent affair, not one in which inequality and war were fundamentally solved. And now we have the added environmental challenges that are complex, global in scale, and without precedent for our species. We are endangering the planet in ways we have never done before, without a guidebook on how to move forward.

The Challenge of Inequality

Technological advances contain within them the seeds of rising inequality, as new technologies create winners and losers in the marketplace. The advent of the spinning jenny and power loom displaced and impoverished multitudes of spinners and weavers in India. The mechanization of agriculture impoverished countless smallholder farmers around the world who desperately fled to the cities to find a livelihood. The introduction of robots on the assembly lines of automobile plants have created unemployment and falling wages for workers laid off from those factories. And now comes the digital economy, with even smarter machines and systems to do the tasks currently carried out by workers. Who will win and who will lose?

Generally, the future labor-market winners will be those with higher skills that machines cannot displace, or with the skills to work alongside the new intelligent machines, such as the tech skills to program the new machines. The losers will be the workers whose tasks are more easily replaced by robots and artificial intelligence. In the past forty years, job losses have been concentrated in the goods-producing sectors, notably in agriculture, mining, and manufacturing. Those job losses will continue in the future. Both agriculture and mining are increasingly being automated, with self-driving vehicles such as tractor-combines and large digging and transport equipment at mining sites. Robots are continuing to replace workers on factory floors in several manufacturing sectors. And it seems clear that other jobs in the service sector will also vanish in the future. Trucks and taxis may well become self-driving, thereby displacing millions of professional drivers. Warehouses are increasingly operated with robots carrying, stacking, and packaging the merchandise. And retail stores are giving way to e-commerce and direct delivery of purchases, again with expert systems and potentially self-driving delivery vehicles.

In recent decades, lower-skilled workers displaced by machines have seen their earnings stagnate or decline, while higher-skilled workers have been made more productive by those same machines and have seen their earnings rise. These trends have been a key reason for the rising inequality of income in many countries, notably including the United States. Yet the ultimate effect of this tendency depends on two additional factors. To the extent that low-skilled workers can gain higher skills through increased education and training, the proportion of the workforce suffering from stagnant or declining earnings can be reduced. And even when market wages are pushed down, governments can compensate for those adverse market forces through increased taxation of those with high and rising incomes and increased transfers to those with low and falling incomes, so that all segments of society share in the gains from technological advance.

The development challenges may also be amplified for the poorest countries in the world, since those countries generally depend on labor-intensive export earnings to finance their future economic growth. Yet the digital revolution is replacing low-cost labor with smart machines. The rapid advances in robotics, for example, are resulting in the automation of jobs in textiles and apparel that in the past were the stepping-stone industries for low-wage countries climbing the ladder of economic development. While the digital revolution will surely help the poorest countries in certain areas—such as low-cost health care, expanded educational opportunities, and improvements in infrastructure—the digital revolution may also cut off traditional pathways for economic development. In that case, global solidarity, wherein rich countries provide added development assistance to enable the poorest countries to invest in the new digital technologies and the accompanying skills, may become vital.

The Challenge of Planetary Boundaries

The environmental challenges may seem even more daunting and, in the view of many observers, insoluble. Is there not an inherent contradiction between endless growth of the world economy and a finite planet? The world economy has increased roughly a hundredfold over the past two centuries: roughly ten times the population and ten times the GDP per capita. Yet the physical planet has remained constant, and the human impact on the environment has therefore intensified dramatically.

One basic calculation puts it this way: The human impact is equal to the population times GDP/population times impact/GDP, sometimes summarized as $I = P \times A \times T$, where I is impact, P is population, A is affluence (GDP per capita), and T is technology (impact/GDP).[10] What is clear from this equation is that per capita economic growth (a rise in A) or population growth (a rise in P) must lead to a greater human impact (I) on the planet unless offset by an improvement in technology (lower T), in the sense of a lower environmental impact per unit of GDP.

Some kinds of technological advances, such as the steam engine, raise A but also raise T because of greenhouse-gas emissions and air pollution. Other kinds of technological advances, such as improvements in photovoltaic solar cells, raise A and *lower* the environmental impact per unit of GDP (a fall in T), with a net overall effect of *lowering* rather than raising the human impact on the planet. Economic growth is therefore sustainable if the rise in P and A are offset by a sufficiently large decline in T—that is, by technologies that lower the impact on the planet per unit of GDP.

The bad news is that global growth during the past two hundred years has tended to be neutral or increasing in T. Dependence on fossil fuels, land clearing for agriculture, bottom trawling for fish, clear-cutting of tropical hardwoods, and fracking for oil and gas are all examples of technological advances that *intensify* the human impact on the environment. We have arrived in the twenty-first century, therefore, with a planet at the very limits of habitability as a result of two centuries of rapid growth combined with intensifying environmental impacts.

The good news is that there are plenty of opportunities today for major technological shifts to lower T, the human impact per unit of GDP. These include the shift from fossil fuels to renewable energy (wind, solar, hydro, geothermal, and others), which would provide more energy with lower greenhouse-gas emissions. Another opportunity is the shift in diet from heavy meat eating, especially beef eating, toward the use of more plant proteins, which would improve human health while also reducing the pressures on land for feed grains and pastures. A third opportunity is improved building designs, which can greatly reduce the need for heating and cooling and thereby the demand for energy. A fourth opportunity is precision agriculture, meaning more precise applications of water and fertilizers—for example, through drip irrigation and fertigation (direct injection of the fertilizers via the irrigation system).

The key to sustainability, in short, is the transformation of technologies and behaviors (such as plant-based diets, or choosing walking over driving) that can deliver the same GDP or higher GDP with a lower environmental impact. Recent breakthroughs in technology, such as dramatic cost reductions in photovoltaics, the development of biodegradable plastics, the development of plant-based substitutes for meats, and the improvement of agricultural methods to reduce the use of pesticides, water, and chemical fertilizers, are all examples of trajectories that combine higher GDP with lower environmental costs. Throughout most of history, humanity has been profligate with nature: use it, lose it, and move on. Yet in our time, there is no possibility of simply moving on. We have filled every nook and cranny of the planet and pushed the environmental crisis to a global scale. The scale of the sustainability challenge is therefore unprecedented, threatening all of the planet, and all of humanity, in ways that we have never before faced. We must therefore lower T, our impact on the planet per unit of GDP.

The framework of *Planetary Boundaries* helps us keep track of the key environmental challenges and the needed technologies and behaviors to address them. In the iconic depiction of planetary boundaries shown in figure 8.10, there are nine main planetary boundaries. Starting from due north and moving counter-clockwise around the circle, the planetary boundaries are climate change (from greenhouse-gas emissions); biospheric integrity (both genetic diversity and functional diversity); land-system change (notably deforestation); freshwater use (heavily related to irrigation); biogeochemical flows (notably nitrogen and phosphorus from fertilizer use); ocean acidification (from the high concentration of CO_2 in the atmosphere); atmospheric aerosol loading (from burning

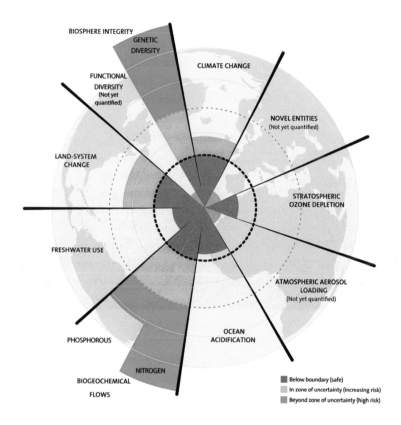

8.10 Planetary Boundaries

Source: J. Lokrantz/Azote based on Will Steffen, Katherine Richardson, Johan Rockström, Sarah E. Cornell, Ingo Fetzer, Elena M. Bennett, Reinette Biggs, et al. "Planetary Boundaries: Guiding Human Development on a Changing Planet." *Science* 347, no. 6223 (2015): 1259855.

fossil fuels and biomass); stratospheric ozone depletion (from the use of chlorofluorocarbons); and novel entities (chemical pollutants including pesticides and plastics).

These planetary boundaries are threatened mainly by greenhouse-gas emissions, poor agricultural practices and diets, and chemical pollutants and inadequate waste management. All of these problems have technological and behavioral solutions that can raise or sustain output while lowering environmental impacts. Our challenge is to plan carefully and soundly, and

8.11 Smog in Guangzhou, China

Source: Stefan Leitner. "Guangzhou," licensed under CC BY-NC-SA 2.0

then regulate businesses methodically, to diminish or ban those technologies that are exacerbating the environmental crises.

The global challenge is not only the range of changes needed, but also their urgency and global scale. Everywhere we look on the planet we see dire and rising threats. The air across Asia, for example, is chronically polluted from fossil-fuel use and often from biomass burning. Figure 8.11 shows Guangzhou, China, beset by smog. Life-threatening air pollution afflicts major cities around the world.

Figure 8.12, a scene of desperation along the Kenya-Somalia border in the drought of 2011, reminds us of the growing intensity of droughts in many of the world's most impoverished drylands, creating conditions of famine and displacement that threaten the survival of the poorest of the poor. Figure 8.13 shows vividly the hazards of excessive nitrogen and phosphorous flows from farms to the coasts, in this case in northeastern China. The beaches are covered in algal blooms that will lead to

8.12 Drought in Kenya-Somalia Border Region, 2011

Source: Sodexo USA, "IMG_0748_JPG," licensed under CC BY 2.0

8.13 Young Boy Swimming in Algal Bloom in Shandong, China

Source: Photo: Reuters/China Daily

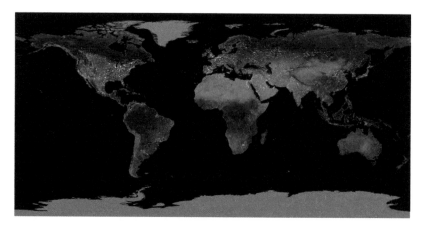

8.14 Areas (in red) That Will Be Submerged by a Six-Meter
Sea Level Rise

Source: NASA

oxygen-deficient waters and a die-off of marine life. Figure 8.14 is a global
map prepared by the U.S. space agency NASA. The red coastal areas show
the parts the planet that would be inundated by a six-meter sea-level rise,
a scale of sea-level rise that is alas consistent with our current trajectory
of global warming.

The Risks of Conflict

The transition from one age of globalization to the next has often been
accompanied by war. The passage from the Neolithic Age to the Equestrian
Age was marked by cavalry wars arriving from the steppes. The transition to
the Ocean Age of global empires was marked by the violence of European
conquerors toward native populations and African slaves in the Americas.
The transition to the Industrial Age was marked by Britain's conquests of
India and its wars against China, and the mass suffering that ensued. Now
the transition to the Digital Age threatens conflict anew, with one of the
biggest risks being a possible clash between the two largest economies,
China and the United States.

There is, of course, nothing inevitable about such a clash. Indeed, the consequences would be so dire as to make such a conflict almost unimaginable. Yet the structural conditions of our age pose an obvious risk. China is a rising power that will end America's recent status as the sole superpower. As the political scientist Graham Allison has noted, historical cases in which a dominant power has been challenged by a rising power have raised the risks of conflict.[11] Either the dominant power (in the current case, the United States) attacks the rising power (in this case, China) to put down a competitive challenge "before it's too late," or the rising power peremptorily attacks the dominant power out of fear of otherwise being blocked on its path of growth. These threats ring true. Already, many U.S. politicians speak of China as an inherent threat to U.S. interests, or to U.S. "primacy," while China not unreasonably views the United States as trying to "contain" China's progress.

If history provides lessons, it is to think the unthinkable, and then to work assiduously to head off the worst cases. China and the United States are already circling each other warily, each believing the worst of the other. Some Chinese strategists believe that the United States will never accept a strong and powerful China, while some American strategists believe that China is out for world conquest. Both of these views are far too deterministic and pessimistic. We should be endeavoring to cultivate the conditions for trust and peace between these two nations, and indeed among the world's major powers, rather than standing by and putting our bets on war. How to cultivate peace in the twenty-first century is one of the core questions of the next and final chapter.

Some Lessons from the Digital Age

The very success of economic growth in the Digital Age has laid several traps for an unwary world. The world economy is producing vast wealth, but failing in three other dimensions of sustainable development. Inequalities are soaring, in part because of the differential effects of digital technologies on high-skilled and low-skilled workers. Environmental degradation is rampant, a reflection of a global economy that has reached nearly $100 trillion in annual output without taking care to ensure that the impacts on the planet are kept to a safe and sustainable level. And the risk of conflict is rising, especially given the rapid shifts in geopolitics, and the anxieties that are being created in the US, China, and elsewhere.

All is not lost—not by a longshot. Humanity has the low-impact technologies (such as renewable energy and precision agriculture) and the policy knowhow needed to head off the environmental crises. We also have the benefit of global experience, if we choose to use it, to redistribute income from the rich to the poor, while finding diplomatic solutions to rising geopolitical tensions. We even have a new globally agreed approach to governance—sustainable development—that can provide a roadmap for action. The next and final chapter looks forward to see how we can achieve the goals of prosperity, social justice, environmental sustainability, and peace, that all the world has adopted.

9

Guiding Globalization in the Twenty-First Century

Each age of globalization has given rise to new tensions and wars. In the Paleolithic Age, *Homo sapiens* drove to extinction the other hominins, Neanderthals and Denisovans, they encountered. In the Neolithic Age, migrating herdsmen and farmers replaced the hunter-gatherers they encountered, perhaps violently, in competition for scarce resources. In the Equestrian Age, horsemen from the steppes raided and plundered the temperate-zone societies of Eurasia. In the Classical Age, great land empires battled for domination of Eurasia. In the Ocean Age, European conquerors largely replaced the indigenous populations of the Americas, who were driven to near elimination by disease and subjugation. In the Industrial Age, European imperialists fought their way to political rule over most of Africa and much of Asia. Today we are again in flux, as the Anglo-American-led world gives way to something else yet to be determined.

Each age has also invented new forms of governance, and that can give us hope. The Paleolithic Age forged the strong bonds of local nomadic clans. The Neolithic Age brought village life and local politics. The Equestrian Age brought the first states. The Classical Age brought the first multi-ethnic empires. The Ocean Age brought ocean-spanning global empires. The Industrial Age brought the beginnings of global governance, including the birth of the United Nations, as well as two hegemonic powers, the United Kingdom and the United States. Now, the Digital Age calls on us to invent more effective ways to govern a globally interconnected world.

In the previous chapter, I outlined three enormous challenges for the Digital Age: rising inequality, massive environmental degradation, and the risks arising from major geopolitical change. These daunting challenges could overload our political institutions and provoke a devastating conflict. Such has been the pattern of the past. Surely the prime task of our age is to resist a slide toward war, as our capacity for mutual destruction exceeds any past limits of history. And while maintaining the peace, our goals must also include keeping the planet habitable and our societies inclusive and just. More than ever, we need to manage globalization with these large goals in mind. Several concepts can help us. The first is sustainable development, meaning the holistic approach to governance that combines economic, social, and environmental objectives. The second is the social-democratic ethos, meaning an inclusive and participatory approach to political and economic life. The third is subsidiarity, meaning that we solve problems at the proper level of governance. The fourth is a reformed United Nations. The fifth is a world safe for diversity.

Sustainable Development

In *The Wealth of Nations*, Adam Smith largely defined the ethos of the Industrial Age: the quest for national wealth. Since the early nineteenth century, sovereign governments have competed for wealth and power through industrialization and technological advancement. A global-scale market economy emerged in which privately owned companies aggressively pursue profits on a global scale. The result has been two centuries of economic growth, albeit punctuated by wars and economic crises. The world economy today is at least one hundred times larger than at the start of the Industrial Age. With annual growth in world output averaging around 3 percent, the world economy continues to double in size roughly every twenty years, that is, in a single generation.

This economic growth has produced startling gains in living standards and has brought the end of extreme poverty within reach. But it has also generated two stark results. First, inequalities of income and wealth are intense and increasing. Not only do we still have extreme poverty in the midst of global wealth; we also have rising inequalities within rich societies that threaten to become much worse in the age of smart machines. Second, we have violated the planetary boundaries with human-induced climate change, loss of biodiversity, and pervasive pollution that threaten the well-being of billions of people and the survival of millions of species.

The key to wellbeing, therefore, is a combination of objectives—not just the pursuit of wealth, but the *combination* of prosperity, lower levels of inequality, and environmental sustainability. The triple bottom line of economic, social, and environmental objectives is the concept of sustainable development. It must be the essential vision for our time. The equivalent of Adam Smith's text for this century should be "The Sustainable Development of Nations."

Dr. Gro Harlem Brundtland, prime minister of Norway in the 1980s, brought the new concept of sustainable development to the world's attention through the Commission on Environment and Development that she chaired. In the commission's 1987 report, *Our Common Future*, sustainable development was defined as development that "meets the needs of the present generation without compromising the ability of future generations to meet their own needs." The new concept was adopted by the UN member states at the 1992 UN Conference on Environment and Development in Rio de Janeiro, otherwise known as the Rio Earth Summit.

At the time, the Rio Earth Summit was heralded as a definitive break-through for global governance. It produced three major environmental agreements—on climate change, biodiversity conservation, and the fight against the spread of deserts. The UN member states adopted the concept of sustainable development and a road map for its implementation known as Agenda 21. Yet the follow-up results were distressingly small. The environmental treaties were not effectively implemented. Human-induced global warming continued unabated; the destruction of biodiversity accelerated; and the spread of degraded lands and desertification in the world's drylands continued apace.

At a follow-up conference in 2012, on the twentieth anniversary of the Rio Earth Summit, the world's governments reconvened and surveyed the global landscape with dismay. Environmental degradation was running out of control, and Agenda 21, the purported guidebook for sustainable development, had fallen into the void. The concept of sustainable development was more urgent than ever, but new means had to be found to bring it to the forefront of public policy. In that context, the governments decided to launch a set of Sustainable Development Goals (SDGs) to bring sustainable development to the forefront of daily politics, civil-society activism, and the strategies of the business sector.

Between 2012 and 2015, the UN member states negotiated the SDGs, which culminated in adoption of the seventeen SDGs shown in figure 9.1 as part of an agreed 2030 Agenda for Sustainable Development. The concept of sustainable development was somewhat recast from its original formulation. Now, instead of emphasizing the harmonization of present and future needs, as in the Brundtland Commission report, sustainable development is now described as meeting the triple bottom line of economic prosperity, social inclusion, and environmental sustainability.

The seventeen goals, and the accompanying 169 detailed targets, are time-bound and quantifiable objectives (mostly) for the year 2030, embodying various economic, social, and environmental objectives. The main economic objectives are to end extreme poverty (SDG 1) and

9.1 UN Sustainable Development Goals

Source: United Nations Department of Global Communications. "Sustainable Development Goals." 2019.

hunger (SDG 2), ensure universal health coverage (SDG 3) and schooling (SDG 4), and provide access to safe water (SDG 6), electricity (SDG 7), decent jobs (SDG 8), and modern infrastructure (SDG 9). The social objectives include gender equality (SDG 5), reduced inequality of income (SDG 10), and peaceful, lawful and inclusive societies (SDG 16). The environmental objectives include sustainable cities (SDG 11), sustainable production and consumption (SDG 12), control of climate change (SDG 13), and the protection of marine ecosystems (SDG 14) and terrestrial ecosystems (SDG 15). The final goal, SDG 17, calls for a global partnership to accomplish the first sixteen SDGs.

To find the ways to achieve these seventeen goals, we need to look to the future in a systematic and rational manner. Most importantly, we need a kind of dynamic and adaptive planning—that is, planning with an explicit account of uncertainty that allows for updating of policies and strategies along the way. Because we do not know with precision what the technologies of the future will offer, we can plan ahead but not rigidly. In this regard, we should consider the very wise statement of President Dwight D. Eisenhower, who served as the supreme allied commander in World War II. Eisenhower liked to say that "plans are useless, but planning is everything." He meant that specific plans will not be followed in practice because unexpected circumstances will surely arise, yet planning—the logical process of looking ahead in a systematic manner—is crucial for success.

Part of successful planning will be multidimensional systems thinking. We have to integrate our understanding of agriculture, healthcare, land use, carbon management, energy systems, and biodiversity conservation. For example, we will have to reconsider land use in order to accomplish several simultaneous objectives: food security, biodiversity conservation, the biological storage of carbon to fight climate change, and economic wellbeing of rural communities. This will require multidimensional systems thinking.

To plan successfully, the world will need an active interchange of ideas, global cooperation in research and development, and the rapid dissemination of best practices across countries. At a time when there are so many centers of excellence in learning, there will be huge advantages of global knowledge networks on the various dimensions of sustainable development. The global research agenda should adopt the concept of *directed technical change*, meaning that R&D efforts should be targeted toward goals of high priority, such as low-cost and plentiful zero-carbon energy, biodegradable waste products, food crops that are resilient to environmental stresses, more efficient means of irrigation, and better climate modeling and forecasts.

Governance for sustainable development will require a tremendous amount of consensus building. That will be hard work. Vested interests and diverse perspectives and cultures often make it difficult to achieve a national much less a global consensus on how to make needed changes—for example, on energy systems, land use, and urban planning. Multi-stakeholder deliberations and consensus building efforts will be needed to implement the good ideas that arise through research and development.

We will also need to hold governments and businesses accountable for their commitments to the SDGs. That kind of accountability will depend on accurate and timely metrics to track progress on the SDGs. Investors too will need to be held accountable for directing new investment funds toward sustainable projects. Fortunately, "ESG Investing," meaning the use of environmental, social, and governance (ESG) indicators in investment allocations, is on the rise. In fact, all investments in the future should satisfy ESG standards.

Finally, we need excitement and inspiration. Sustainable development must be our generation's moonshot—a galvanizing adventure that draws forth the talents, resources, and energies to get the job done. I can recall from my youth the thrill of the moonshot, when U.S. President John F. Kennedy called on Americans to back a space adventure of high risk and daring. In May 1961, President Kennedy declared, "I believe that this nation should commit itself to achieving the goal before the decade is out of land-ing a man on the moon and returning him safely to the earth. No single space project in this period will be more impressive to mankind, or more important for the long-range exploration of space. And none will be so difficult or expensive to accomplish." Those riveting words set the United States on the path to the moon. President Kennedy's goal was accom-plished a mere eight years later.

The future trajectory of the world's population will also make a differ-ence. According to the most recent UN forecasts, the world population in 2100 might be anywhere between 7 billion and 16 billion people, depend-ing on the future path of fertility rates (figure 9.2). Sustainable develop-ment will be vastly harder to achieve if the world population soars to 10 billion or more. The low-population trajectory, fortunately, is the one we would expect if we honor the commitments to healthcare for all (SDG 3),

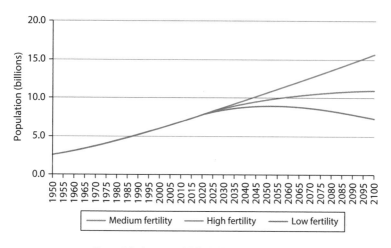

9.2 Low, Medium and High Fertility Projections

Source: United Nations, Department of Economic and Social Affairs, Population Division (2019). World Population Prospects 2019, Online Edition

education for all (SDG 4), and gender equality (SDG 5). That combination would mean that both girls and boys will stay in school longer, marry later, join the labor force in greater numbers, and voluntarily choose to have smaller families, while investing more in the health, nutrition, and education of each child. That so-called demographic transition would lead to a peaking of the world population in this century of perhaps 9 billion, a faster reduction in poverty, and far less adverse stress on the natural environment than if the world population continues to rise throughout the century to more than 10 billion.

Social-Democratic Ethos

The 193 UN member states are pursuing sustainable development with widely varying degrees of consistency and commitment. Some countries are on track to achieve most or all of the SDGs, including the decarbonization of their energy systems and reduced levels of inequality. Others continue on the path of highly polluting fossil fuels and growing inequality.

An examination of the relative progress and commitment of different countries can provide evidence of "what works" to achieve the SDGs.

The countries in the global forefront of achieving the SDGs are the countries of northern Europe. In 2019, the ranking of countries according to SDG progress showed that the world's top five countries were Denmark, Sweden, Finland, France, and Austria.[2] Interestingly, the 2019 rankings of countries by their self-reported levels of life satisfaction ("subjective wellbeing") were similar: Finland, Denmark, Norway, Iceland, and the Netherlands.[3] Indeed, when we compare the full rankings of SDG achievement and the rankings of life satisfaction, we find a strong degree of correlation, with the countries of northern Europe at the top of both sets of world rankings.

The key to this dual success in sustainable development and life satisfaction is a long-standing style of governance and social ethos in the northern European countries. The top-ranked countries all share a philosophy of "social democracy," including long periods during the past century in which social-democratic political parties led the governments of these nations. In this context, a social-democratic ethos signifies a set of ideas for organizing politics and the economy. These include a commitment to a market economy with private ownership combined with a high level of worker unionization, labor rights, a healthy work-life balance (including paid family leave and ample vacation time), and the universal provision of public services, including quality healthcare and education financed by the budget. This strategy has sometimes been called "the middle way" between free-market capitalism on one side and state ownership of industry on the other side. By all accounts, this middle way produces the most successful combination of prosperity, social inclusion, and environmental sustainability of any political-economic system on the planet today.

The social-democratic ethos will become even more important during the Digital Age as more and more jobs are displaced by smart machines. Workers with more job skills, typically requiring more education, will find that their jobs are empowered by the smart machines, while workers with lesser skills will be displaced by the machines. The result will be a further increase in earnings inequality and economic insecurity for lower-skilled workers. In order to ensure that all parts of society benefit from the ongoing technological advances, public policies will have to tax the "winners" and use the proceeds to ensure universal access to quality healthcare, education, and social protection as a matter of human right—the core idea of the social-democratic ethos.

Subsidiarity and the Public Sphere

A key to good policy making is the distinction between private goods and public goods. Private goods are goods that the marketplace efficiently provides under the incentives of profit maximization. Public goods are those that the marketplace underprovides because the profit motive will send the wrong signals. Public goods include quality education and healthcare for all, new scientific knowledge, access to new technologies, protection of the environment, and infrastructure such as highways and long-distance transmission lines for electric power. Private goods (such as housing, furnishings, automobiles, personal appliances, tourism, etc.) operate mostly on a market basis, with households generally spending their own incomes to purchase goods from profit-oriented businesses. Public goods, by contrast, are typically provided through public budgets, with government revenues covering the costs of public investments and services.

A major policy challenge is to set the right boundaries between the private and public sectors, and between the public sectors at varying political scales. Some public goods are local, meaning that they can be effectively provided by local governments, such as cities or towns. Schools, clinics, police protection, and local roads are all examples of local public goods. Other public goods are national in character, such as national defense or a national highway system. Still other public goods are transnational or regional, including at least two countries, such as the management of a river that runs through several countries. Matters such as the diversion of river flows, flood control, hydroelectric power, and navigation rights along the riverway are all public goods that should generally be handled by a transnational authority with representatives from all of the affected countries. Still other public goods are continental in scale, such as major transport systems (highways and railways throughout Europe and Asia), long-distance power transmission lines, transboundary pollution control, and the protection of biodiversity and ecosystems shared by many nations (such as the Amazon Basin, with nine countries having territory in the basin). A growing number of public goods are global in nature, such as the end of human-induced climate change, the control of epidemic diseases, development assistance for the poorest countries, the crackdown on international tax evasion, and nuclear non-proliferation.

The doctrine of subsidiarity provides an important framework for the provision of public goods. It holds that the provision of public goods (and services) should be managed at the lowest scale of governance feasible for the particular goods and services in question. When the goods and services can be effectively left to the marketplace, it is good to do so. For those goods that are inherently public in nature, it is best to provide them at the most local level of governance feasible. National governments could in principle be put in charge of operating schools and clinics, for example, but there is usually no compelling case to do so, as schools and clinics can be provided effectively by local governments taking into account the specific needs of each local community. Local governance enables more local participation in decision making by the people directly affected and more attention to local conditions. At the same time, it does not make sense to assign local governments to provide services or solve problems that can only be addressed at a larger geographical scale, such as rivershed management or the control of transboundary pollution. Those problems require transnational authorities. Similarly, it would be impossible to control human-induced climate change by the disaggregated efforts of individual cities or even nations, without the benefit of an overarching global framework, namely the UN Framework Convention on Climate Change (UNFCCC) and the Paris Climate Agreement, both of which include all nations of the world.[4]

The failure to understand the subsidiarity doctrine leads to endless confusion in public policies. Some free-market ideologists, for example, object to the government's role in the economy without appreciating the difference between private and public goods. Advocates of local governance often fail to realize that certain public goods cannot be provided by local governments alone. Nationalists who are opposed to global treaties and UN regulations often assume that all necessary public goods can be provided by national governments, without reflecting on the realities of transboundary challenges such as transnational infrastructure and global environmental management of challenges such as climate change.

In the twenty-first century, many dimensions of sustainable development will require public goods on a multi-country or global scale. Rivers, ecosystems, pollution, climate control, international financial flows, the Internet, power transmission, highway systems, railroad networks, and aviation all require strong regional and global cooperation. None can be managed effectively at the level of a single country. Regional groupings of nations, such as the European Union, the African Union, ASEAN, Mercosur, the Shanghai Cooperation Organization, the Regional Comprehensive Economic Partnership (in Asia), and others, will be even more important in the future than they are today.

China has been promoting large-scale transnational cooperation in infrastructure in two major initiatives. The first is the Belt and Road Initiative (BRI), to provide land-based infrastructure for the "belts" connecting Asia and Europe, and for the sea "roads" connecting Asia, Europe, and Africa through the Indian Ocean. The second is the Global Energy Interconnection (GEI) initiative led by an organization called GEIDCO (Global Energy Interconnection Development and Cooperation Organization). GEI aims to connect high-quality sites of renewable energy (wind, solar, and hydro) around the world through long-distance power transmission. Both BRI and GEI are creative approaches to governance of transboundary infrastructure for the twenty-first century. Indeed, the two initiatives should be combined, since the BRI should be based on renewable energy if it is to serve the true interests of the countries involved and of the world. Figure 9.3 shows a map of the existing and planned infrastructure the Belt and Road Initiative entails.

As regional public goods rise in importance, regional groupings such as the European Union, the African Union, and ASEAN will become even more important than they are today. We can imagine that twenty-first-century governance will increasingly involve cooperation among multi-national groups rather than between individual nations. We can suppose that there will be eight major regional *groupings*: North America, South America, European Union, African Union, South Asia, East Asia, Commonwealth of Independent States, and Western Asia. These eight regional groupings could begin to constitute the core of global diplomacy. Currently, the UN is an organization of individual member states, now totaling 193 countries. With 193 countries, there are more than 18,000 *pairwise* combinations of countries. With eight regions, there are only twenty-eight pairwise combinations of regions, a much more manageable number for effective international cooperation.

Existing/Planned
Railroads
Oil pipeline
Gas pipeline
Port
Silk Road Economic Belt
Maritime Silk Road
Economic Corridor

9.3 Map of Belt and Road Initiative

Source: Map adapted from Mercator Institute for China Studies (MERICS), May 2018

Reforming the United Nations

As historian Mark Mazower describes in his important intellectual history *Governing the World*, the idea of global governance first took hold among the intellectual leaders of the European Enlightenment.[5] The German philosopher Immanuel Kant foresaw a "perpetual peace" on the basis of a global confederation of republics. After the Napoleonic Wars, the conservative states of Europe entered into the Concert of Europe to try to maintain peace and stability, and especially to avoid revolutionary ideas such as parliamentary democracy and republicanism. In the second half of the nineteenth century, the European powers collaborated to avoid conflicts among themselves as they incorporated large swathes of Africa and Asia into their respective empires. They also established new international institutions to govern the increasingly interconnected world, including the International Telegraph Union (1865) and the International Postal Union (1874).

The first comprehensive attempt at global governance among the world's nation-states came in the wake of World War I with the establishment of the League of Nations, heaquartered in Geneva, in 1920. The League was a remarkable breakthrough in concept, giving representation to nations in order to maintain the peace. There were forty-two initial members, later joined by another twenty-one countries. Though the League was established at the behest of U.S. president Woodrow Wilson, the United States itself did not join because of opposition in the Senate. Without the United States, and in the face of unremitting financial and political turmoil in Europe and neighboring Western Asia and Africa, the League proved unable to respond to the growing geopolitical and socioeconomic crises of the 1930s. With the outbreak of World War II, the League's technical staff mostly transferred to the United States. The League itself was dissolved in 1946, its functions taken over by the new United Nations.

The term United Nations was originally applied to the anti-fascist alliance in World War II led by the United States, the United Kingdom, and the Soviet Union. It then became the appellation for the successor body to the League of Nations. The new United Nations organization was established in 1945 under the UN Charter and assumed its home in New York City the following year. The moral charter of the UN, the Universal Declaration of Human Rights, was adopted in 1948.

As I recounted briefly in the previous chapter, the UN represented the internationalist side of post–World War II U.S. foreign policy. The United States strongly supported its creation from the 1940s through the 1960s, for three main reasons. First, it could be used as an instrument to advance U.S. foreign policy—for example, in the Korean War, where the United States and its allies operated as a UN-mandated force. Second, the UN offered an effective way to create a global agenda for economic development under the aegis of the United States. Third, the UN offered an important venue for the United States to compete with the Soviet Union for the "hearts and minds" of the newly independent postcolonial states.

As the power, voice, and influence of the developing countries increased at the UN, and as the competition with the Soviet Union waned toward the end of the Cold War, the U.S. attitude toward the UN became ambivalent and at times hostile. When the developing countries called for a New International Economic Order (NIEO) in the 1970s, the United States opposed the NIEO and instead demanded that the countries fall into line with the U.S.-led global capitalist system. Since the 1990s, the United States has become increasingly resistant to ceding authority to UN initiatives, and a growing number of UN treaties have been left unsigned or unratified by the US.

As of today, there are 193 UN member states, covering nearly the entire world population. Yet in important operational ways, the UN remains a twentieth-century institution guided by rules laid down by the United States in 1945. Most importantly, at the end of World War II, the five victorious allied powers (the Soviet Union, United Kingdom, and United States, together with France and China) were given special status as the five permanent members of the UN Security Council. These P5 countries not only were granted permanent seats on the Security Council but were also accorded a veto over its decisions and over subsequent changes in the UN Charter.

The problem, of course, is that the world has changed significantly since 1945, when the United States reigned supreme. The P5 countries are no longer the decisive forces in geopolitics, and no longer the obvious candidates for extraordinary privilege in global governance. One way to see that is in table 9.1, which measures the "size" of countries according to their share of world population and world output. For purposes of the calculations, a nation's share of world output is defined as the simple average of two

**Table 9.1 Largest Countries Ranked by Population and Output, 2018
(percent of world total)**

Country	Share of Output	Share of Population	Average Share
China	17.2	18.7	17.9
United States	19.7	4.4	12.0
India	5.5	17.9	11.7
Japan	5.0	1.7	3.3
Indonesia	1.9	3.5	2.7
Brazil	2.3	2.8	2.6
Germany	3.9	1.1	2.5
Russia	2.5	2.0	2.3
United Kingdom	2.8	0.9	1.8
France	2.7	0.9	1.8

Source: IMF World Economic Outlook, October 2019. Output share is the simple average of the share of national output measured in world output at U.S. dollars and at international dollars.

measures: its share of world output measured at market prices and its share measured at purchasing-power-adjusted prices.

The table shows the ten largest countries as of 2018. While all of the P5 countries are among the ten largest countries, three of the P5—the UK, France, and Russia—are in fact smaller than five other countries: India, Japan, Germany, Brazil, and Indonesia. The allocation of permanent seats on the Security Council represents decisions taken in 1945 rather than today's realities. Note that three of the five large countries without permanent seats are in Asia: India, Japan, and Indonesia.

The UN Security Council currently has fifteen members, the P5 plus ten rotating seats with two-year terms and no veto power. The rotating members are elected by five regional groupings: Asia (two seats), Latin America (two seats), Africa (three seats), Western Europe and Others Group (WEOG) (two seats), and Eastern Europe (one seat). Thus, combining the permanent and rotating members, Asia currently holds three seats, or a mere 20 percent of the Security Council, despite having 60 percent of the world's population and accounting for nearly 50 percent of the world's GDP. The underrepresentation of Asia on the UN Security

Council is one of the most glaring weaknesses of the UN system today. The UN was designed for North Atlantic leadership, yet the global center of gravity of population, economics, and geopolitics is shifting toward Asia and Africa.

Table 9.2 presents a reform proposal that would help to rebalance the UN Security Council. In my proposed reform, the Security Council would expand to twenty-one members, with Asia holding six seats, or around 30 percent. Six new permanent members would be added, the large five underrepresented countries mentioned above (Brazil, Germany, India, Indonesia, and Japan) plus Nigeria, Africa's largest country. The problem of course is that even this modest change would involve a relative diminution of power of the United States and the other P5 countries, which they can block by veto. In fact, reform of the UN Security Council has been stymied for many years by exactly this problem, the opposition of the P5 to needed reforms. And with its relative weakening in the global scene, the United States may well seek to hobble rather than reform the UN in the years ahead. Reform will come when the United States and the other P5 members finally appreciate that a healthy and vibrant UN is essential for global peace and security, including of the P5 countries themselves.

Table 9.2 Proposed Reform of the UN Security Council

Region	Current seats	Revised seats	Permanent	Rotating
Latin America and Caribbean	2	3	Brazil	2
Eastern Europe	2	2	Russia	1
Asia-Pacific	3	6	China, India, Japan, Indonesia	2
Africa	3	4	Nigeria	3
Western Europe and other groups	5	6	United States, United Kingdom, France, Germany	2
World Total	15	21	11	10

Ethics in Action for a Common Plan

In his 2015 encyclical *Laudato Si'*, Pope Francis wrote:

> Interdependence obliges us to think of one world with a common plan. Yet the same ingenuity which has brought about enormous technological progress has so far proved incapable of finding effective ways of dealing with grave environmental and social problems worldwide. A global consensus is essential for confronting the deeper problems, which cannot be resolved by unilateral actions on the part of individual countries. Such a consensus could lead, for example, to planning a sustainable and diversified agriculture, developing renewable and less polluting forms of energy, encouraging a more efficient use of energy, promoting a better management of marine and forest resources, and ensuring universal access to drinking water.[6]

The challenge of globalization from the earliest days of humanity has been the lack of consensus. Our species, exquisitely evolved for cooperation within our clan, is equally primed for conflict with the "other." In a world that has the ability to "end all forms of human poverty and all forms of human life," as President John F. Kennedy eloquently stated in his Inaugural Address, can we actively find a consensus for a common plan?

To take up Pope Francis's challenge and explore the possibilities and limits of consensus, I recently co-led in a multifaith effort to find the common basis for global action for sustainable development. Religious leaders and practitioners across the world's major faiths—Christianity, Shia and Sunni Islam, Judaism, Hinduism, Confucianism, and First Nation beliefs—as well as secular philosophers, gathered over two years seeking Ethics in Action for sustainable development. We asked ourselves: Is there a common framework that could engage communities across the divisions of faith, culture, race, and ethnicity?

Our answer, tentatively, is yes. The religious leaders repeatedly chastised politicians for misusing religion in their cynical quest for power. Religious beliefs are frequently misused and misquoted by politicians in order to stoke fear and division. In fact, the religious leaders readily found common ground on the key precepts of sustainable development. The challenge, then, is not an unbridgeable divide of human belief but rather the clash of interests and ambitions. The problem is one of politics rather than irreconcilable human differences.

The faith leaders and ethicists identified three moral precepts common to all of the world's faiths. The first is the Golden Rule, the principle of reciprocity: Do not do unto others what you would not have them do to you. The Golden Rule is found in the teachings of Confucius and of Jesus, in Hindu texts, and in Kant's categorical imperative. The second principle is the preferential option for the poor—that is, giving due attention to the poorest members of society. Ethics consists in the protection of human dignity, and human dignity requires that each person in society have the economic means to meet basic needs. In United Nations parlance, it is "to leave no one behind." The third precept is protection of creation—the physical Earth on which our own survival, and that of millions of other species, depends. These principles can be the building blocks of a common global plan for sustainable development, if politics does not get in the way.

Politics, indeed, has two faces. For the ancient Greek philosopher Aristotle, politics is the quest for the common good of the citizenry, the members of the *polis* (the political community). Aristotle defined this as a quest for *eudaimonia* (a flourishing life). For the Renaissance-era political theorist Niccolò Machiavelli, by contrast, politics is the struggle for power by the prince. Kant believed that global peace would be possible when princes could no longer march their citizens off to war. Kant described war as a plaything of princes who are not accountable to their subjects:

> In a constitution which is not republican, and under which the subjects are not citizens, a declaration of war is the easiest thing in the world to decide upon, because war does not require of the ruler, who is the proprietor and not a member of the state, the least sacrifice of the pleasures of his table, the chase, his country houses, his court functions, and the like. He may, therefore, resolve on war as on a pleasure party for the most trivial reasons, and with perfect indifference leave the justification which decency requires to the diplomatic corps who are ever ready to provide it.[7]

One hundred fifty years after Kant, an evil and cynical Nazi war leader, Hermann Goering, while imprisoned at Nuremburg for Nazi war crimes, described how demagogues can use propaganda to launch wars—even, alas, in democracies. Interviewed in his jail cell, he told his interviewer:

> Why, of course, the people don't want war. Why would some poor slob on a farm want to risk his life in a war when the best that he can get out of it is to come back to his farm in one piece. Naturally, the common people don't want war; neither in Russia nor in England nor in America, nor for that matter in Germany. That is understood. But, after all, it is the leaders of the country who determine the policy and it is always a simple matter to drag the people along, whether it is a democracy or a fascist dictatorship or a Parliament or a Communist dictatorship.[8]

"There is one difference," Goering's interviewer pointed out. "In a democracy the people have some say in the matter through their elected representatives, and in the United States only Congress can declare wars." Goering replied:

> Oh, that is all well and good, but, voice or no voice, the people can always be brought to the bidding of the leaders. That is easy. All you have to do is tell them they are being attacked and denounce the pacifists for lack of patriotism and exposing the country to danger. It works the same way in any country.

We are left, in the end, with a need, a hope, and a conundrum. The need is to steer the new age of globalization so that our energies are directed toward ending human poverty rather than human life. The hope is that across the world's societies and religions there are common ethical underpinnings. The conundrum is how easily we nonetheless fall prey to our small differences, which can be stirred into virulent hatreds by demagogic leaders in their quest for power.

I have mentioned many times one modern leader whose leadership I admire and whose words continue to inspire. President Kennedy lived through the closest brush with global nuclear annihilation that we have ever experienced: the 1962 Cuban Missile Crisis. In the wake of that horrifically close call, Kennedy urged peace between the United States and the Soviet Union and achieved a first step toward that peace by negotiating the Partial Nuclear Test Ban Treaty in 1963. In making the case for peace rather than war, Kennedy explained our common human interests in words that still guide us today in managing our interdependent world:

> So, let us not be blind to our differences—but let us also direct attention to our common interests and to the means by which those differences can be resolved. And if we cannot end now our differences, at least we can help make the world safe for diversity. For, in the final analysis, our most basic common link is that we all inhabit this small planet. We all breathe the same air. We all cherish our children's future. And we are all mortal.[9]

Globalization reflects the fundamental fact that the human journey, from our common roots in Africa until today, has always been a shared one. Our reality as a global species was not self-evident through most of our history, because life seemed to be local and because other tribes, races, and empires seemed to be implacable foes. Yet the great religions portrayed a common origin and destiny of humanity, and today we can envision our common fate more clearly than ever before in the images sent home daily by orbital satellites mapping the Earth. Our common fate does not mean homogeneity and an end of differences. It means a global society strengthened by distinctive cultures in a world made safe for diversity.

We are, as throughout our species' long saga and adventure, facing the interactions of geography, technology, and institutions. The great evolutionary biologist E. O. Wilson is no doubt correct when he notes that we have stumbled into the twenty-first century with our "Stone Age emotions, medieval institutions, and godlike technology." We are out of synch, out of kilter. Yet we also have our capacities to reason and to cooperate, formed on the African savanna more than a hundred thousand years ago. We have a much clearer understanding today of our common interests. Our greatest hope is to use the lessons of history and of our common human nature to forge a new era of cooperation at the global scale.

Acknowledgments

This book originated as a series of three lectures hosted by Professor Gordon L. Clark at the Oxford School of Geography and the Environment in May 2017. I am most grateful to Prof. Clark and his colleagues and students for the warm hospitality, stimulating environment, and insightful feedback on the ideas presented here.

In turning the lectures into this book, I am especially grateful to Ms. Ismini Ethridge for her superb and comprehensive assistance in the research and preparation of the manuscript. She carried this project forward at every stage, and without her excellent support, the book simply could not have been written. She has been very ably assisted in the home stretch by Ms. Juliana Bartels.

Prof. Gordon McCord at UC San Diego shared his insights, ideas, and invaluable support of the geographic analysis. Of course, any and all remaining errors are solely my own.

I am thrilled and grateful that Columbia University Press is once again publishing my work. The Press's great attention to detail, superb editorial support, and constant encouragement are an author's dream. I would like particularly to thank Bridget Flannery-McCoy for her great confidence in the project and Ms. Caelyn Cobb for her exceptional editorial support at all stages of preparing the book.

My wife, Sonia Ehrlich Sachs, is an intellectual partner in every aspect of my work and thinking and, as always, was indispensable for this book. Thank goodness for her wisdom, infinite patience, and deep interest in the material.

Data Appendix

This appendix describes the major data sources used in the calculations, graphs, and maps throughout the book.

Climate Zones

The climate classification used in this book is the Köppen-Geiger system, which classifies the major world climate zones into five main categories based on temperature and precipitation, and a sixth (highland) category based on elevation.

Summary of the Köppen-Geiger Classification system

Type	Description
A	Equatorial climates
Af	Equatorial rainforest, fully humid
Am	Equatorial monsoon
As	Equatorial savannah with dry summer
Aw	Equatorial savannah with dry winter
B	Arid climates
BS	Steppe climate
BW	Desert climate
C	Warm temperate climates
Cs	Warm temperate climate with dry summer
Cw	Warm temperate climate with dry winter
Cf	Warm temperate climate, fully humid
D	Snow climates
Ds	Snow climate with dry summer
Dw	Snow climate with dry winter
Df	Snow climate, fully humid
E	Polar climates
ET	Tundra climate
EF	Frost climate
H	Highland climates (varied)

Source: Markus Kottek, Jürgen Grieser, Christoph Beck, Bruno Rudolf, and Franz Rubel, "World Map of the Köppen-Geiger climate classification updated," *Meteorologische Zeitschrift* 15, no. 3 (2006): 259–63. https://doi.org/10.1127/0941-2948/2006/0130.

The GIS climate files used in this book were digitized from the climate-zone map in A. Strahler, and A. H. Strahler. 1992. *Modern Physical Geography*, 4th ed. New York: Wiley. The data set can be found at https://sites.hks.harvard.edu/cid/ciddata/geog/gisdata.html.

The Strahler and Strahler map, in turn, is based on:

R. Geiger and W. Pohl. 1954. Revision of the Köppen-Geiger *Klimakarte der Erde Erdkunde*, Vol. 8: 58–61.

Since the climate has changed over time, projecting today's climate map back to conditions of past millennia is only an approximation.

Population Data

Historical Population Data

Much of the historical population data draws on Kees Klein Goldewijk, Arthur Beusen, and Peter Janssen's study on the HYDE 3.1 project data. The study estimates "total and urban/rural population numbers, densities and fractions (including built-up area) for the Holocene, roughly the period 10000 BCE to AD 2000 with a spatial resolution of 5 min longitude/latitude." Details may be found here:

Kees Klein Goldewijk, Arthur Beusen, and Peter Janssen. "Long-Term Dynamic Modeling of Global Population and Built-up Area in a Spatially Explicit Way: HYDE 3.1." *The Holocene* 20, no. 4 (2010): 565–73. https://doi.org/10.1177/0959683609356587.

World population, GDP and per capita GDP from 1–2008 CE

The historical economic data draw on the Maddison Project Database. While this database has been adapted and updated during the last decade, I chose to use the 2010 release version as it provides the most comprehensive coverage by countries, regions and years. The 2010 dataset was the final version provided by the late economic historian Angus Maddison himself, covering world population, GDP and per capita GDP from 1 to 2008 CE. For further information on the project see:

Maddison Project Database, version 2010. Jutta Bolt, Robert Inklaar, Herman de Jong and Jan Luiten van Zanden (2010), "Rebasing 'Maddison': new income comparisons and the shape of long-run economic development," Maddison Project Working paper 10

Gridded Population Data for 2015

The spatially explicit population data for 2015 is from the Center for International Earth Science Information Network (CIESIN) Columbia University. 2016. Gridded Population of the World, Version 4 (GPWv4): Population Count. Palisades, NY: NASA Socioeconomic Data and Applications Center (SEDAC). http://dx.doi.org/10.7927/H4X63JVC.

Ancient Cities data

The data on ancient cities is based on Meredith Reba, Femke Reitsma, and Karen C. Seto, "Spatializing 6,000 Years of Global Urbanization from 3700 BC to AD 2000," *Scientific Data* 3 (2016): 160034. https://doi.org/10.1038/sdata .2016.34. I deeply thank Dr. Reba for assistance in accessing these very insightful data.

Data Used in the Creation of Maps and Geospatial Analysis

The maps draw on shapefiles from the following sources.

Coastal and river boundaries:

Made with Natural Earth, naturalearthdata.com. (Note that I apply present data coastal and river boundaries to ancient civilizations. This is of course only an approximation in view of changes in coastlines and river flows.)

Ancient Empire/Regional outlines:

worldmap.harvard.edu

Figure 5.2 Empire of Alexander the Great

http://awmc.unc.edu/awmc/map_data/shapefiles/cultural_data/political _shading/alexander_extent/

Figure 5.3 Roman Empire

http://worldmap.harvard.edu/geoserver/wfs?outputFormat=SHAPE -ZIP&service=WFS&request=GetFeature&format_options

=charset 3AUTF-8&typename=geonode 3Aroman_empire_117_ce
_9sa&version=1.0.0

Figure 5.4 Han Dynasty

http://worldmap.harvard.edu/geoserver/wfs?outputFormat=SHAPE
-ZIP&service=WFS&request=GetFeature&format_options=charset
3AUTF-8&typename=geonode 3Aeastern_han_dynasty_in_73_ce
_lg4&version=1.0.0

Figure 5.6 Map of Silk Road

https://worldmap.harvard.edu/data/geonode:silk_road_8h3

Figure 5.8 Umayyad Empire

http://worldmap.harvard.edu/geoserver/wfs?outputFormat=SHAPE
-ZIP&service=WFS&request=GetFeature&format_options=charset
3AUTF-8&typename=geonode 3Aumayyad_caliphate_6ds&version
=1.0.0

Figure 5.9 Ottoman Empire

http://worldmap.harvard.edu/geoserver/wfs?outputFormat=SHAPE
-ZIP&service=WFS&request=GetFeature&format_options=charset
3AUTF-8&typename=geonode 3Aottomans_4ra&version=1.0.0

Figure 5.10 Song Dynasty

http://worldmap.harvard.edu/geoserver/wfs?outputFormat=SHAPE
-ZIP&service=WFS&request=GetFeature&format_options=charset
3AUTF-8&typename=geonode 3Asongdynasty_moo&version=
1.0.0

Figure 5.12 Timurid Empire

http://worldmap.harvard.edu/geoserver/wfs?outputFormat=SHAPE
-ZIP&service=WFS&request=GetFeature&format_options=charset
3AUTF-8&typename=geonode 3Atimurid_empire_7so&version=
1.0.0

Tables

Throughout the text, I refer to seven continental regions, Africa (AF), Asia (AS), Commonwealth of Independent States (CIS), Europe (EU), Latin America (LA), North America (NA), and Oceania (OC). Note that for purposes of analysis, the CIS is separated from Europe and Asia, but in standard geographical accounts would be part of those two continents.

Following are supplementary tables that contain calculated data referred to in the text.

Table 1.3a Percent Land and Population Within 100 km of Coasts

Continent	Land Area Within 100 km of Rivers (%)	Population Within 100 km of Rivers (%)			
		3000 BCE	100 CE	1400	2015
AF	9.7	36.8	37.8	25.9	25.2
AS	22.4	28.6	29.0	33.6	39.3
CIS	15.8	9.8	9.5	10.6	14.0
EU	51.3	56.1	52.0	45.0	50.6
LA	17.2	29.1	28.3	28.4	43.7
NA	29.5	26.8	31.4	41.4	49.4
OC	23.8	51.6	64.1	69.5	81.8
Total	20.0	32.4	32.6	32.8	38.0

Source: Author's calculations using HYDE and CIESIN data. See Historical Population Data, Gridded Population Data for 2015, and Data used in the Creation of Maps and Geospatial Analysis for details.

Table 1.3b Percent Land and Population Within 20 Km of Rivers

Continent	Land Area Within 20 Km of Rivers (%)	Population within 20 Km of Rivers (%)			
		3000 BCE	100 CE	1400	2015
AF	11.8	33.6	31.7	25.2	21.9
AS	17.9	29.5	29.6	32.2	28.6
CIS	18.9	35.0	31.6	34.2	38.7
EU	25.0	29.3	31.3	35.4	35.0
LA	17.0	27.3	26.3	26.3	21.4
NA	20.1	51.5	43.9	33.9	28.9
OC	4.3	13.3	11.9	11.1	8.9
Eurasia (AS+CIS+EU)	18.4	30.3	30.4	33.5	30.3
Total	16.3	30.1	29.9	31.1	27.7

Source: Author's calculations using HYDE and CIESIN data. See Historical Population Data, Gridded Population Data for 2015, and Data used in the Creation of Maps and Geospatial Analysis for details.

Table 1.3c Percent Land and Population Within 20km Rivers and/or 100km of Coast

Continent	Land Area within 20 Km of Rivers and/or 100km of Coast (%)	Population within 20 Km of Rivers and/or 100km of Coast (%)			
		3000 BCE	100 CE	1400	2015
AF	20.0	60.5	59.2	45.4	42.1
AS	36.4	52.6	53.0	58.6	59.8
CIS	33.2	43.0	39.5	42.5	48.8
EU	69.0	76.4	74.5	71.3	74.0
LA	32.3	51.6	50.0	50.0	57.3
NA	46.8	70.9	67.9	68.6	68.6
OC	27.0	60.5	70.8	75.3	84.4
Total	33.8	56.3	56.2	57.1	58.0

Source: Author's calculations using HYDE and CIESIN data. See Historical Population Data, Gridded Population Data for 2015, and Data used in the Creation of Maps and Geospatial Analysis for details.

Table 3.1 Percent Land Area and Population Within the Lucky Latitudes (Old World)

Continent	Land Area within the Lucky Latitudes (%)	Population within the Lucky Latitudes (%) 3000 BCE	100 CE	1400	2015
AF	14.2	48.1	51.5	14.6	15.0
AS	57.8	73.3	70.6	63.1	56.8
CIS	10.1	49.1	47.6	27.9	32.2
EU	29.8	51.4	47.7	32.3	28.7
Total Old World	28.1	65.7	63.8	49.2	45.4

Source: Author's calculations using HYDE and CIESIN data. See Historical Population Data, Gridded Population Data for 2015, and Data used in the Creation of Maps and Geospatial Analysis for details.

Notes

1. Seven Ages of Globalization

1. For a dazzling analysis of culture and behavior from the viewpoint of evolutionary biology, see Edward O. Wilson, *The Social Conquest of Earth* (New York: Liveright, 2012).

2. For a riveting accounting of these late-nineteenth-century famines, see Mike Davis, *Late Victorian Holocausts* (Brooklyn: Verso, 2001).

3. Kees Klein Goldewijk, Arthur Beusen, and Peter Janssen, "Long-Term Dynamic Modeling of Global Population and Built-up Area in a Spatially Explicit Way: HYDE 3.1," *Holocene* 20, no. 4 (2010): 565–73.

4. Extreme poverty signifies a level of deprivation at which basic human needs (nutritious diet, safe water, sanitation, clothing, shelter, and so forth) are not ensured. The World Bank has regularly established metrics to measure extreme poverty. The World Bank's current poverty line is per capita consumption at or below $1.90 per day measured in 2011 prices using purchasing-power parity (PPP) exchange rates. Academic studies of poverty throughout history propose their own respective poverty lines for coherence with the recent World Bank data.

5. For the scale of forager communities, see Tobias Kordsmeyer, Pádraig Mac Carron, and R. I. M. Dunbar, "Sizes of Permanent Campsite Communities Reflect Constraints on Natural Human Communities," *Current Anthropology* 58, no. 2 (2017): 289–94.

6. In fact, the replacement rate is slightly above 2 children per woman to account for the slight mortality risk of the next generation.

7. The official U.S. employment data for 2018 may be found at https://www.bls.gov/emp /tables/employment-by-major-industry-sector.htm. Note that in the calculations in

the text I have added "non-agricultural self-employed" to the tertiary sector. The total sums to 99.9 because of rounding.

8. David McGee and Peter B. deMenocal, "Climatic Changes and Cultural Responses During the African Humid Period Recorded in Multi-Proxy Data," in *Oxford Research Encyclopedia of Climate Science*, 2017.

9. Jutta Bolt, Robert Inklaar, Herman de Jong, and Jan Luiten van Zanden, "Rebasing 'Maddison': New Income Comparisons and the Shape of Long-Run Economic Development," GGDC Research Memorandum 174, January 2018.

10. Adam Smith, *An Enquiry Into the Nature and Causes of the Wealth of Nations* [1776] (New York: Random House, 1937).

11. For further information on the sources of these data and other data used throughout the text, please see the data appendix at the end of the book.

12. Two leading economists, Ronald Findlay and Kevin O'Rourke, offer a deeply informed global history of trade, technology, and warfare during the 1000 years from 1000 AD to 2000 AD in *Power and Plenty: Trade, War, and the World Economy in the Second Millennium*.

2. The Paleolithic Age (70,000–10,000 BCE)

1. The Paleolithic period dates from the time that hominins first used stone tools, approximately 3.3 million years ago to the end of the last ice age at the conclusion of the Pleistocene epoch, some 11,700 years ago. The Paleolithic period is divided into three sub-periods, the lower Paleolithic (to around 200,000 year ago), the Middle Paleolithic (200,000 years ago to around 50,000 years ago), and the Upper Paleolithic (50,000 years ago to around 11,700 years ago). The timing of the emergence of anatomically modern humans is subject to considerable debate and uncertainty. A recent publication, using genetic evidence, suggests a date of 200,000 years ago for the emergence of modern humans. E. K. F. Chan, A. Timmermann, B. F. Baldi, et al. "Human Origins in a Southern African Palaeo-Wetland and First Migrations." *Nature* 575 (2019).

2. Edward O. Wilson, *Genesis: The Deep Origin of Societies* (New York: Liveright, 2019).

3. Israel Hershkovitz, Gerhard W. Weber, Rolf Quam, Mathieu Duval, Rainer Grün, Leslie Kinsley, et al., "The Earliest Modern Humans Outside Africa," *Science* 359, no. 6374 (2018): 456–59.

4. B. M. Henn, L. L. Cavalli-Sforza, and M. W. Feldman, "The Great Human Expansion," *Proceedings of the National Academy of Sciences* 109, no. 44 (2012): 17758–64.

5. James F. O'Connell, Jim Allen, Martin A. J. Williams, Alan N. Williams, Chris S. M. Turney, Nigel A. Spooner, et al., "When Did *Homo sapiens* First Reach Southeast Asia and Sahul?," *Proceedings of the National Academy of Sciences* 115, no. 34 (2018): 8482–90.

6. For recent evidence on this debate, see Sander van der Kaars, Gifford H. Miller, Chris S. M. Turney, et al., "Humans Rather Than Climate the Primary Cause of Pleistocene Megafaunal Extinction in Australia," *Nature Communications* 8, January 20, 2017.

Notes

7. Pita Kelekna, "The Politico-Economic Impact of the Horse on Old World Cultures: An Overview," *Sino-Platonic Papers*, no. 190 (June 2009).

8. Tibetan gene variants that are adaptive for high altitude seem to be from Denisovans. See Emilia Huerta-Sanchez, Xin Jin, Rasmus Nielsen, et al., "Altitude Adaptation in Tibetans Caused by Introgression of Denisovan-like DNA," *Nature* 512 (2014), 194–197.

9. For a survey of the debate, see Ofer Bar-Yosef, "The Upper Paleolithic Revolution," *Annual Review of Anthropology* 31, no. 1 (2002): 363–93.

10. A recent study suggesting that the structure of the human brain continued to evolve during the transition from the Middle Paleolithic to the Upper Paleolithic is Simon Neubauer, Jean-Jacques Hublin, and Philipp Gunz, "The Evolution of Modern Human Brain Shape," *Science Advances* 4, no. 1 (2018).

11. There remains considerable uncertainty and heated debate about the timing and methods of the earliest migrations from Asia to North America. The uncertainties include the timing, the number of waves of migration, and now even the question of whether the new arrivals came over a land corridor, as long surmised, or perhaps instead by boat along the coastline. Recent evidence that early migrants came by coastal waters is presented in Loren G. Davis et al., "Late Upper Paleolithic occupation at Cooper's Ferry, Idaho, USA, ~16,000 years ago," *Science* 365, no. 6456 (2019): 891–897.

12. Martin Sikora, Andaine Seguin-Orlando, Vitor C. Sousa, Anders Albrechtsen, Thorfinn Korneliussen, Amy Ko, et al., "Ancient Genomes Show Social and Reproductive Behavior of Early Upper Paleolithic Foragers," *Science* 358, no. 6363 (2017): 659–62.

13. H. Gintis, C. van Schaik, and C. Boehm, "Zoon Politikon: The Evolutionary Origins of Human Socio-Political Systems," *Behavioural Processes* 161 (2019): 17–30.

3. The Neolithic Age (10,000–3000 BCE)

1. Dolores R. Piperno, "A Model of Agricultural Origins," *Nature Human Behaviour* 2, no. 7 (2018): 446–47.

2. An excellent recent study of the change in living standards and health during the transition to farming may be found in Alison A Macintosh, Ron Pinhasi, and Jay T Stock. "Early Life Conditions and Physiological Stress Following the Transition to Farming in Central/Southeast Europe: Skeletal Growth Impairment and 6000 Years of Gradual Recovery," *PloS one* 11, no. 2 (2016): e0148468.

3. Kees Klein Goldewijk, Arthur Beusen, and Peter Janssen, "Long-Term Dynamic Modeling of Global Population and Built-up Area in a Spatially Explicit Way: HYDE 3.1," *Holocene* 20, no. 4 (2010): 565–73.

4. David Reich, *Who We Are and How We Got Here* (New York: Random House, 2018), 100.

5. Reich, *Who We Are and How We Got Here*, 113.

6. Jared Diamond, *Guns, Germs, and Steel* (New York: Norton, 1997), xx.

7. A famous and influential account of the distinctive geographical, political, and social features of these early alluvial societies is Karl S. Wittfogel's *Oriental Despotism: a Comparative Study of Total Power* (New Haven, CT: Yale University Press, 1957).

Wittfogel argued that the need for major public works to control river flooding and irrigation gave rise to strong, indeed despotic, states. The thesis garnered many followers and also considerable criticism for making hasty over-generalizations.

8. For a fascinating account of the long-term patterns of river flow and their implications, see Mark G. Macklin and John Lewin, "The Rivers of Civilization," *Quaternary Science Reviews* 114 (2015): 228–44.

9. See Ian Morris, *Why the West Rules—For Now: The Patterns of History, and What They Reveal About the Future* (New York: Picador, 2011).

10. The total land area of Old World Lucky Latitudes is 23.4 million km². The shares of this land area by continent are as follows: Africa, 18.1 percent; Asia, 66.2 percent; CIS, 9.4 percent; and Europe, 6.4 percent. For further data on climate and population in the Lucky Latitudes, see the data appendix.

4: The Equestrian Age (3000–1000 BCE)

1. On the domestication of the donkey, see Stine Rossel, Fiona Marshall, Joris Peters, Tom Pilgram, Matthew D. Adams, and David O'Connor, "Domestication of the Donkey: Timing, Processes, and Indicators," *Proceedings of the National Academy of Sciences* 105, no. 10 (2008): 3715–20

   On the domestication of the dromedarey, see Ludovic Orlando, "Back to the Roots and Routes of Dromedary Domestication," *Proceedings of the National Academy of Sciences* 113, no. 24 (2016): 6588–90; Faisal Almathen, Pauline Charruau, Elmira Mohandesan, Joram M. Mwacharo, Pablo Orozco-terWengel, Daniel Pitt, Abdussamad M. Abdussamad, et al., "Ancient and Modern DNA Reveal Dynamics of Domestication and Cross-Continental Dispersal of the Dromedary," *Proceedings of the National Academy of Sciences* 113, no. 24 (2016): 6707–12; Barat ali Zarei Yam and Morteza Khomeiri, "Introduction to Camel Origin, History, Raising, Characteristics, and Wool, Hair and Skin: A Review," *Research Journal of Agriculture and Environmental Management* 4, no. 11 (2015): 496–508.

   For the South American camelids, see Juan C. Marín Romina Rivera, Valeria Varas, Jorge Cortés, Ana Agapito, Ana Chero, et. al., "Genetic Variation in Coat Colour Genes MC1R and ASIP Provides Insights Into Domestication and Management of South American Camelids," *Frontiers in Genetics* 9 (2018): 487.

2. Peter Mitchell, "Why the Donkey Did Not Go South: Disease as a Constraint on the Spread of Equus Asinus into Southern Africa," *African Archaeological Review* 34, no. 1 (2017): 21–41.

3. Jack M. Broughton and Elic M. Weitzel, "Population Reconstructions for Humans and Megafauna Suggest Mixed Causes for North American Pleistocene Extinctions," *Nature Communications* 9, no. 1 (2018): 5441.

4. Rossel et al., "Domestication of the Donkey."

5. Pita Kelekna, *The Horse in Human History* (Cambridge: Cambridge University Press, 2009), xx.

6. Ralph W. Brauer, "The Camel and Its Role in Shaping Mideastern Nomad Societies," *Comparative Civilizations Review* 28, no. 28 (1993): 47.

7. Kelekna, *The Horse in Human History*, 45–49.

8. David Reich, *Who We Are and How We Got Here* (New York: Random House, 2018), 120.

9. Meredith Reba, Femke Reitsma, and Karen C. Seto, "Spatializing 6,000 Years of Global Urbanization from 3700 BC to AD 2000," *Scientific Data* 3 (2016): 160034.

5. The Classical Age (1000 BCE–1500 CE)

1. Karl Jaspers, *The Origin and Goal of History* (London: Routledge, 1953).

2. Violet Moller, *The Map of Knowledge: A Thousand-Year History of How Classical Ideas Were Lost and Found* (New York: Doubleday, 2019), 61.

3. L. Carrington Goodrich, *A Short History of the Chinese People* (New York: Courier, 2002), 31.

4. Pita Kelekna, *The Horse in Human History* (Cambridge: Cambridge University Press, 2009), 390.

5. Dieter Kuhn, *The Age of Confucian Rule* (Cambridge: Harvard University Press, 2009), 29.

6. Neil Pederson, Amy E. Hessl, Nachin Baatarbileg, Kevin J. Anchukaitis, and Nicola Di Cosmo, "Pluvials, Droughts, the Mongol Empire, and Modern Mongolia," *Proceedings of the National Academy of Sciences* 111, no. 12 (2014): 4375–79.

7. Kees Klein Goldewijk, Arthur Beusen, and Peter Janssen, "Long-Term Dynamic Modeling of Global Population and Built-up Area in a Spatially Explicit Way: HYDE 3.1," *The Holocene* 20, no. 4 (2010): 565–73.

6. The Ocean Age (1500–1800)

1. For a wonderful account of the voyages, see Louise Levathes, *When China Ruled the Seas: The Treasure Fleet of the Dragon Throne, 1405–1433* (New York: Simon and Shuster, 1994).

2. Adam Smith, *An Enquiry Into the Nature and Causes of the Wealth of Nations* [1776] (New York: Random House, 1937).

3. Alfred W. Crosby, *Germs, Seeds and Animals: Studies in Ecological History* (New York: Routledge, 2015).

4. For a recent discussion, see Nathan Nunn and Nancy Qian, "The Columbian Exchange: A History of Disease, Food, and Ideas," *Journal of Economic Perspectives* 24, no. 2 (2010): 163–88.

5. Alexander Koch, Chris Brierley, Mark M. Maslin, and Simon L. Lewis, "Earth System Impacts of the European Arrival and Great Dying in the Americas After 1492," *Quaternary Science Reviews* 207 (2019): 13–36, https://doi.org/10.1016/j.quascirev.2018.12.004.

6. For an informative recent history, see John W. O'Malley, *The Jesuits: A History from Ignatius to the Present* (Lanham, MD: Rowman & Littlefield, 2014).

7. A recent critical history of the East India Company carries a descriptive title, see William Dalrymple, *The Anarchy: The East India Company, Corporate Violence, and the Pillage of an Empire* (New York: Bloomsbury, 2019).

8. Alfred Thayer Mahan, *The Influence of Sea Power Upon History, 1660–1783* (Boston: Little, Brown, 1890).

9. Joyce Chepkemoi, "Largest Empires in Human History by Land Area," *World Atlas*, May 11, 2017, https://www.worldatlas.com/articles/largest-empires-in-human-history -by-land-area.html.

10. Kees Klein Goldewijk, Arthur Beusen, and Peter Janssen, "Long-Term Dynamic Modeling of Global Population and Built-up Area in a Spatially Explicit Way: HYDE 3.1," *Holocene* 20, no. 4 (2010): 565–73.

11. Sven Beckert, *Empire of Cotton: A Global History* (New York: Knopf, 2014), 85.

12. Beckert, *Empire of Cotton*, 105.

13. Smith, *Wealth of Nations*.

7. The Industrial Age: (1800–2000)

1. The most authoritative demographic data on population, longevity, urbanization, and age structure for all nations since 1950 is provided by the UN Population Division, accessible here: https://www.un.org/en/development/desa/population/publications /database/index.asp. Data on national and world incomes after 1980 are provided by the IMF in the World Economic Outlook database, https://www.imf.org/external /pubs/ft/weo/2019/01/weodata/index.aspx.

2. For a captivating history of the British industrial revolution with a strong focus on technological advances, including the steam engine, see the classic study by David Landes, *Unbound Prometheus: Technological Change and Industrial Development in Western Europe from 1750 to the Present*, (Cambridge: Cambridge University Press, 1969).

3. Jutta Bolt, Robert Inklaar, Herman de Jong, and Jan Luiten van Zanden, "Rebasing 'Maddison': New Income Comparisons and the Shape of Long-Run Economic Development," GGDC Research Memorandum 174, January 2018.

4. E. A. Wrigley, *Energy and the English Industrial Revolution* (Cambridge University Press, 2010).

5. For pioneering theoretical investigations of GPTs and economic growth, see Bresnahan and Trajtenberg (1995) and Helpman (1998).

6. Martin Weitzman, "Recombinant Growth," *Quarterly Journal of Economics* 113, no. 2, (May 1998): 331–60.

7. Markku Wilenius and Sofi Kurki, "Surfing the Sixth Wave: Exploring the Next 40 Years of Global Change," in *6th Wave and Systemic Innovation for Finland: Success Factor for the Years 2010–2050 Project*. University of Turku: Finland Futures Research Centre, 2012.

8. Klaus Schwab, *The Fourth Industrial Revolution* (Geneva: World Economic Forum, 2016).

9. Prasannan Parthasarathi, *Why Europe Grew Rich and Asia Did Not: Global Economic Divergence, 1600–1850* (Cambridge: Cambridge University Press, 2011), 131.

10. For estimates of illiteracy for India and other countries around 1950, see Statistical Division of UNESCO, World Illiteracy Mid-Century: A Statistical Study" (1957); for life expectancy, see the data of the UN Population Division, https://population .un.org/wpp/Download/Standard/Mortality/.

11. See John Iliffe, *Africans: The History of a Continent*, (New York: Cambridge University Press, 1995), 198–99.

12. Bolt et al., "Rebasing 'Maddison.'"

13. John Maynard Keynes, *The Economic Consequences of the Peace* [1919] (Jersey City, N.J.: Start Kindle Edition, 2014).

14. Keynes, *The Economic Consequences of the Peace*.

15. David Vine, *Base Nation: How U.S. Military Bases Abroad Harm America and the World* (New York: Metropolitan Books, 2015); Nick Turse, "U.S. Military Says It Has a 'Light footprint' in Africa," *The Intercept*, December 1, 2018, https://theintercept .com/2018/12/01/u-s-military-says-it-has-a-light-footprint-in-africa-these-documents -show-a-vast-network-of-bases/.

16. Defense Manpower Data Center, "DoD Personnel, Workforce Reports & Publications," DMDC.osd.mil: USA.gov, 2019.

17. The most recent estimate by the World Bank is 736 million in extreme poverty in 2015, down from 1.85 billion in 1990. See "Poverty: Overview," https://www.worldbank.org /en/topic/poverty/overview, accessed November 11, 2019.

8. The Digital Age (Twenty-First Century)

1. World Economic Forum, "How Much Data is Generated Each Day?," April 17, 2019, https:// www.weforum.org/agenda/2019/04/how-much-data-is-generated-each-day-cf4bddf29f/.

2. Data as of November 20, 2019, from the following sources: Facebook log-ons, "The Top 20 Valuable Facebook Statistics—Updated November 2019," https://zephoria.com /top-15-valuable-facebook-statistics/; Google searches, https://www.internetlivestats .com/google-search-statistics/; YouTube videos, Omnicore, "YouTube by the Numbers: Stats, Demographics & Fun Facts," September 5, 2019, https://www.omnicoreagency .com/youtube-statistics/; Internet users, Internet World Stats, "Top 20 Countries in Internet Users vs. Rest of the World—June 30, 2019," https://www.internetworld stats.com/top20.htm; Swift settlements, swift.com, "The SWIFT-CLS Partnership in FX Reduces Risk and Adds Liquidity," April 4, 2019, https://www.swift.com /news-events/news/the-swift-cls-partnership-in-fx-reduces-risk-and-adds-liquidity.

3. See David Silver, Thomas Hubert, Julian Schrittwieser, Ioannis Antonoglou, Matthew Lai, and Arthur Guez, et. al., "Mastering Chess and Shogi by Self-Play with a General Reinforcement Learning Algorithm," *arXiv.org* (2017).

4. Jeffrey D. Sachs, *The End of Poverty: Economic Possibilities for Our Time* (New York: Penguin, 2006).

5. World Bank, *Poverty and Shared Prosperity 2018: Piecing Together the Poverty Puzzle* (Washington, D.C.: World Bank, 2018), http://documents.worldbank.org/curated

Notes

/en/104451542202552048/Poverty-and-Shared-Prosperity-2018-Piecing-Together
-the-Poverty-Puzzle.

6. The World Bank reports that China is on track to end poverty according to the national definition of rural poverty (per capita rural net income of RMB 2,300 per year in 2010 constant prices). See https://www.worldbank.org/en/country/china
/overview, accessed November 15, 2019.

7. The data are for China's GDP at constant prices from the IMF World Economic Outlook database, October 2019.

8. Data from World Intellectual Property Corporation, "World Intellectual Property Report 2018," https://www.wipo.int/export/sites/www/pressroom/en/documents/pr
_2018_816_annexes.pdf#annex1.

9. See the report of the Intergovernmental Science-Policy Platform on Biodiversity and Ecosystem Services (IPBES), 2019, https://ipbes.net/system/tdf/ipbes_7_10_add.1_en
_1.pdf?file=1&type=node&id=35329.

10. For the intellectual history of this equation, see Marian R. Chertow, "The IPAT Equation and Its Variants," *Journal of Industrial Ecology* 4, no. 4 (2000), 13–29.

11. See Graham Allison, *Destined for War: Can America and China Escape Thucydides's Trap?* (New York: Houghton Mifflin Harcourt, 2017).

9. Guiding Globalization in the Twenty-First Century

1. World Commission on Environment and Development, *Our Common Future* (Oxford: Oxford University Press, 1987).

2. The SDG rankings are available in the UN report by Jeffrey Sachs, Guido Schmidt-Traub, Christian Kroll, Guillaume Lafortune, and Grayson Fuller, *Sustainable Development Report 2019: Transformations to Achieve the Sustainable Development Goals* (New York: Bertelsmann Stiftung and Sustainable Development Solutions Network [SDSN], 2019).

3. The life satisfaction rankings can be cound in the 2019 world happiness report: John F. Helliwell, Richard Layard, and Jeffrey D. Sachs, *The UN World Happiness Report 2019.* (New York: SDSN, 2019).

4. In 2019, President Donald Trump announced his intention to withdraw the United States from the Paris Climate Agreement but not from the UNFCCC.

5. Mark Mazower, *Governing the World: The History of an Idea, 1815 to the Present* (New York: Penguin, 2013).

6. Pope Francis, *Laudato si'* (Vatican City: Vatican Press, 2015), sec. 23.

7. Immanuel Kant, *Perpetual Peace: A Philosophical Sketch* [1795] (Cambridge: Cambridge University Press, 1970).

8. G. M. Gilbert, interview with Hermann Goering, April 18, 1946, in *Nuremberg Diary* (New York: Farrar, Strauss, 1947), 278.

9. John F. Kennedy, "Commencement Address at American University," Washington, D.C., June 10, 1963, https://www.jfklibrary.org/archives/other-resources/john-f-kennedy
-speeches/american-university-19630610.

Further Readings

1: Seven Ages of Globalization

Davis, Mike. *Late Victorian Holocausts: El Niño Famines and the Making of the Third World.* Brooklyn: Verso, 2001.

Diamond, Jared. *Guns, Germs, and Steel.* New York: Norton, 1997.
Jared Diamond's book is a masterpiece of concision, insight, and sheer joy of discovery. He explains beautifully the deep role of physical geography in shaping our world.

Kordsmeyer, Tobias L., Pádraig Mac Carron, and R. I. M. Dunbar. "Sizes of Permanent Campsite Communities Reflect Constraints on Natural Human Communities." *Current Anthropology* 58, no. 2 (2017.): 289–94.

Morris, Ian. *Why the West Rules—For Now: The Patterns of History, and What They Reveal About the Future.* New York: Picador, 2011
Ian Morris offers a fascinating and provocative account of the interactions of geography, technology, and geopolitics in shaping globalization over millennia.

Wilson, Edward O. *The Social Conquest of Earth.* New York: Liveright, 2012.

2: The Paleolithic Age

Davis, Loren G., David B. Madsen, Lorena Becerra-Valdivia, Thomas Higham, David A. Sisson, and Sarah M. Skinner. "Late Upper Paleolithic Occupation at Cooper's Ferry, Idaho, USA, ~16,000 Years Ago." *Science* 365 (2019): 891–97.

van der Kaars, Sander, Gifford H. Miller, Chris S. M. Turney, Ellyn J. Cook, Dirk Nürnberg, Joachim Schönfeld, *et. al.* "Humans Rather than Climate the Primary Cause of Pleistocene Megafaunal Extinction in Australia." *Nature Communications* 8, no. 14142 (2017). https://doi.org/10.1038/ncomms14142.

Further Readings

Bar-Yosef, Ofer. "The Upper Paleolithic Revolution." *Annual Review of Anthropology* 31, no. 1 (2002): 363–93. https://doi.org/10.1146/annurev.anthro.31.040402.085416.

Reich, David. *Who We Are and How We Got Here*. New York: Random House, 2018.
David Reich is a leader of the revolution in genomics that is untangling the history of human populations and their migrations in prehistory. He presents a scintillating account of the science and reveals recent findings.

Wilson, Edward O. *Genesis: The Deep Origin of Societies*. New York: Liveright, 2019.
E. O. Wilson is the world's greatest evolutionary biologist, our age's leading heir to Darwin, and the progenitor of many fundamental ideas about human nature, the consilience of knowledge, and the interactions of culture and genetics in shaping our behavior.

3. The Neolithic Age

Macklin, Mark G, and John Lewin. "The Rivers of Civilization." *Quaternary Science Reviews* 114 (2015): 228–44.

Morris, Ian. *Why the West Rules – for Now: The Patterns of History, and What They Reveal About the Future*. New York: Picador, 2011.

Pulleyblank, EG. "Karl S. Wittfogel: Oriental Despotism: A Comparative Study of Total Power. New Haven: Yale University Press; London: Oxford University Press, 1957. 60s." *Bulletin of the School of Oriental and African Studies* 21, no. 3 (1958): 657–60.

Robinson, Andrew. *The Story of Writing*. London: Thames & Hudson, 2007.
Andrew Robinson's account helps us understand "the Internet of 3000 BCE"—that is, the breakthrough technologies of early writing systems that were fundamental in the rise of civilizations across Eurasia.

Smith, Richard L. *Premodern Trade in World History*. New York: Routledge, 2009.
Richard Smith opens our eyes to the fundamental role and means of long-distance trade in human prehistory and the way trade has long shaped societies.

4: The Equestrian Age

Cunliffe, Barry. *By Steppe, Desert, and Ocean*. Oxford: Oxford University Press, 2015.
Barry Cunliffe offers a wonderful vision of the interaction of human biomes—settlements of the steppes, desert, and oceans—in shaping early history.

Kelekna, Pita. *The Horse in Human History*. Cambridge: Cambridge University Press, 2009.
Pita Kelekna has produced a remarkably comprehensive and authoritative study of the role of the horse in early history and the implications of the absence of the domesticated horse in the early Americas.

Peter Mitchell. "Why the Donkey Did Not Go South: Disease as a Constraint on the Spread of Equus Asinus into Southern Africa." *African Archaeological Review* 34, no. 1 (2017): 21–41. https://doi.org/10.1007/s10437-017-9245-3.

Further Readings

5: The Classical Age

Beard, Mary. *SPQR: A History of Ancient Rome*. New York: Norton, 2015.
    Leading classicist Mary Beard gives a fresh, vivid, and fascinating account of the rise of the Roman Empire, a history that remains absolutely vital to understanding Western history and the history of ideas of the past 2,500 years.

Harris, W. V. *Roman Power: A Thousand Years of Empire*. Cambridge: Cambridge University Press, 2016.
    W. V. Harris, one of the great modern historians of the Greco-Roman world, offers an expert, detailed, and remarkably insightful account of the rise and decline of the Roman Empire, including a vivid discussion of the interactions of politics, demography, military technology, and culture.

Frankopan, Peter. *The Silk Roads: A New History of the World*. New York: Knopf, 2017.
    Peter Frankopan brilliantly elucidates the dynamics of Silk Road trade and the steppe empires in world history.

Moller, Violet. *The Map of Knowledge: A Thousand-Year History of How Classical Ideas Were Lost and Found*. New York: Doubleday, 2019.
    Violet Moller provides a scintillating account of how the knowledge of ancient Greece and Rome was transmitted to the modern world through countless civilizations, including the Arabs, Byzantines, Almohads, Venetians, and others.

6: The Ocean Age

Beckert, Sven. *Empire of Cotton: A Global History*. New York: Knopf, 2014.
    Sven Beckert has written a brilliant and original account of perhaps the world's first truly transoceanic industry and the powerful forces of early modern capitalism, greed, empire, and slaveholding that built it.

Dalrymple, William. *The East India Company, Corporate Violence, and the Pillage of an Empire*. London: Bloomsbury, 2019.

Hugill, Peter J. *World Trade Since 1431: Geography, Technology, and Capitalism*. Baltimore: Johns Hopkins University Press, 1993.
    Peter Hugill provides an extremely lucid account of the interactions of naval technology, physical geography, and the institutions of global commerce.

Levathes, Louise. *When China Ruled the Seas: The Treasure Fleet of the Dragon Throne, 1405–1433*. New York: Simon and Shuster, 1994.

Mann, Charles C. *1491: New Revelations of the Americas Before Columbus*. New York: Knopf, 2005.

Mann, Charles C. *1493: Uncovering the New World Columbus Created*. New York: Random House, 2011.
    Charles Mann's volumes aim to elucidate the profound changes for the entire world brought about by Columbus's discovery of the sea route from Europe to the Americas. Adam Smith

declared this discovery one of the most important events of human history, and Mann's
superb volumes help us understand Smith's assessment with much deeper insight.

Parthasarathi, Prasannan. *Why Europe Grew Rich and Asia Did Not: Global Economic Divergence, 1600–1850.* Cambridge: Cambridge University Press, 2011.
Prasannan Parthasarathi provides an invaluable look at the rise of the British Empire
through the lens of India. The rise of the West was far from inevitable and far from fair.
Britain bested India's leadership in early modern textile production and trade through
protectionism and force.

7: The Industrial Age

Landes, David. *The Unbound Prometheus: Technological Change and Industrial Development in
Western Europe from 1750 to the Present.* Cambridge: The Cambridge University Press, 1969.
Pollard, Sidney. *Peaceful Conquest: The Industrialization of Europe 1760–1970.* Oxford: Oxford
University Press, 1981.
Sidney Pollard brilliantly describes the west-to-east diffusion of industrialization across
Europe during the two centuries after Watt's steam engine and other British technological breakthroughs. This is a vivid story of the interactions of geography, technology,
and politics, both national and Europe-wide.
Statistical Division of UNESCO. *World Illiteracy Mid-Century: A Statistical Study.*
Paris: United Nations Educational, Scientific, and Cultural Organization, 1957.
Wrigley, E. A. *Energy and the English Industrial Revolution.* Cambridge: Cambridge University Press, 2010.
E. A. Wrigley is a powerful historical voice making clear that coal truly changed everything in the world economy, allowing humanity to break free of the constraints of the
"organic economy." This is interpretive history at its finest.

8: The Digital Age

Allison, Graham. *Destined for War: Can America and China Escape Thucydides's Trap?* Boston:
Houghton Mifflin Harcourt, 2017.
Chertow, Marian. "The IPAT Equation and Its Variants." *Journal of Industrial Ecology* 4,
no. 4 (2000): 13–29.
Sachs, Jeffrey D. *The Age of Sustainable Development.* New York: Columbia University Press,
2015.
I cite my own book because in it I attempted to synthesize the lessons of countless
original works that aim to interpret our age as the interaction of pathbreaking technologies and deepening ecological and social crises.

9: Globalization in the Twenty-First Century

Sachs, Jeffrey D. *A New Foreign Policy: Beyond American Exceptionalism.* New York: Columbia
University Press, 2018.

Further Readings

There is certainly no shortage of excellent writing about our present global predicament, in which rising geopolitical tensions are combined with growing ecological and demographic challenges (including aging, urbanization, and mass migration). My own brief account is a plea to Americans to recognize that America should not aim for "primacy" in the twenty-first century, but rather for global cooperation, the rule of law, and security for all nations under the UN Charter.

Bibliography

Allison, Graham. *Destined for War: Can America and China Escape Thucydides's Trap?* New York: Houghton Mifflin Harcourt, 2017.

Almathen, Faisal, Pauline Charruau, Elmira Mohandesan, Joram M. Mwacharo, Pablo Orozco-terWengel, Daniel Pitt, Abdussamad M. Abdussamad, et al. "Ancient and Modern DNA Reveal Dynamics of Domestication and Cross-Continental Dispersal of the Dromedary." *Proceedings of the National Academy of Sciences* 113, no. 24 (2016): 6707–12. https://doi.org/10.1073/pnas.1519508113.

Andrade, Tony. *The Gunpowder Age: China, Military Innovation, and the Rise of the West in World History.* New Jersey: Princeton University Press, 2017.

Barros Damgaard, Peter de, Rui Martiniano, Jack Kamm, J. Víctor Moreno-Mayar, Guus Kroonen, Michaël Peyrot, Gojko Barjamovic, et al. "The First Horse Herders and the Impact of Early Bronze Age Steppe Expansions into Asia." *Science* 360, no. 6396 (2018): eaar7711. https://doi.org/10.1126/science.aar7711.

Bar-Yosef, Ofer. "The Upper Paleolithic Revolution." *Annual Review of Anthropology* 31, no. 1 (2002): 363–93. https://doi.org/10.1146/annurev.anthro.31.040402.085416.

Beard, Mary. *SPQR: A History of Ancient Rome.* New York: Norton, 2015.

Beckert, Sven. *Empire of Cotton: A Global History.* New York: Knopf, 2014.

Benítez-Burraco, A. "Commentary: Ancient Genomes Show Social and Reproductive Behavior of early Upper Paleolithic Foragers." *Frontiers in Psychology* 8, no. 2247 (2017). https://doi.org/10.3389/fpsyg.2017.02247.

Bolt, J., R. Inklaar, H. de Jong, and J. L. van Zanden. "Rebasing 'Maddison': New Income Comparisons and the Shape of Long-Run Economic Development." *GGDC Research Memorandum* 174 (2018).

Bibliography

Bouckaert, R., P. Lemey, M. Dunn, S. J. Greenhill, A. V. Alekseyenko, A. J. Drummond, R. D. Gray, M. A. Suchard, and Q. D. Atkinson. "Mapping the Origins and Expansion of the Indo-European Language Family." *Science* 337, no. 6097 (2012): 957–60. https://doi.org/10.1126/science.1219669.

Bourguignon, François and Christian Morrisson. "Inequality Among World Citizens: 1820–1992." *American Economic Review* 92, no. 4 (2002): 727–44.

Brauer, Ralph W. "The Camel and Its Role in Shaping Mideastern Nomad Societies." *Comparative Civilizations Review* 28, no. 28 (1993): 47.

Bresnahan, Timothy F., and Manuel Trajtenberg. "General Purpose Technologies 'Engines of growth'?." *Journal of Econometrics* 65, no. 1 (1995): 83–108.

Broughton, Jack M. and Elic M. Weitzel, "Population Reconstructions for Humans and Megafauna Suggest Mixed Causes for North American Pleistocene Extinctions." *Nature Communications* 9, no. 1 (2018): 5441.

Browning, Sharon R., Brian L. Browning, Ying Zhou, Serena Tucci, and Joshua M. Akey. "Analysis of Human Sequence Data Reveals Two Pulses of Archaic Denisovan Admixture." *Cell* 173, no. 1 (2018): 53–61. https://doi.org/10.1016/j.cell.2018.02.031.

Bulliet, Richard. *The Camel and the Wheel*. Cambridge, MA: Harvard University Press, 1975.

Carter, William, Ramesh Shrestha, and Juan Fernandez-Diaz. "Estimating Ancient Populations by Aerial Survey." *American Scientist* 107, no. 1 (2019): 30. https://doi.org/10.1511/2019.107.1.30.

Chan, Eva K.F., Axel Timmermann, Benedetta F. Baldi, Andy E. Moore, Ruth J. Lyons, Sun-Seon Lee, et al. "Human Origins in a Southern African Palaeo-Wetland and First Migrations." *Nature* 575 (2019): 185–89.

Chan, K. S. "Foreign Trade, Commercial Policies and the Political Economy of the Song and Ming Dynasties of China." *Australian Economic History Review* 48, no. 1 (2008): 68–90.

Chepkemoi, Joyce. "Largest Empires in Human History by Land Area." worldatlas.com May 11, 2017. Accessed July 27, 2019. https://www.worldatlas.com/articles/largest-empires-in-human-history-by-land-area.html.

Cieslak, Michael, Melanie Pruvost, Norbert Benecke, Michael Hofreiter, Arturo Morales, Monika Reissmann, and Arne Ludwig. "Origin and History of Mitochondrial DNA Lineages in Domestic Horses." *PLoS ONE* 5, no. 12 (2010): e15311. https://doi.org/10.1371/journal.pone.0015311.

Comin, Diego, William Easterly, and Erick Gong. "Was the Wealth of Nations Determined in 1000 BC?." *American Economic Journal: Macroeconomics* 2, no. 3 (2010): 65–97.

Crosby, A.W. *Germs, Seeds and Animals: Studies in Ecological History: Studies in Ecological History*. New York: Routledge, 2015.

Cunliffe, Barry. *By Steppe, Desert, and Ocean*. Oxford: Oxford University Press, 2015.

Dalrymple, William. *The Anarchy: The East India Company, Corporate Violence, and the Pillage of an Empire*. New York: Bloomsbury, 2019.

Davis, Loren G., David B. Madsen, Lorena Becerra-Valdivia, Thomas Higham, David A. Sisson, and Sarah M. Skinner. "Late Upper Paleolithic Occupation at Cooper's Ferry, Idaho, USA, ~16,000 Years Ago." *Science* 365 (2019): 891–97.

Bibliography

Davis, Mike. *Late Victorian Holocausts: El Niño Famines and the Making of the Third World*. New York: Verso, 2000.

Defense Manpower Data Center. "DoD Personnel, Workforce Reports & Publications." DMDC.osd.mil: USA.gov, 2019.

Defense Manpower Data Center, "DoD Personnel, Workforce Reports & Publications," DMDC.osd.mil: USA.gov, 2019. der Erde Erdkunde, Vol. 8: 58–61.

Diamond, Jared. *Guns, Germs, and Steel*. New York: Norton, 1997.

Dow, Gregory K., and Clyde G. Reed. "The Origins of Sedentism: Climate, Population, and Technology." *Journal of Economic Behavior & Organization* 119 (2015): 56–71. https://doi.org/10.1016/j.jebo.2015.07.007.

d'Errico, F., and C. B. Stringer. "Evolution, Revolution or Saltation Scenario for the Emergence of Modern Cultures?" *Philosophical Transactions of the Royal Society B: Biological Sciences* 366, no. 1567 (2011): 1060–69. https://doi.org/10.1098/rstb.2010.0340.

Eltis, David, and David Richardson. *Atlas of The Transatlantic Slave Trade*. New Haven, CT: Yale University Press. Map 1 from accompanying web site, Overview of Slave Trade out of Africa, 1500–1900. Reproduced with the permission of Yale University Press.

Everson, S. ed. *Aristotle: The Politics and the Constitution of Athens*. Cambridge: Cambridge University Press, 1996.

Fernihough, Alan, and Kevin Hjortshøj O'Rourke. *Coal and the European Industrial Revolution*. No. w19802. National Bureau of Economic Research, 2014.

Findlay, Ronald, and Kevin H. O'Rourke. *Power and Plenty: Trade, War, and the World Economy in the Second Millennium*. Princeton, NJ: Princeton University Press, 2009.

Food and Agriculture Organization of the United Nations, 1998, G. Uilenberg, A Field Guide for the Diagnosis, Treatment and Prevention of African Animal Trypanosomosis. www.fao.org/3/X0413E/X0413E00.htm#TOC. Reproduced with permission.

Francis. *Laudato Si'*. Washington DC: United States Conference of Catholic Bishops, 2015.

Frankopan, Peter. *The Silk Roads: A New History of the World*. New York: Knopf, 2015.

Geiger, R. and W. Pohl. 1954. Revision of the Köppen-Geiger *Klimakarte der Erde*. Darmstadt: Justus Perthes.

Gibbs, Kevin, and Peter Jordan. "A Comparative Perspective on the 'Western' and 'Eastern' Neolithics of Eurasia: Ceramics; Agriculture and Sedentism." *Quaternary International* 419 (2016): 27–35. https://doi.org/10.1016/j.quaint.2016.01.069.

Gifford-Gonzalez, Diane, and Olivier Hanotte. "Domesticating Animals in Africa: Implications of Genetic and Archaeological Findings." *Journal of World Prehistory* 24, no. 1 (2011): 1–23. https://doi.org/10.1007/s10963-010-9042-2.

Gilbert, G.M. Interview with Hermann Goering. April 18, 1946, in *Nuremberg Diary* (New York: Farrar, Strauss, 1947), 278.

Gilpin, William, Marcus W. Feldman, and Kenichi Aoki. "An Ecocultural Model Predicts Neanderthal Extinction Through Competition with Modern Humans." *Proceedings of the National Academy of Sciences* 113, no. 8 (2016): 2134–39. https://doi.org/10.1073/pnas.1524861113.

Gintis, H., C. van Schaik, and C. Boehm. "Zoon Politikon: The Evolutionary Origins of Human Socio-Political Systems." *Behavioural Processes* 161 (2019): 17–30.

Bibliography

Goldfield, Anna E., Ross Booton, and John M. Marston. "Modeling the Role of Fire and Cooking in the Competitive Exclusion of Neanderthals." *Journal of Human Evolution* 124 (2018): 91–104. https://doi.org/10.1016/j.jhevol.2018.07.006.

Goodrich, Luther Carrington. *A Short History of the Chinese People.* New York: Courier, 2002.

Guilmartin, John. "Military Technology." *Encyclopædia Britannica.* 2019. https://www.britannica.com/technology/military-technology.

Gregory, Michael D., J. Shane Kippenhan, Daniel P. Eisenberg, Philip D. Kohn, Dwight Dickinson, Venkata S. Mattay, Qiang Chen, Daniel R. Weinberger, Ziad S. Saad, and Karen F. Berman. "Neanderthal-Derived Genetic Variation Shapes Modern Human Cranium and Brain." *Scientific Reports* 7, no. 1 (2017): 6308. https://doi.org/10.1038/s41598-017-06587-0.

Haak, Wolfgang, Iosif Lazaridis, Nick Patterson, Nadin Rohland, Swapan Mallick, Bastien Llamas, Guido Brandt, et al. "Massive Migration from the Steppe Is a Source for Indo-European Languages in Europe." *bioRxiv* (2015): 013433. doi:10.1101/013433.

Hare, Brian. "Survival of the Friendliest: *Homo Sapiens* Evolved via Selection for Pro-sociality." *Annual Review of Psychology* 68, no. 1 (2017): 155–86. https://doi.org/10.1146/annurev-psych-010416-044201.

Harris, W. V. *Roman Power: A Thousand Years of Empire.* Cambridge: Cambridge University Press, 2016.

Helliwell, John F., Richard Layard, and Jeffrey D. Sachs, eds. *The UN World Happiness Report 2019.* New York: Sustainable Development Solutions Network: 2019.

Helpman, Elhanan, ed. *General Purpose Technologies and Economic Growth.* Cambridge, MA: MIT Press, 1998.

Henn, B. M., L. L. Cavalli-Sforza, and M. W. Feldman. "The Great Human Expansion." *Proceedings of the National Academy of Sciences* 109, no. 44 (2012): 17758–64.

Hershkovitz, Israel, Gerhard W. Weber, Rolf Quam, Mathieu Duval, Rainer Grün, Leslie Kinsley, Avner Ayalon, et al. "The Earliest Modern Humans Outside Africa." *Science* 359, no. 6374 (2018): 456–59.

Hoffman, Phillip. *Why Did Europe Conquer the World?.* Princeton, NJ: Princeton University Press, 2017.

Hofmanová, Zuzana, Susanne Kreutzer, Garrett Hellenthal, Christian Sell, Yoan Diekmann, David Díez-del-Molino, Lucy van Dorp, et al. "Early Farmers from Across Europe Directly Descended from Neolithic Aegeans." *Proceedings of the National Academy of Sciences* 113, no. 25 (2016): 6886–91. https://doi.org/10.1073/pnas.1523951113.

Huerta-Sánchez, Emilia, Xin Jin, Asan, Zhuoma Bianba, Benjamin M. Peter, and Nicolas Vinckenbosch, *et. al.* "Altitude Adaptation in Tibetans Caused by Introgression of Denisovan-Like DNA." *Nature* 512 (2014).

Hugill, P. J. *World Trade Since 1431: Geography, Technology, and Capitalism.* Baltimore: Johns Hopkins University Press, 1995.

Iliffe, John. *Africans: The History of a Continent.* New York: Cambridge University Press, 1995.

International Monetary Fund, World Economic Outlook Database, October 2019.

International Monetary Fund. "China: Gross domestic product based on purchasing-power-parity (PPP) share of world total (Percent)." World Economic Outlook (April 2019).

Bibliography

Jandora, J. W. "Developments in Islamic Warfare: The Early Conquests." *Studia Islamica*, no. 64 (1986): 101. https://doi.org/10.2307/1596048.

Jaspers, Karl. *The Origin and Goal of History*. London: Routledge, 1953. Reprint, New York: Routledge, 2010.

Kant, Immanuel. *Perpetual Peace: A Philosophical Sketch*. Cambridge: Cambridge University Press, 1970.

Kelekna, Pita. *The Horse in Human History*. Cambridge: Cambridge University Press, 2009.

——. "The Politico-Economic Impact of the Horse on Old World Cultures." *Sino-Platonic Papers* 190 (2009).

Kennedy, John F. "Commencement Address at American University." Washington DC, June 10, 1963.

Keynes, John Maynard. *The Economic Consequences of Peace*. London: Routledge, 2017.

Kirby, Richard Shelton. *Engineering in History*. Mineola, NY: Dover, 1990.

Klein Goldewijk, Kees, Arthur Beusen, and Peter Janssen. "Long-Term Dynamic Modeling of Global Population and Built-up Area in a Spatially Explicit Way: HYDE 3.1." *The Holocene* 20, no. 4 (2010): 565–73. https://doi.org/10.1177/0959683609356587.

Knoppers, Gary, and Bernard M. Levinson. *The Pentateuch as Torah: New Models for Understanding Its Promulgation and Acceptance*. Winona Lake, IN: Eisenbrauns, 2007.

Ko, Kwang Hyun. "Hominin Interbreeding and the Evolution of Human Variation." *Journal of Biological Research-Thessaloniki* 23, no. 1 (2016): 17. https://doi.org/10.1186/s40709-016-0054-7.

Koch, Alexander, Chris Brierley, Mark M. Maslin, and Simon L. Lewis. "Earth System Impacts of the European Arrival and Great Dying in the Americas after 1492." *Quaternary Science Reviews* 207 (2019): 13–36. https://doi.org/10.1016/j.quascirev.2018.12.004.

Kordsmeyer, Tobias L., Pádraig Mac Carron, and R. I. M. Dunbar. "Sizes of Permanent Campsite Communities Reflect Constraints on Natural Human Communities." *Current Anthropology* 58, no. 2 (2017.): 289–94.

Kottek, Markus, Jürgen Grieser, Christoph Beck, Bruno Rudolf, and Franz Rubel. "World Map of the Köppen-Geiger climate classification updated." *Meteorologische Zeitschrift* 15, no. 3 (2006): 259–63. https://doi.org/10.1127/0941-2948/2006/0130.

Kuhn, Dieter. *The Age of Confucian Rule*. Cambridge, MA: Harvard University Press, 2009.

Lane, Kevin. "Through the Looking Glass: Re-Assessing the Role of Agro-Pastoralism in the North-Central Andean Highlands." *World Archaeology* 38, no. 3 (2006): 493–510. https://doi.org/10.1080/00438240600813806.

Landes, David. *The Unbound Prometheus: Technological Change and Industrial Development in Western Europe from 1750 to the Present*. Cambridge: Cambridge University Press, 1969.

Larson, Greger, Dolores R. Piperno, Robin G. Allaby, Michael D. Purugganan, Leif Andersson, Manuel Arroyo-Kalin, Loukas Barton, et al. "Current Perspectives and the Future of Domestication Studies." *Proceedings of the National Academy of Sciences* 111, no. 17 (2014): 6139–46. doi: 10.1073/pnas.1323964111.

Levathes, Louise. *When China Ruled the Seas: The Treasure Fleet of the Dragon Throne, 1405–1433*. New York: Simon and Shuster, 1994.

Bibliography

Lokrantz, J./Azote based on Will Steffen, Katherine Richardson, Johan Rockström, Sarah E. Cornell, Ingo Fetzer, Elena M. Bennett, Reinette Biggs, et al. "Planetary Boundaries: Guiding Human Development on a Changing Planet." *Science* 347, no. 6223 (2015): 1259855.

Macintosh, Alison A, Ron Pinhasi, and Jay T Stock. "Early Life Conditions and Physiological Stress Following the Transition to Farming in Central/Southeast Europe: Skeletal Growth Impairment and 6000 Years of Gradual Recovery." *Plos one* 11, no. 2 (2016): e0148468.

Macklin, Mark G, and John Lewin. "The Rivers of Civilization." *Quaternary Science Reviews* 114 (2015): 228–44.

Maddison Project Database, version 2010. Bolt, Jutta, Robert Inklaar, Herman de Jong, and Jan Luiten van Zanden (2010). "Rebasing 'Maddison': New Income Comparisons and the Shape of Long-Run Economic Development." Maddison Project Working Paper 10.

Maddison, Angus. "Statistics on World Population, GDP and Per Capita GDP, 1–2008 AD." *Historical Statistics* 3 (2010): 1–36.

Mahan, Alfred Thayer. *The Influence of Sea Power Upon History, 1660–1783*. Boston: Little, Brown, 1890.

Malthus, Thomas Robert. *An Essay on the Principle of Population*. Edinburgh and London: Ballantyne and Company, 1872.

Mandeville, Bernard. *The Grumbling Hive: or, knaves Turn'd Honest*. 1705.

Mann, Charles C. *1491: New Revelations of the Americas Before Columbus*. New York: Knopf, 2005.

"Mobile Phone Market Forecast - 2019." areppim: information, pure and simple, 2019, https://stats.areppim.com/stats/stats_mobilex2019.htm

——. *1493: Uncovering the New World Columbus Created*. New York: Random House, 2011.

Marín, Juan C., Romina Rivera, Valeria Varas, Jorge Cortés, Ana Agapito, Ana Chero, Alexandra Chávez, Warren E. Johnson, and Pablo Orozco-terWengel. "Genetic Variation in Coat Colour Genes MC1R and ASIP Provides Insights into Domestication and Management of South American Camelids." *Frontiers in Genetics* 9 (2018): 487. https://doi.org/10.3389/fgene.2018.00487.

Martinón-Torres, María, Xiujie Wu, José María Bermúdez de Castro, Song Xing, and Wu Liu. "*Homo Sapiens* in the Eastern Asian Late Pleistocene." *Current Anthropology* 58, no. S17 (2017): 434–48. https://doi.org/10.1086/694449.

Mazower, Mark. *Governing the World: The History of an Idea, 1815 to the Present*. New York: Penguin, 2013.

McGee, David, and Peter B. deMenocal. "Climatic Changes and Cultural Responses During the African Humid Period Recorded in Multi-Proxy Data." In *Oxford Research Encyclopedia of Climate Science*, ed. Matthew C. Nisbet, Shirley S. Ho, Ezra Markowitz, Saffron O'Neill, Mike S. Schäfer, and Jagadish Thaker. Oxford: Oxford University Press, 2017.

Metcalf, Jessica L., Chris Turney, Ross Barnett, Fabiana Martin, Sarah C. Bray, Julia T. Vilstrup, Ludovic Orlando, et al."Synergistic Roles of Climate Warming and Human Occupation in Patagonian Megafaunal Extinctions During the Last Deglaciation." *Science Advances* 2, no. 6 (2016): e1501682. https://doi.org/10.1126/sciadv.1501682.

Bibliography

Mitchell, Peter. "Why the Donkey Did Not Go South: Disease as a Constraint on the Spread of Equus Asinus into Southern Africa." *African Archaeological Review* 34, no. 1 (2017): 21–41. https://doi.org/10.1007/s10437-017-9245-3.

Moller, Violet. *The Map of Knowledge: A Thousand-Year History of How Classical Ideas Were Lost and Found.* New York: Doubleday, 2019.

Morris, E. "From Horse Power to Horsepower." 2007. https://www.accessmagazine.org/wp-content/uploads/sites/7/2016/07/Access-30-02-Horse-Power.pdf.

Morris, Ian. *Why the West Rules—for Now: The Patterns of History, and What They Reveal About the Future.* New York: Picador, 2011.

Naish, Darren. "Domestic Horses of Africa." *Scientific American Blog Network.* 2015. https://blogs.scientificamerican.com/tetrapod-zoology/domestic-horses-of-africa/.

National Science Board. Science and Engineering Indicators 2018. Alexandria, VA: National Science Foundation, 2018.

Naundrup, Pernille Johansen, and Jens-Christian Svenning. "A Geographic Assessment of the Global Scope for Rewilding with Wild-Living Horses (Equus Ferus)." Ed. Marco Festa-Bianchet. *PLoS ONE* 10, no. 7 (2015): e0132359. https://doi.org/10.1371/journal.pone.0132359.

Neubauer, Simon, Jean-Jacques Hublin, and Philipp Gunz. "The Evolution of Modern Human Brain Shape." *Science Advances* 4, no. 1 (2018): eaao5961. https://doi.org/10.1126/sciadv.aao5961.

Northrup, David. "Globalization and the Great Convergence: Rethinking World History in the Long Term." *Journal of World History* 16, no. 3 (2005): 249–67. https://doi.org/10.1353/jwh.2006.0010.

Norwich, John Julius. *A Short History of Byzantium.* New York: Vintage, 1999.

Nunn, Nathan, and Nancy Qian. "The Columbian Exchange: A History of Disease, Food, and Ideas." *Journal of Economic Perspectives* 24, no. 2 (2010): 163–88.

O'Connell, James F., Jim Allen, Martin A. J. Williams, Alan N. Williams, Chris S. M. Turney, Nigel A. Spooner, Johan Kamminga, Graham Brown, and Alan Cooper. "When Did Homo Sapiens First Reach Southeast Asia and Sahul?" *Proceedings of the National Academy of Sciences* 115, no. 34 (2018): 8482–90.

O'Malley, John W. *The Jesuits: A History from Ignatius to the Present.* Lanham, MD: Rowman & Littlefield, 2014.

Orlando, Ludovic. "Back to the Roots and Routes of Dromedary Domestication." *Proceedings of the National Academy of Sciences* 113, no. 24 (2016): 6588–90. https://doi.org/10.1073/pnas.1606340113.

Paine, Lincoln. *The Sea and Civilization: A Maritime History of the World.* New York: Knopf, 2013.

Parthasarathi, Prasannan. *Why Europe Grew Rich and Asia Did Not: Global Economic Divergence, 1600–1850.* Cambridge: Cambridge University Press, 2011.

Pederson, N., A. E. Hessl, N. Baatarbileg, K. J. Anchukaitis, and N. Di Cosmo. "Pluvials, Droughts, the Mongol Empire, and Modern Mongolia." *Proceedings of the National Academy of Sciences* 111, no. 12 (2014): 4375–79. https://doi.org/10.1073/pnas.1318677111.

Piperno, Dolores R. "A Model of Agricultural Origins." *Nature Human Behaviour* 2, no. 7 (2018): 446–47. https://doi.org/10.1038/s41562-018-0390-8.

Bibliography

Pollard, Sidney. *Peaceful Conquest: The Industrialization of Europe 1760–1970*. Oxford: Oxford University Press, 1981.

Pulleyblank, EG. "Karl S. Wittfogel: Oriental Despotism: A Comparative Study of Total Power" (review). *Bulletin of the School of Oriental and African Studies* 21, no. 3 (1958): 657–60.

Reba, Meredith, Femke Reitsma, and Karen C. Seto. "Spatializing 6,000 Years of Global Urbanization from 3700 BC to AD 2000." *Scientific Data* 3 (2016): 160034. https://doi .org/10.1038/sdata.2016.34.

Reich, David. *Who We Are and How We Got Here*. New York: Random House, 2018

Riley, James C. "Estimates of regional and global life expectancy, 1800–2001." *Population and Development Review* 31, no. 3 (2005): 537–43.

Rito, Teresa, Daniel Vieira, Marina Silva, Eduardo Conde-Sousa, Luísa Pereira, Paul Mellars, Martin B. Richards, and Pedro Soares. "A Dispersal of Homo Sapiens from Southern to Eastern Africa Immediately Preceded the Out-of-Africa Migration." *Scientific Reports* 9, no. 1 (2019): 4728. https://doi.org/10.1038/s41598-019-41176-3.

Robinson, Andrew. *The Story of Writing*. London: Thames & Hudson, 2007.

Rossel, Stine, Fiona Marshall, Joris Peters, Tom Pilgram, Matthew D. Adams, and David O'Connor. "Domestication of the Donkey: Timing, Processes, and Indicators." *Proceedings of the National Academy of Sciences* 105, no. 10 (2008): 3715–20. https://doi .org/10.1073/pnas.0709692105.

Sachs, Jeffrey. *The End of Poverty*. New York: Penguin, 2006.

——. *The Age of Sustainable Development*. New York: Columbia University Press, 2014.

——. *A New Foreign Policy: Beyond American Exceptionalism*. New York: Columbia University Press, 2018.

Sachs, Jeffrey, Guido Schmidt-Traub, Christian Kroll, Guillaume Lafortune, and Grayson Fuller. *Sustainable Development Report 2019: Transformations to Achieve the Sustainable Development Goals*. (New York: Bertelsmann Stiftung and Sustainable Development Solutions Network [SDSN]: 2019).

Schlebusch, Carina M., Helena Malmström, Torsten Günther, Per Sjödin, Alexandra Coutinho, Hanna Edlund, Arielle R. Munters, et al. "Southern African Ancient Genomes Estimate Modern Human Divergence to 350,000 to 260,000 Years Ago." *Science* 358, no. 6363 (2017): 652–55. https://doi.org/10.1126/science.aao6266.

Schwab, Klaus. *The Fourth Industrial Revolution*. New York: Crown Business, 2016.

Sikora, Martin, Andaine Seguin-Orlando, Vitor C. Sousa, Anders Albrechtsen, Thorfinn Korneliussen, Amy Ko, Simon Rasmussen, et al. "Ancient Genomes Show Social and Reproductive Behavior of Early Upper Paleolithic Foragers." *Science* 358, no. 6363 (2017): 659–62.

Silver, David, Thomas Hubert, Julian Schrittwieser, Ioannis Antonoglou, Matthew Lai, and Arthur Guez *et. al.* "Mastering Chess and Shogi by Self-Play with a General Reinforcement Learning Algorithm." *arXiv.org* (2017), https://arxiv.org/abs/1712.01815.

Smith, Adam. *The Wealth of Nations* [1776]. (1937).

Smith, Richard. *Premodern Trade in World History*. New York: Routledge, 2008.

Spickler, AR. *African Animal Trypanosomiasis: Nagana, Tsetse Disease, Tsetse Fly Disease, African Animal Trypanosomosis*. Iowa State University (The Center for Food Security and Public Health: 2018).

Bibliography

Stahl, P. W. "Animal Domestication in South America." In *The Handbook of South American Archaeology*, 121–30. New York: Springer, 2008.

Stringer, Chris. "Evolution: What Makes a Modern Human." *Nature* 485, no. 7396 (2012): 33.

Surovell, Todd A., Spencer R. Pelton, Richard Anderson-Sprecher, and Adam D. Myers. "Test of Martin's Overkill Hypothesis Using Radiocarbon Dates on Extinct Megafauna." *Proceedings of the National Academy of Sciences* 113, no. 4 (2016): 886–91. https://doi.org/10.1073/pnas.1504020112.

Thayer Mahan, Alfred. "*The Influence of Sea Power upon History*." 1900.

Thucydides. *The History of the Peloponnesian War*. Trans. Richard Crawley, rev. Donald Lateiner. New York: Barnes and Noble Classic, 2006.

Troncoso, Victor Alonso. "The Hellenistic gymnasium and the pleasure of 'paideia.'" *Symbolae Philogorum Posnaniensium* 19 (2009): 71–84.

Turse, Nick. "U.S. Military Says It Has a "Light Footprint" in Africa. These Documents Show a Vast Network of Bases." *The Intercept*, December 1, 2018.

UNESCO, Statistical Division *World Illiteracy Mid-Century: A Statistical Study*. Paris: UNESCO, 1957.

United Nations, Department of Economic and Social Affairs, Population Division (2019). World Population Prospects 2019, Online Edition.

U.S. Bureau of Labor Statistics. "Table 2.1 Employment by Major Industry Sector." Office of Occupational Statistics and Employment Projections, 2019.

van der Kaars, Sander, Gifford H. Miller, Chris S. M. Turney, Ellyn J. Cook, Dirk Nürnberg, Joachim Schönfeld, A. Peter Kershaw, and Scott J. Lehman. "Humans Rather than Climate the Primary Cause of Pleistocene Megafaunal Extinction in Australia." *Nature Communications* 8, no. 14142 (2017). https://doi.org/10.1038/ncomms14142.

Vine, David. *Base Nation: How U.S. Military Bases Abroad Harm America and the World*. New York: Metropolitan Books, 2015.

Violatti, Cristian. "Indus Valley Civilization." In *Ancient History Encyclopedia*, 2013. https://www.ancient.eu/Indus_Valley_Civilization/.

Weitzman, Martin. "Recombinant Growth." *Quarterly Journal of Economics* 113, no. 2 (May 1998): 331–60.

Wilenius, Markku, and Sofi Kurki. "Surfing the Sixth Wave: Exploring the Next 40 Years of Global Change." In *6th Wave and Systemic Innovation for Finland: Success Factor for the Years 2010–2050 Project*. University of Turku: Finland Futures Research Centre, 2012.

Wilson, Edward O. *Genesis: The Deep Origin of Societies*. New York: Norton, 2018.

Wittfogel, Karl S. *Oriental Despotism: a Comparative Study of Total Power*. New Haven, CT: Yale University Press, 1957.

——. *The Social Conquest of Earth*. New York: Liveright, 2012.

World Bank. "Poverty: Overview." 2019, accessed November 11, 2019, 2019, https://www.worldbank.org/en/topic/poverty/overview.

World Bank, Poverty and Shared Prosperity 2018: Piecing Together the Poverty Puzzle (Washington, D.C.: World Bank, 2018), http://documents.worldbank.org/curated/en/104451542202552048/Poverty-and-Shared-Prosperity-2018-Piecing-Together-the-Poverty-Puzzle.

World Economic Forum."How Much Data is Generated Each Day?," April 17, 2019, https://www.weforum.org/agenda/2019/04/how-much-data-is-generated-each-day-cf4bddf29f/.

World Intellectual Property Corporation, "World Intellectual Property Report 2018," https://www.wipo.int/export/sites/www/pressroom/en/documents/pr_2018_816_annexes.pdf#annex1.

——. *"Poverty and Shared Prosperity 2018: Piecing Together the Poverty Puzzle."* Washington, DC: World Bank, 2018.

——. *"*The World Bank in China: Overview." 2019, accessed November 15, 2019, https://www.worldbank.org/en/country/china/overview.

World Commission on Environment and Development. *Our Common Future.* Oxford: Oxford University Press, 1987.

Wrigley, E. A. *Energy and the English Industrial Revolution.* Cambridge: Cambridge University Press, 2013.

Yam, Barat ali Zarei, and Morteza Khomeiri. "Introduction to Camel Origin, History, Raising, Characteristics, and Wool, Hair and Skin: A Review." *Research Journal of Agriculture and Environmental Management* 4, no. 11 (2015): 496–508.

Index

Page numbers in *italics* indicate figures or tables.

Index

Xiognu Khanate, 80, 86

Yamnaya people, 45, 62–65
yellow fever, 102
yersinia pestis (the plague), 45
Yongle emperor, 97
Younger Dryas, 36, 41

zebras, 58
zero-carbon energy, 28, 199
Zheng He, 95, *96*, 97
zones. *See* climate zones; cold zones;
    ecological zones; mountain zones;
    temperate zones
Zoroastrianism, 71